SPORTS CAR GRAPHIC

MARCH 1965   50¢

NASSAU SPEED WEEK

ROAD TEST: 4.2-LITER E-TYPE JAGUAR

SHELBY AMERICAN MUSTANG GT

SHELBY
MUSTANG

THE TOTAL PERFORMANCE PONY CAR

COLIN COMER FOREWORD BY LEE IACOCCA

For Remy and Briggs, my two favorite future Shelby Mustang drivers.

Contents

Acknowledgments — 6

Foreword
Lee Iacocca — 7

Introduction
The Birth of the Pony Car — 8

Chapter 1
Turning a Gelding into a Stud — 10

Chapter 2
Shelby Builds a Racehorse — 56

Chapter 3
Gelding the Pony — 80

Chapter 4
Go Big or Go Home — 122

Chapter 5
The Beginning of the End — 162

Chapter 6
The Second Coming — 200

Index — 238

Acknowledgments

I never wanted to be a writer. My first magazine gig, with *Sports Car Market*, was a result of a late-night "debate" with its publisher Keith Martin wherein I accused him of printing inaccurate information on the muscle car market. His response? "Well why don't you come and write for us then?" Be careful what you argue about, kids. My first book, written in 2006, was a result of my writing in *SCM*, which was noticed by the fine folks at Motorbooks. They literally showed up on my doorstep with a book contract. I accepted mainly because I don't know how to say no and because I had no idea that writing a book would try to eat my face. I swore I'd never do another one after the experience. But an odd thing happened after that first book was published: people I didn't know thanked me for writing it. So for all of the extremely kind people who have gone out of their way to tell me they have enjoyed something I, the kid who almost flunked eighth-grade English class, wrote—thank you. I can't describe how much your kind words motivate me when deadlines loom, the computer screen burns brightly, and I wonder, "what have I done?".

For Mr. Lee Iacocca, who had a vision for the Mustang as a performance car, whose drive made him force Carroll Shelby to make that a reality, and who kindly shared those memories with me. Thank you, Lee. I know I speak for us all when I say your work ethic and pride in this country serve as the example every American should attempt to live up to.

I also think I am the luckiest guy on earth to have met so many of my heroes. These guys could have rightfully told me to go fly a kite but instead have always gone above and beyond to help, and in the process they have become some of my closest friends. So for Chuck Cantwell, Peter Brock, Allen Grant, Dan Gurney, John Morton, Bob Bondurant, Lew Spencer, and of course the late Carroll Hall Shelby and his dream that brought us all together, thank you. Without your accomplishments there would be nothing for me to write about, and without your help I would be truly lost even trying.

For my hero emeritus, Phil Remington, who taught me more than I could ever explain. I miss him greatly, and rarely a day goes by that I don't ask myself, "What would Rem do?" Rem, you will live forever in Shelbys, motorsports, and our hearts.

For Jim Farley, Bill Ford, Henry Ford III, and the rest of my friends at the Ford Motor Company who continue to make us all proud to be "Ford Guys." You guys rock!

For Scott Black, Gary Patterson, and the entire crew of Shelby American who work hard every day to keep Shelby's dream alive (and tire companies in business), thank you.

And, as we all know, there are no better multiplier of words than photographs, and I am extremely thankful for photos and support so generously given by Jeff Burgy; Austin Craig; John Atzbach; Sam Smith and all of my former co-workers at *Road & Track* who allowed me to raid the great *R&T* archives; David Newhardt; Dana Mecum, Sam Murtaugh, John Hollansworth Jr., and the whole Mecum Auction family; Marty Schorr; Will Brewster; Michael Darter; Vernon Estes; Joshua Taff; Stuart Shoen; and probably about 20 people I am forgetting. My sincere thanks to you all. I hope I did your work justice.

It would be impossible to offer the detailed car information in this book without the decades of effort spent by the Shelby American Automobile Club (www.saac.com) documenting each and every Shelby ever built. I couldn't have done it without my SAAC Registries (buy the set!) and the tireless support offered by Rick and Colleen Kopec, Howard Pardee, Ned Scudder, Greg Kolasa, and the entire Shelby American Automobile Club. These folks are the real deal. If you like Shelbys and aren't a SAAC member, well, shame on you!

I am extremely thankful for my family, who always encourage and support me no matter how stupid the choices I may make are: my extremely tolerant (or brainwashed?) wife, Cana and our two incredible kids Remington and Briggs, all three of whom are the reason I can't wait to wake up every day; my mom Deila Mangold, who never got too upset at my using her cookware to change my oil; Ann Comer; Carl Mangold; Cara, Mike, and Miles Dickmann; Shelagh and Jim Weiss; and for my late Granddad Michael and Nana Mary Comer; and my late Grandpa Ernie and Grandmother Renata Wolff; and all of my (usually) wonderful in-laws and extended family that are a part of that "until death do us part" deal I entered into.

The following have gone above and beyond to help with this book, especially when I was certain there was not only no light but not even a tunnel in which it may appear. In no particular order: Kati (Remington), Dave and Brady Blackledge; Jim Farley; Jay Leno; McKeel and Soon Hagerty and all of my friends at Hagerty Insurance (the best in the business!); Peter "P.D." Cunningham; Chuck Wegner; Gino Carini; Mike and Ivy Guarise; Tony "TFG" Gaples; Lester and Lisa Quam; Courtney Quam; Dana and Patti Mecum; Boris Said; Dan Binks; Phil Binks; Norma Saken; Craig and Carolyn Jackson; Jason Billups; Brant and Laura Halterman; Roger Morrison; Richard Morrison; Nick Esayian; Angie Kozleski; Carol Connors; Craig Conley; Bruce Meyer; Gayle Brock; Tim Magnusson; Lee and Felicia Cross; Richard Baum; Martin and Audrey Gruss; Paul Burkhardt; Olaf Abel; Keith Martin, Jim Pickering, Chester Allen, David Tomaro and the entire SCM gang; Mr. and Mrs. Joe Bruno Jr.; Frank and Victoria Boucher; Gordie Boucher; George and Cheri Forge; Keith, Shannan, and Sean McLaine; Kelly Whitton; Scott McPherson; the Men's Art Council of the Phoenix Art Museum; Mike and Dawn Fisher; Chris Hines; Al Pinkowsky; Darwin Holmstrom; publisher Zack Miller and everybody at Motorbooks who makes me look a lot better than I actually am; and likely dozens of others I have forgotten. I can only hope to be as good of a friend to you as you all are to me. Thank you.

For my friends Steven Juliano and Tynan Blackledge, two incredible guys that left this earth far too soon.

And lastly, something I hoped I'd never have to write but for my late father, Brendan Michael Comer, who somehow perfected the art of being a parent, a hero and a best friend all in one. Beyond encouraging my love of cars from an early age he also gave me not only the ability to write but also the courage to do so. For these reasons, and a million more, this book is dedicated to you, Dad. We miss you every day.

—Colin Comer

Foreword by Lee Iacocca

As General Manager of the Ford Division in the early 1960s, I believed there was an undefined new demographic reality: the average age of the United States population was falling at a rapid pace; the Baby Boom generation was our new power demographic. They didn't want the cars their parents drove. These young buyers desired sporty cars with great styling and performance at a price that represented value.

The answer was the 1964½ Mustang, a car I am credited with being the "father" of. However, it was a team effort by my staff at Ford. The Mustang broke all previous sales records. As it turned out men, women, old, young, it didn't matter—everybody loved the Mustang. The car created frenzy when introduced and quickly grew into a cultural icon.

I knew the Mustang had legs, but it needed more. Performance was key to our new demographic. The Mustang needed to get a performance image nobody could top. I called on my friend Carroll Shelby, creator of the two-seat, race-winning Cobra to make the Mustang into a world-beating sports car. Like me, Carroll came up by virtue of working hard and never giving up. I knew there wasn't a better man for the job. In typical Shelby fashion, Carroll told me, "Lee you can't make a racehorse out of a mule." But I knew he couldn't resist a challenge.

Carroll was a dear friend of mine and, as great as the Mustang was, he helped us deliver a Mustang performance image. What he built symbolizes all that is great with this country. Hard work and shooting straight is the key to success. People are smart, they see through hype and empty promises. Carroll was larger than life, with charisma and swagger. He made big promises but he always delivered on them. And, that's what made him great. Under that Stetson was a man who embodied the American Dream.

My years as General Manager and President of the Ford Division were challenging and some of the happiest years of my life. I was at the helm of the company everybody else was chasing. I owe thanks for a big part of that to Carroll and his Shelby Mustang. Carroll helped us build a brand with longevity and a loyal following that is unmatched. It warms my heart that Colin Comer, another one of Shelby's friends, is here to give this well-deserved tribute to Carroll and his Shelby Mustang. I'm as proud today as I was 50 years ago to call Carroll Shelby one of my best friends. This one is for you, Carroll.

Lee Iacocca

Lee Iacocca
April 2014

Introduction
The Birth of the Pony Car

Ford's Falcon was an exceptional appliance. Introduced in 1960, it was a sturdy, reliable, inexpensive, and extremely economical compact car that did everything that was expected of it—that is, as long as you simply expected it to get you from point A to point B. It might be fair to say the only people who truly loved the Falcon were Robert McNamara (the Ford general manager who fathered the Falcon), Henry Ford II, and Ford's corporate bean counters. After all, the Falcon, while inexpensive to buy, was even cheaper to build. And build them Ford did, by the millions. The Falcon handily outsold every other compact car on the market at that time.

But simply selling a lot of Falcons didn't satisfy Ford Vice President Lee Iacocca. He knew Ford needed something different from what was offered by anyone else to capture the attention of the emerging baby-boom market. They needed a car that these young buyers could not only afford, but also relate to, a vehicle with which they could make a personal statement. They didn't want four-wheeled appliances like the soulless Falcon or their parents' cars; they wanted something that stood out. Something young, energetic, exciting. Iacocca was quick to identify this market, and along with Ford Product Planning Manager Don Frey, set out to build a Falcon-based sporty car that would become not only the first Pony Car, but also a pop culture phenomenon. That car, while nothing more than a Falcon under its sexy new sheet metal, was the Mustang.

The Mustang's legendary story is often told, one of the few that is actually bigger than even the most creative marketing hyperbole can convey. Ford had hoped to sell 100,000 Mustangs in their first year of production. The Mustang was introduced on April 17, 1964, and Ford received orders for one-quarter of that 100,000-car goal on that first day alone. By the end of the first year of production, more than 400,000 had been sold, making the Mustang's inaugural year one of the most successful in automotive history.

Mustang sales remained on fire, with credit going not only to Ford's impressive marketing skills, but also to the variety of Mustangs Ford offered; Ford produced the Mustang in coupe, convertible, and fastback body styles. Ford kept the Mustang's standard features to a minimum, thereby holding its base price at a level that made it possible for almost anybody to justify buying one. The real magic, especially when it came to Ford's profit margin, involved the Mustang's extensive options list. While it was possible, rarely did anybody drive out of a Ford dealership with a base model, no-option Mustang; if they did, it was certainly a loss leader unit for Ford. By allowing buyers to build their own unique Mustang, selecting everything from powertrains right through light-up "Pony Corral" grille badge surrounds, Ford catered to a buyer's every whim and also got into the ever-profitable options business.

But as successful as the Mustang was in its first year, there was one very influential segment of the car-buying population that wasn't exactly head over heels for Ford's new Pony Car: power-hungry gearheads. The dyed-in-the-wool car guys saw through the sharply creased designer suit the Mustang wore and recognized the chassis' humble beginnings as the econo-compact Falcon. While Ford was selling every Mustang it could build, a dark storm was brewing—the Mustang was gaining a reputation as a "secretary's car," a car purchased by a buyer more interested in looking sporty rather than in driving in a sporting fashion. Of particular threat was another genre born just months before the Mustang and was taking off like a Saturn rocket: the newly minted muscle car. As good as the Mustang was, even in its highest tune with the solid-lifter 289-cubic-inch "Hi-Po" V-8, it was no match for the likes of Pontiac's new GTO.

Thankfully, Ford was quick to recognize that unless they gave the Mustang some teeth—and did so quickly—it could very easily become last year's fashion accessory rather than a model line that would endure. The Mustang needed the kind of street cred that only comes from kicking ass and taking names. And they knew just the guy to help get the secretary's car there—the same guy who had been giving the sports car world a proper flogging with Ford power for the past few years in his Cobra sports cars: Carroll Shelby.

If you are holding this book, I bet you know what Ol' Shel did for the cute little Mustang. He took off everything it didn't need and added what it did: attitude. By turning simple K-code Mustang fastbacks into all-conquering Sports Car Club of America (SCCA) B Production racers that could also sport license plates, he created a legend, and in the process literally saved not only the Mustang, but also himself. How? The Shelby Mustang created the performance halo the Mustang sorely needed, and in the process turned Shelby American from a small boutique sports car builder into a bona fide automobile manufacturer. While Shelby American produced a total of just 998 of its legendary Cobras from 1962 to 1967, from 1965 to 1970 there were almost 14,000 Shelby Mustangs produced. Shelby Mustangs, over this original five-year span of production, defined high performance.

So strong was this performance image that it only snowballed when the original Shelby Mustang production era ended after the 1970 model year. When buyers could no longer purchase new Shelby Mustangs, values of used ones began to creep up as they gained cult status and became sought-after collectibles. Owner's clubs were formed in these pre-Internet days to network and help preserve these prized automobiles. And while Carroll

Shelby went off to other projects, even following Iacocca over to Chrysler for a stint, Ford never forgot the magic that Shelby Mustangs created. So after over three decades of no new Shelby–Ford projects, Ford and Carroll Shelby were back together, and in 2006 the Shelby Mustang returned. Even though we lost Carroll in 2012, his name and his quest to kick serious ass live on in the Shelby Mustangs of today. For example, 700-plus horsepower Ford Shelby GT500s with world-class handling and braking that even 'Ol Shel couldn't have dreamed of are available right off the showroom floor. With a bumper-to-bumper warranty to boot!

Shelby Mustang celebrates the car and the people who made it happen and also those who keep the Shelby Mustang and its legend alive today. This isn't about the nuts and bolts of the cars; it isn't intended to be a boring textbook account of every part number or tune-up specification known for Shelby Mustangs. These cars deserve more than a dry regurgitation of the same old facts and figures.

Instead, with *Shelby Mustang*, my goal is to take you, the reader, deep into the world of the Shelby Mustang and introduce you to people you may not know but should. To show you the passion that people have for these fantastic cars, the lifestyle, and even Shelby Mustang memorabilia. To look back and see, all these years later, that the prom queen and king are still together, and to find out just what their family is like. It's a hell of a story. From humble economy-vehicle beginnings emerged cars that are far more than the sum of their parts. It is that rare blend of ingredients, people, luck, and success that somehow makes magic. And that, as much as horsepower, is what truly makes Shelby Mustangs and all that surrounds them kick ass. Ready to dig in?

Turning a Gelding into a Stud

Before we get into what Carroll Shelby did for the Mustang, we need to look at why it was Carroll Shelby who did it. Most of you know the story, so we'll paint it only in the broadest strokes here. The bio is one you almost certainly know. Born January 11, 1923, Carroll Hall Shelby enlisted in the US Army Air Corps, later known as the US Air Force, served as a pilot and flight instructor during World War II, and dabbled in a few businesses after the war, including his infamous stint as a chicken farmer. He soon became bored with his post–fighter-pilot life. Since there wasn't much call for flying fighter planes in civilian life, he chose the second best option and decided to race cars.

At that time, hot sports cars from England dominated amateur sports car road racing in the United States. Shelby first raced in 1952, driving a borrowed MG TC. From the start he knew that racing cars was the perfect drug with which to appease the fighter-plane monkey on his back. Displaying impressive raw talent, Shelby achieved considerable success with the underpowered TC and soon earned a place behind the wheel of a Jaguar XK-120 and then an Allard J2. Sydney Allard's J2 was a hybrid of Allard's own cycle-fendered sports car and an American V-8 engine. Allard purchased V-8 engines from various sources, but the J2 that Shelby drove had THE engine of choice under its hood: a 331-cubic-inch Cadillac. The Cadillac-powered Allard and Shelby's natural driving ability combined to earn the Texan a first-place finish at an SCCA event in Caddo Mills, Texas.

More importantly, the J2 showed Shelby the potential of mounting an American V-8 lump under the hood of an agile British sports car. Shelby went on to race—and win— in Aston Martins, Austin Healeys, Maseratis, and Ferraris. Shelby won the 1956 SCCA National Championship and was named Sports Car Driver of the Year in 1957 by *Sports Illustrated*. On June 24, 1959, Shelby and co-driver Roy Salvadori took first place at the 24 Hours of Le Mans in an Aston Martin DBR/1.

Snakes on a Track

But the idea of a V-8–powered sports car kept percolating in the peripheries of Shelby's consciousness. He kept his foot in the business end of things, opening a car dealership, Carroll Shelby Sports Cars, in Dallas in 1957. The business side became more important in 1960, when Shelby began to experience chest pain. Shelby had been diagnosed with heart valve leakage at the age of seven. By his teenage years, Shelby's heart condition was thought to have disappeared, but in 1960 it resurfaced. Shelby was diagnosed with angina and advised by his doctor to stop racing for good. He last raced in the *Los Angeles Times* Grand Prix at Riverside Raceway in California in December 1960, winning that year's USAC Championship in the process.

After he stopped racing, Shelby started the Carroll Shelby School of High Performance Driving at Riverside International Raceway in California. But teaching aspiring race drivers was just a pastime to keep him occupied until he could realize his true ambition: building his own car. He knew the basic formula: combine a proven chassis with a powerful and reliable American V-8. Now all he needed was a car and an engine.

Shelby approached General Motors about the possibility of using Chevrolet's compact small-block V-8, but GM management viewed Shelby's project as a direct competitor with Chevrolet's Corvette—which, of course, it was. Likewise, Donald Healey refused to sell Shelby rolling chassis for his new sports car because he feared it would best his Austin-Healey sports cars in competition—which, of course, it did.

Ford Motor Company's early V-8s were no match for the fast-revving, lightweight Chevrolet small-block, but in 1962 Ford introduced its new Windsor V-8, a lightweight, 221-cubic-inch engine that was a potential match for the Chevy small-block. While Ford brought V-8 power to the masses with its flathead in 1932, the company was slow to develop a competitive overhead-valve V-8. The original Y-block design was primitive at best, and while the FE engines that replaced the Y-blocks in 1958 used more efficient designs, they were heavy and slow revving. Though Shelby would later put the big FE to good use in the coil-spring Cobras and Shelby GT500 Mustangs, he had no interest in the design for his lightweight sports car. The new Windsor design, however, looked very promising. Shelby contacted Ford's representative for competition engines, Dave Evans, who assured Shelby that the Windsor engine had been extensively tested and had lots of room left for future development. Evans arranged for Shelby to receive two experimental 221 Ford V-8s.

By that time, Shelby had a chassis in which to put those engines. He'd learned that the Bristol Aeroplane Company had ceased selling engines to the AC Car Company in England, leaving AC with a surplus of Ace sports car chassis. The Ace was a stout, good-looking, and

continued on page 18

ABOVE: Factory PR shot of the prototype Cragar/Shelby mag wheel. Note the center cap.

BELOW: A later Shelby PR photo showing the final version of the optional Cragar mag wheel with finished center cap.

TRACK TEST: SHELBY AM

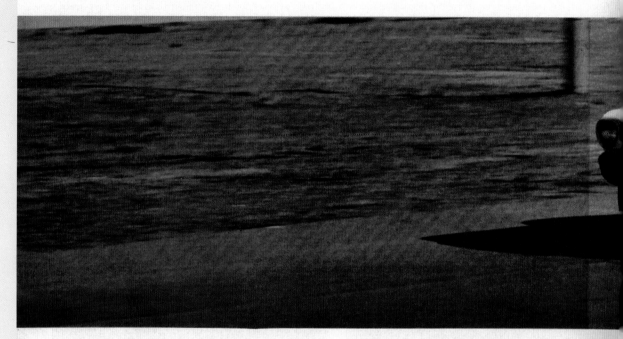

BY JERRY TITUS

Shelby converts the Ford Mustang into a fierce charger for International competition!

Shown in various attitudes on the Willow Springs course, the third and final prototype of the GT350 is close to production form. The vent ducts in the fastback roof will be blanked off only on the competition version. Light and easy to control at maximum speed, the car exhibits slight understeer on high-speed bends.

IN THREE SHORT YEARS, Shelby-American has progressed from a rented stall in Moon Equipment's shop to a monster facility on the grounds of Los Angeles Int'l Airport — a parcel so vast that North American used to assemble their Saberliners there, until the contract ran out. It will now be used for the assembly of the "427" Cobras and the Mustang GT350. Shelby's alliance with Ford Motor Company has been a successful one for both concerns. The bib-overalled chicken-farmer put far more teeth in Ford's "Total Performance" theme than any other competition ventures. In turn, he is being given a bigger and bigger slice of the performance pie.

The story of the Shelby-ized Mustang GT350 started many months ago and reached a climax when SCCA recognized it as a Production Sports Car, assigned it to Class B. Familiar with some of the circumstances surrounding homologation of the original Cobra, we suspected 'Ole Shel' had pulled another slickie. The normal production Mustang is a Com-

pact. SCCA didn't buy it quite that way, either. They would only accept it as a sports car *IF* 100 chassis were built by last January 1st that were decidedly special two-seaters, sold as an individual model, and delivered in raceable form. Knowing that Shelby had committed himself to a new model Cobra and the Ford GT (see page 50-53), we figured he'd at last backed himself in a corner, and were wondering how he was going to get out. The answer came as we were driving down the freeway in mid-December and passed a whole caravan of transports, each loaded with white, fastback Mustangs, all missing hoods and in semi-stripped form. They were headed for the Venice, Calif., facility. Ole Shel had taken over the San Jose assembly line for a couple of days. Numbering well over 100, these cars were more than enough to convince the SCCA that Carroll wasn't kidding. Had they tested a prototype as we did, they'd have been even *more* convinced.

Development of the GT350 has more-or-less become the "baby" of

58

Jerry Titus' track test of the new GT350 Competition model in the March 1965 *Sports Car Graphic* really helped put Shelby's new Mustang on the map. The car Titus used was 5R002. He was joined by Ken Miles. Note all of the prototype features on 002 that never saw production.

RICAN MUSTANG GT350

PHOTOS: DARRYL NORENBERG

MUSTANG

an English immigrant (now a citizen) alternately known under such aliases as "The Beak," "The Hawk," and "The Flyin' Limey"—Ken Miles. A Shelby employee for over a year now, he brings to the organization as much, if not more, road-racing savvy than any other man on this continent possesses. His official title is "Competition Consultant," but he wears a couple of other hats, too; he goes like hell in any kind of race car, and is a recognized suspension set-up artist. The latter two talents have been well applied to the Mustang GT350, as we had ample opportunity to discover during a track test on the challenging Willow Springs circuit.

With a high center of gravity, a butt-headed silhouette, a theoretically unsophisticated suspension system, a heavy forward weight bias, and a pot full of other limitations when considered as a race car, the Mustang is no "piece of cake" to convert to such an application. However, there are a bunch of imported sports cars with the same limitations, so Miles had plenty of experience to draw on, combined with many of the recent developments to come out of Shelby-American as a result of their intense racing and research programs. While held to the basic Mustang configuration, their hands were relatively free to alter as they saw fit. After all, it *was* to be a separate model. Cost was a primary consideration, as they hope to hold the price of the street version to under $4,000 and the ready-to-race machine to under $6,000.

The first move was to reduce the weight. Replacing the rear seats and upholstery with light pressed-paper trim, and having the racing model assembled in San Jose less all sound-deadening and undercoating, amounted to a huge chunk. In the racing version, the side windows are replaced with pull-up plexi-glass units and all the internal regulator mechanism removed. The hood is duplicated in fiberglass, as is the rear bumper. The front bumper is removed and the gravel guard behind it is replaced with a reshaped fiberglass covering that greatly increases air intake to the radiator. The small and somewhat functional vents in the fastback are removed and blanketed out via a fiberglass insert. These fancy little grill assemblies weigh 14 pounds each. The front seats are replaced by glass buckets, very light and efficient ones that retain the adjustment tracks.

(continued on page 75)

Ken Miles buckles up, well supported by the fiberglass bucket. Wood-rim steering wheel and special instrument panel will be part of the special Mustang package.

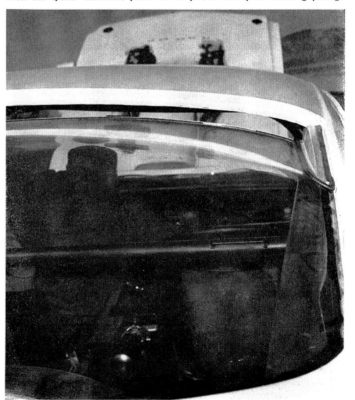

Rear window has been bent at top to allow an air-gap for ventilation on the competition model, also reduces some drag and turbulence in the rear section of the car.

SHELBY MUSTANG

With just about the maximum in weight-saving accomplished, it was then necessary to put pounds back into the car in the form of competition options. The street car will have six-inch rims on steel wheels. The race car uses seven-inch wide magnesium wheels. Both are 15 inches in diameter. Goodyear 6.50/6.70 "Red Dots" are mounted for competition. Brakes are disc in front and 10 x 2.5 drums in the rear. These are borrowed from bigger cars in the Ford family. The live rear-end is of Galaxie derivation, with limited-slip and heavy-duty axles. The street model gets an "export" or heavy-duty radiator. The racing version uses a Galaxie HD/Air Conditioning radiator with a very large oil cooler mounted directly behind it. Both have the Mustang HD suspension, with an extra fat front sway bar and Koni shocks. For better rear-axle control, the race car has special radius rods or torque arms in the rear that run above the leaf springs and into the unitized body near the front pivots of these springs. For better geometry in the front, the inner pivot points of both upper and lower control arms are altered — the top arm lowered and the lower arm moved outboard. Despite these additions, the racing model tips the scales at a mere 2153 pounds.

The 289 Hi-Performance Fairlane is the powerplant in both models, but the racing version is a hand-assembled unit with a special camshaft; roughly the same except for a grand's worth of tender, loving care that net it a 20-percent increase in performance. Both use the new Holley four-barrel with a special intake manifold. A very efficient set of side-routed headers are used for racing. The competition engine has a large, steel sump, the street version a cast-aluminum pan with extra capacity and big fins. Both connect to Ford's close-ratio four-speed transmission.

About the only item not finalized at test time was the configuration of the intake scoop in the hood. It will be a reversed scoop that draws high-pressure air from forward of the windshield. Just how big and how far back it will be is what's yet to be decided. Attention to the interior of the car is elaborate. To assure proper ventilation on the racing machine, air is drawn in through the small grille just below the windshield, through the plenum chamber normally used for the heater. To get it OUT of the car, the rear window is heated and allowed to droop down above the transverse centerline. Thus it leaves a two-inch gap at the top, right where boundary air coming over the roof will draw it out, cutting drag and reducing turbulence in the process.

While a centrally-mounted tachometer is the only addition to the street model's dash, the race car gets a complete panel of new and business-like instruments. In addition to the bucket seats, this model also comes equipped with a rollbar, seat belts and shoulder harness. Again, the street car has the production bucket seats and the majority of trim intact. It does, however, have the rear seating blanked off and the spare tire mounted atop it.

Ken Miles, Bob Bondurant, and this writer took the prototype race car to Willow, combining a six-hour, 'let's-see-what-breaks' run with our test. For the type of car, Willow is one of the least advantageous circuits. If it looked good here, it would almost anywhere. Miles suited up and proceeded to tour around holding a roughly 6000-rpm redline, to get time on a fresh engine. Except in a tight, uphill switchback, the car looked to be every inch a thoroughbred. It tended to tail-wag in that particular segment, but so do the vast majority of cars. What really impressed us was that Ken was soon turning 1:40's — faster than the existing A-Production times, with the exception of the Team Cobras. He handed over to us and we were turning 1:41's within four laps. We were impressed, and plenty. While the optioned production Mustang is a VERY strong understeerer, the Shelby car very lightly understeers and is quite easy to bring to dead neutral or even to a slight oversteer. Except for braking IN a turn, it is an embarrassingly simple car to drive at competition speeds. Under full power, it uses quite a bit of road — a real drifter — but gets a surprising amount of bite when cornered in a neutral or closed-throttle attitude. The brakes work great in a straight line, but the tail-end is very sensitive if you try the same thing with the wheel turned. The ride is impressively soft, probably much of this due to the large tire cross-section, and the car negotiates rough surfaces with a minimum of skitterishness that would do credit to a very sophisticated racing machine. Only in the last few 'tenths' does the car take some getting used to. Still holding the revs down but using everything else, Miles clipped a 1:39.9 before we left. The run terminated about the fifth hour when an ominous howl developed in the rear end; the differential bolts had loosened, something a simple lock-tab arrangement will eliminate.

The Shelby American Ford Mustang GT350 has a bright future. It is really a fun race car and should prove equally enjoyable in street form. Class B-Production should be swamped by it and any stragglers in AP will be quickly gobbled up. Due to frontal area, it is doubtful that the Mustang will have as high a top speed as some of its competition — especially in FIA racing — but it's far from wanting in the acceleration department. If they can hold the price down to their target, Shelby will sell a bunch! ♣

One of the most effective changes Shelby made to the Mustang was the now-famous upper control arm drop. Devised by Ford engineer Klaus Arning, this simple modification alters the roll center and camber curve of the front suspension, transforming the "tippy toe" Mustang geometry into that of a performance car. But since most people have no idea what this modification actually consists of here's a Shelby PR photo to help. Note the stock (Ford) holes where the upper control arm used to mount, and the 1-inch lower holes where the control arm is relocated to.

continued from page 13

(in the finest British tradition) underpowered sports car. Shelby had engines but no chassis; AC had chassis but no engines. No worries: snake oil was applied, resulting in negotiations going fairly smoothly, and Shelby soon had a steady supply of AC chassis at his disposal. Shelby shipped his two experimental engines to England, where they were tested in Ace chassis that had been modified to accept the Ford V-8.

The first test car, later numbered CSX 2000, arrived at Dean Moon's shop in Santa Fe Springs, California, on February 2, 1962. By then the original 221-cubic-inch Windsor had been punched out to 260 cubic inches by Ford. According to legend, the crew at Moon's shop had CSX 2000 ready to roll in less than eight hours, and on that same day they had the car out street racing.

The resulting car, the Shelby Cobra, proved so dominant in sports car racing that its success took even Carroll Shelby by surprise. From the first Cobra race car, which was simply a modified version of street chassis CSX 2002, the Cobra proved itself to be virtually unbeatable in competition, rarely losing any events in which they were entered. The entire world took notice, including the powers that be at Ford Motor Company.

Gelded Pony
When Ford introduced the Mustang in 1964, Ford was promoting itself as the "Total Performance" company. While the Mustang performed like no car before it in the sales charts, selling over one million units in its first 18 months, the car was lacking in the traditional sense of performance. The car was a nifty device for day-to-day transportation, but it didn't exactly make any serious performance junkies' red blood boil with excitement.

The Mustang contributed record amounts of money to corporate coffers but did little to enhance Ford's Total Performance image. And in the mid-1960s, performance equaled profit. Ford worried that Mustang sales would taper off once the novelty of its crisp sheet metal wore off. The company needed to bolster the Mustang's performance image, and bolster it fast. And the quickest way to improve the car's performance image was to go racing.

This task proved more difficult than it would seem, in hindsight, mostly due to the economy-car underpinnings of the Mustang. The main problem, from a racing standpoint, was the bargain-basement suspension, lifted directly from the Ford Falcon, that provided the car's baseline—part of the reason that Ford was able to offer such a low base price for the car.

Mustangs manufactured between April and July of 1964 are referred to as "1964½" cars. Officially they are 1965 models, according to Ford's records, and have 1965 serial numbers, but there are differences between a 1964½ and a 1965 car. As far as a performance freak was concerned, the main difference was that the top engine offering, which in the early cars was only a 210-horsepower, D-code 289-cubic-inch V-8; it was several months before the 271-horsepower K-code version of the engine was available.

But the Mustang did possess the most important—and hardest to attain—attribute of a race car: a low curb weight. The compact Mustang, which rode on a 108-inch wheelbase and measured just 181 inches long and 68.2 inches wide, weighed a mere 2,556 pounds in notchback coupe form. The fastback version that would form the basis of the original Shelby GT350 was a bit heavier, but still only weighed 2,606 pounds. To put that into perspective, the 2014 Mazda Miata, one of the smallest two-seat sports cars on the market, weighs 2,447 pounds, and a 2014 Mustang weighs a whopping 3,618 pounds. It costs a lot less to build up an engine and suspension for racing than it does to trim down excess flab, so right from the start, the Mustang intrigued racers.

Joe Mulholland, an engineer working for Ford, was one such racer. As an insider at Ford, he knew that the K-code engine was coming from the start. Within weeks of the Mustang's introduction, Mulholland was working his connections within Ford's product-development department and arranged to have a couple of production cars delivered to the Waterford Hills raceway in Clarkston, Michigan. His partner in this scheme was Ford Product Planner John Onken, who had been instrumental in developing the Mustang. The cars performed as well as could be expected of vehicles with suspensions from the

The company needed to bolster the Mustang's performance image, and bolster it fast.

The now legendary 1965 tachometer and oil pressure gauge. Spotter's tip: Reproductions abound today, but only the originals have the tiny checkered flag at the very tip of the "C" on the face; the reproduction ones are lacking this detail. *Road & Track/ Hearst Magazines*

This 1965 Ford PR shot is clearly using the GT350 to add some street cred to the standard Mustang in the foreground. After all, that was the original plan. *Road & Track/Hearst Magazines*

humble Ford Falcon—they were virtually impossible to drive. Australian racer Allan Moffat, who was doing the development driving, went off the track in nearly every corner. Moffat trashed both cars on the first day.

Though no single Mustang held up to the rigors of track use especially well, the brakes in particular proved problematic, overheating and becoming virtually useless almost immediately. The 210-horsepower D-code engine wasn't much better. In addition to being hopelessly underpowered, its carburetor design inhibited the flow of fuel under heavy cornering forces, stalling the engine.

Car Life magazine puts an early GT350 through its paces. At least this time they were flogging it on pavement. *Road & Track/Hearst Magazines*

While Peter Brock's wild Le Mans stripes were a completely new concept for a street car in 1965, today is there a more instantly recognizable car that a 1965 GT350 wearing them? *Road & Track/Hearst Magazines*

Grafting on a Pair

When developing the Mustang, Lee Iacocca had tasked Don Frey with creating a car that would appeal to women because of its cute looks and men because it was fun to drive. The experience at Waterford Hills had shown that while women might indeed dig the new Mustang's looks, men would be less enamored of its driving dynamics. Onken wanted to rectify that situation, but spending money to develop the Mustang as a performance car would be a tough sell at corporate headquarters. Fortunately, Onken had a better idea—sell performance as safety. Under the management of Robert McNamara, Ford had developed a reputation for building safe cars, so Onken would sell the company on developing a Mustang with "safer" handling.

Shelby's explosive growth meant they needed more space. The move to this facility at 6501 West Imperial Highway, with 12 acres adjacent to the Los Angeles International Airport, solved that problem. At least for a while. *Road & Track Hearst Magazines*

Onken's plan wasn't as hard a sell as he'd initially anticipated. Ford itself had decided to make a serious racing Mustang almost as soon as the car hit the showroom floor. Peter Proctor and co-driver Andrew Cowan won the touring-car class of the 1964 Tour de France, a grueling 5,000 mile, 10-day endurance event, in a T-5, which was the European name for the Mustang (the name *Mustang* being already trademarked by a heavy-equipment company). Winning some snobby European rally was all well and good and impressed the semi-soft cheese crowd to no end, but in its home market, it meant very little. The Mustang needed to earn its chops in the land of Velveeta, not the land of Camembert. The SCCA ran a popular production car racing series, a venue that would sell a lot more cars in the US market than any European rally. Ford needed the Mustang to race, or more precisely, the company needed its pony car to win races. The company decided to homologate the Mustang for SCCA B/Production competition, the same class in which Chevrolet's small-block Corvettes was racing, believing that beating GM's flagship sports car in B/Production racing would create instant credibility among buyers.

This assembly line photo shows just how labor intensive welding in the "over ride" traction bars was. *SAAC Archives*

continued on page 28

Take a 2+2, inject some Cobra venom, tone up the leg muscles, add lightness, and you get a...

MUSTANG GT·350

by John Ethridge, *Technical Editor*

Motor Trend wasn't going to ignore the new GT350 street car; they tested it for their May 1965 issue and came away quite impressed. The photos in these old road tests are priceless for us detail freaks, aren't they?

WHEN FORD DECIDED to go racing with the Mustang, they wisely first consulted their oracle for such matters, Carroll Shelby. Shelby's Los Angeles-based company, Shelby American, builds the all-conquering Cobras. Starting with the 1965 season, Shelby has taken over all Ford's road-racing operations. He knew that the first order of business was to get the SCCA to accept a raceable version of the Mustang in a competitive production sports car class. This was ultimately done (Class B), but with the stipulation that at least 100 more-or-less similar models of the proposed two-seater be built. Realizing that at first, anyway, they couldn't find 100 racing customers, they decided to make a street version as well.

Our test car was the street GT-350, which is the model most of Shelby's customers will order. Shelby receives the 2+2 semi-completed from the Ford assembly plant, and this forms the basis for either the street or competition car. Anyone who intends to drive on the street wouldn't want, need, or be willing to pay for the racing goodies and features of the competitive version. Gumball tires, magnesium wheels, oil cooler, plastic rear and side windows, gutted interior, and fiberglass seats are for the race course.

Although the most apparent difference between our test car and an ordinary Mustang is the absence of rear seats and the interior-mounted spare tire, the real difference is in suspension, engine, and weight. Between removal of the rear seats plus cutting and paring here and there, they've trimmed exactly 200 pounds off the weight of the Mustang 2+2 we tested in January. There are 35 more horses under the fiberglass hood, provided by a large Holley four-barrel carb on a special high-riser intake manifold, plus exhaust headers leading into twin pipes and straight-through mufflers.

Suspension has actually gotten the most attention of all. The words here are: control, limit, locate, stiffen, and snub. The Mustang performance handling kit springs are retained for use all around, but the shocks are special Konis. The rear axle got a pair of stabilizer bars, located above and parallel to the forward half of the leaf spring. Each chassis anchor for the bars appears to occupy what would've been part of any rear-seat passenger's anatomy with the standard 2+2 seats. This probably accounts for the absence of rear seats in the street GT-350. Rebound and jounce limiters complete rear suspension modifications.

Most noticeable change in the front suspension is a very substantial-looking anti-roll bar. The Shelby people tell us there are subtle changes in front suspension geometry, but we couldn't detect them by looking.

A weight-transfer program was carried out along with the weight-reduction program. Relocating the battery in the trunk and using the fiberglass hood were the major steps taken to reduce the proportion of weight carried by the front wheels. This permits use of the power-steering ratio in a manual setup. This improved steering transforms the car. It's wonderfully quick and light — even with the big tires.

When you start the engine, you're first impressed with a raucous note from the twin exhausts. These emerge just in front of each rear wheel. They're actually louder *inside* the car, because there's no insulation or undercoating. Not everyone will appreciate the cockpit noise and firm ride, but we're sure no enthusiast will ever complain. The engine's willing and responsive, and the carb/manifold setup hasn't made it temperamental in the least. Maybe it's just a bit cold-

PHOTOS BY PAT BROLLIER, DARRYL NORENBERG

AT NEAR MAXIMUM CORNERING CONDITIONS, THERE'S VERY LITTLE LEAN. BLUE SPOT TIRES STICK AND DON'T ROLL UNDER LIKE ORDINARY ONES.

STRONG LIMITED-SLIP DIFFERENTIAL LETS YOU LEAVE TWO LONG, BLACK STREAKS. BUT TOO MUCH WHEELSPIN WILL HURT ACCELERATION.

Big Holley carb's almost as long as engine block. Added cross-member triangulates engine bay, complicates rotor cap removal.

Custom wheel, designed especially for the GT-350, is sole accessory. Side exhaust's handy for issuing challenges at drags.

Spare perches atop aluminum panel where seats used to be. Tidy cover slips on for appearance. Panel won't support extra weight.

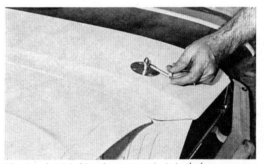

Fiberglass hood is hinged at rear and pin-latched same as racing stock cars. Airscoop actually admits air to the air cleaner!

BRAKES COULD HARDLY BE BETTER. THEY SIMPLY BRING THE CAR TO A STRAIGHT-LINE STOP IN A VERY SHORT DISTANCE, WITH NO WHEEL LOCK.

natured on cold mornings, but it warms up quickly and runs normally within a block or two.

Handling is much improved over even the handling-kit-equipped normal Mustang. The GT-350's best handling qualities won't show with half-hearted cornering, though. You have to corner hard enough to take all the slack out of the suspension in one direction. Then you get (on smooth surface) a sensation of superb stability, and you can feel the tires really bite. The GT-350, in fact, develops so much cornering force that the idiot light came on and the gauge wavered (it has both) on several occasions due to oil surge in the sump. You'd need some baffling if you drove this way regularly.

The car's still a basic understeerer, but nowhere near so much as the regular Mustang. Hard-over-to-hard-over maneuvers, as in a series of esses, produce the most noticeable handling peculiarity. Due to the high center of gravity, the suspension has to deal with some very high dynamic rolling moments under these conditions. When the body rolls from one extreme to the other, it tends to force the tail out momentarily. But with practice, we were able to smooth and tidy up our negotiation of esses considerably.

If you're looking for some justification or excuse for getting a GT-350, it gives very good gas mileage for such a high-performing car. Our best was just under 17 mpg when driving at steady legal speeds on freeways. The low, 11.2, came during performance testing. Average for our 900-mile test was 14 mpg.

The GT-350 is one car that'll never put you to sleep at the wheel. We recommend it as a sure cure for all strains of boredom. It positively exudes character — something rare in this day of follow-the-crowd compromises and design by large committees. The only really unpleasant moment we had with the car was when we had to give it back.

At present, you can have any color GT-350 you want, as long as it's white with blue trim. A no-cost option is 4.11 gears instead of the 3.89 set. The list of extra-cost accessories consists of a set of four custom wheels in place of the standard steel ones. The warranty is the same as Ford's for high-performance stuff: 4000 miles or 90 days. /MT

1965 MUSTANG GT-350
2-door, 2-passenger fastback coupe

OPTIONS ON TEST CAR: Custom wheels
BASE PRICE: $4547
PRICE AS TESTED: $4820 (plus tax and license)
ODOMETER READING AT START OF TEST: 2222 miles
RECOMMENDED ENGINE RED LINE: 6500 rpm

PERFORMANCE

ACCELERATION (2 aboard)

0-30 mph	2.7 secs.
0-45 mph	4.5
0-60 mph	7.0

PASSING TIMES AND DISTANCES

40-60 mph	2.9 secs., 215 ft.
50-70 mph	3.7 secs., 325 ft.

Standing start ¼-mile 15.7 secs. and 91 mph
Speeds in gears @ shift points

1st	56 mph @ 6500 rpm	3rd	108 mph @ 6400 rpm
2nd	82 mph @ 6500 rpm	4th	125 mph @ 6100 rpm
			(observed)

Speedometer Error on Test Car

Car's speedometer reading	32	47	53	64	74	85
Weston electric speedometer	30	45	50	60	70	80

Observed mph per 1000 rpm in top gear........................20.5 mph
Stopping Distances — from 30 mph, 24.5 ft.; from 60 mph, 140 ft.

SPECIFICATIONS FROM MANUFACTURER

Engine
Ohv V-8
Bore: 4.00 ins.
Stroke: 2.87 ins.
Displacement: 289 cu. ins.
Compression ratio: 10.5:1
Horsepower: 306 hp @ 6000 rpm
Horsepower per cubic inch: 1.06
Torque: 329 lbs.-ft. @ 4200 rpm
Carburetion: 1 4-bbl.
Ignition: 12-volt coil

Gearbox
4-speed manual, all synchro; floorshift

Driveshaft
1-piece, open tube

Differential
Hypoid, semi-floating
Standard ratio: 3.89:1

Suspension
Front: Independent SLA, with high-mounted coil springs, double-acting tubular shocks, and heavy-duty anti-roll bar
Rear: Solid axle, with semi-elliptic leaf springs, double-acting tubular shocks, control arms, and rebound straps

Steering
Recirculating ball and nut
Turning diameter: 39 ft.
Turns lock to lock: 3.7

Wheels and Tires
14 x 6.0 J, 5-lug, aluminum center, steel rim wheels
7.75 x 14 4-ply Goodyear Blue Spot tires

Brakes
Hydraulic, front, disc; rear, duo-servo
Front: 9.5-in.-dia. caliper discs
Rear: 10-in. dia. x 1.75 ins. wide
Effective lining area: N.A.
Swept drum area: N.A.

Body and Frame
Unitized; bolt-on front fenders
Wheelbase: 108.0 ins.
Track: front, 56.0 ins.; rear, 56.0 ins.
Overall length: 181.6 ins.
Overall width: 68.2 ins.
Overall height: 52.2 ins.
Curb weight: 2800 lbs.

Cobra steering wheel, oil pressure gauge, and tachometer are added. Horn is on dash.

Heart of suspension modification is rear stabilizer bar, Koni shock, and cable strap.

Relocated battery has tray and drain, but sloppy service attendants could fault it.

ABOVE: Supercharging was an idea tried very early by Shelby. The first GT350 to receive boost was 5S010. Pictured is the unique one-off carburetor pressure box fitted to 5S425, another prototype Paxton car. *SAAC Archives*

OPPOSITE: Shelby American rightfully used every GT350 race win to their advantage for marketing.

continued from page 23

Ford needed to turn the Mustang into a genuine competitor for the Chevrolet Corvette, which was a tall order. Jacques Passino, Ford's special products manager (which was code for "race manager"), looked into the matter of SCCA certification and tasked Ray Geddes with getting the SCCA to classify the Mustang as a "production racecar," but got nowhere. Geddes' background was in business—he had an MBA and a law degree— not racing. Overall, Geddes' presentation to the SCCA seemed not to have been all that well thought-out. For example, Geddes' crew seemed not to have realized that part of what qualified a car for sports car classes was that it only had two seats, and the Mustang, of course, had four. That gaffe alone was enough to keep the Mustang out of B/Production sports car racing. Lee Iacocca realized they needed to call in someone with some experience in this sort of thing, and they already had the best man for the job in their camp: Carroll Shelby. Using Ford's engines Shelby had already set the racing world on its ear with his Cobra, and this association thrilled Ford. With Shelby's connections within the SCCA, the road to homologation would undoubtedly be much smoother, not to mention faster.

IT'S WHAT'S UP FRONT THAT COUNTS!

When you take half a Mustang and half a Cobra, power it with 306 Ford horses (350 in the competition version) and call it the G.T. 350, you end up with a power house from Shelby-American that's unbeatable...on the street or in competition. Take the Pomona ABC Production race on June 20...first overall. Take Elkhart Lake on the same weekend...first in B, fourth overall (the first three, all A Production, were Cobras). Let's take a look at just a small part of the record.

Location	Driver	Result
Kent	Titus	1st overall
Cumberland	Johnson	1st in Bp
Lime Rock	Johnson	1st in Bp
	Donahue	2nd in Bp
	Krinner	3rd in Bp
	Owens	4th in Bp
Willow Springs	Cantwell	1st in Bp
Mid-Ohio	Johnson	1st overall
Dallas	Miles	1st in Bp

G.T. 350 STREET VERSION SPECIFICATIONS Shelby-American prepared 289 cubic inch O.H.V. Cobra V-8 engine equipped with special high riser aluminum manifold, center pivot float four barrel carburetor, hand built tubular "tuned" exhaust system featuring straight through glass-packed mufflers, finned Cobra aluminum valve covers, extra capacity finned and baffled aluminum oil pan; fully synchronized Borg Warner special Sebring close ratio four speed transmission; computer designed competition suspension geometry; one inch diameter front anti-roll bar; fully stabilized, torque controlled rear axle; 6½" wide wheels mounted with Goodyear high-performance low-profile tires; Kelsey Hayes front disc brakes; wide drum rear brakes with metallic linings; competition adjustable shock absorbers; integrally-designed functional hood air scoop; competition instrumentation including tachometer; racing steering wheel; rear quarter panel windows; rear brake air scoop; competition seat belts; 19:1 quick ratio steering.

G.T. 350 COMPETITION VERSION Additions to the street version include: Fiberglass front lower apron panel; engine oil cooler; large capacity water radiator; front and rear brake cooling assemblies; 34 gallon fuel tank, quick fill cap; electric fuel pump; large diameter exhaust pipes; five magnesium bolt-on 7" x 15" wheels, revised wheel openings; interior safety group including roll bar; full Shelby-American competition prepared and dyno-tuned engine; every car track-tested at Willow Springs before delivery.

SHELBY G.T. 350

Contrary to popular belief less than half of all 1965 GT350s received the optional Le Mans stripes at the factory, but here's a photo of one that did. Just think—this entire job was likely completed in less time than most restorers today take to carefully measure where the tape should go. *SAAC Archives*

It was a big job, but big never worried Shelby. The man was a Texan, after all.

To put it mildly, Carroll Shelby had doubts about taking on the racing Mustang project. In fact, as Shelby recounted, when Iacocca asked him to "tighten up" the Mustang Shelby's response was "Lee, you can't make a race horse out of a mule." To which Iacocca apparently responded with "I didn't ask you to do it; you work for me."

From Shelby's perspective, he was busy dominating racetracks around the world with his Cobras, in the process getting long-dreamed-of vengeance against his (and Henry Ford II's) arch nemesis, Enzo Ferrari. His Daytona Cobra Coupe race cars were well on their way to beating the dominant Ferraris and winning Shelby a world manufacturers' championship. But Shelby had the necessary connections to make the Mustang production racer happen. He knew SCCA Executive Director John Bishop, and he knew how to grease the proper wheels. Besides, Shelby owed Ford a favor—the company had sold him competitive engines that made the success of his company possible, something General Motors had been unwilling to do. In late July 1964 Shelby agreed to take on the project and get Ford's cute little secretary's car racing. It was a big job, but big never worried Shelby. The man was a Texan, after all.

Shelby took a different approach than Ford had. As one of the largest corporations in the world, Ford was used to telling others what to do, and that approach hadn't worked with the John Bishop. Bishop knew Shelby, and Shelby knew Bishop, which meant that Shelby had the sense to ask Bishop what he needed to do to make the Mustang qualify for the B/Production class. When Ford told Bishop that it intended to race the Mustang, Bishop had responded with a firm "no." When Shelby asked, Bishop answered: get rid of the back seat. For SCCA homologation of this new Shelby Mustang for the 1965 racing season, Bishop said, the car had to be a two-seater. The SCCA mandated that a production car could have its suspension or engine modified for racing, but not both. This led to Shelby's decision to use the new 2+2 fastback Mustang with Ford's excellent K-code, 271-horsepower, solid-lifter 289 engine as his starting point. He would modify the suspension and chassis but leave the stock K-code alone with the exception of bolt-on

parts. Most importantly, Shelby would have to produce 100 production-version cars ready for inspection by January 1, 1965. Bishop believed this would be an impossible task, but he had no idea how motivated Ford was to make this happen. Plus he should have known better than to underestimate Shelby.

Important decisions about what kind of car they needed to build had to be made quickly. Shelby knew he could never sell 100 pure racing cars, so he decided to build a street version of the car; for the race version, they would just modify the engine to race specs. This decision made perfect sense because Ford would have to warranty the street version: with stock Ford running gear it was no more of a risk than a standard Hi-Po Mustang. Shelby would give the cars racing suspensions that he would warranty himself. After meeting with Bishop, Shelby presented this plan to Iacocca, who approved what was then known as the "Mustang-Cobra program," and both Ford and Shelby got to work.

Doesn't the fellow on the balcony bear an uncanny resemblance to Peter Brock? Hmmm. *SAAC Archives*

ABOVE: This poor model appears to have broken down in her GT350 at LAX. Good thing it looks like she is parked right behind Shelby American. *SAAC Archives*

RIGHT: Maybe our model is smiling because all it took was a quick gapping of the ignition points to get her GT350 up and running? *SAAC Archives*

The Mustang, in stock form, was a less-than-inspiring track car, but with simple modifications it became quite competent. Shelby estimated the costs of converting the Mustang into a serious racer and told Iacocca that development would probably cost about $15,000. In August 1964 Ford sent Shelby two notchback Mustang coupes. That was the good news. The bad news was that Ford was providing him with $1,500 to develop the cars, rather than the $15,000 he'd requested. But Shelby had already proven himself to be one of the most resourceful people in automotive history and was not the kind of man to let something as simple as a lack of funds stop his project. He went to Goodyear and got $5,000 to help defray development costs, then went and got another $5,000 from Castrol.

A major reason why Shelby was able to work on such a shoestring budget was his arsenal of ace California "hot rod" mechanics and fabricators, including Phil Remington. It is one thing to build a pretty good production car, and it is not that much more complex to build a race car that isn't completely embarrassing. But to build a great car, a truly historic car that sets the world on its ear in both competition and road use, it takes more than just great marketing. It takes genius. A few manufacturers have stumbled upon this elusive quality that can turn an average product into one that keeps everybody else playing catch-up for decades. And that, essentially, is the core of the hot rod movement—and was Shelby's secret weapon. Combined with the incredible talent and mechanical aptitude of his drivers, such as Ken Miles, whether he wanted to or not Shelby had the right team to make the Mustang into a race car.

Shelby sent his English development driver Ken Miles to Willow Springs Raceway near Mojave, California, with instructions to develop a car that would stick like glue to the racetrack but wouldn't be unmanageable on the street, and to do this while keeping costs down. Miles rubbed many people the wrong way and is often described as "prickly," but he and Carroll Shelby were more than just employer and employee—they were friends. The man was instrumental in the success of Shelby's racing program. He'd begun his racing career on two wheels, racing motorcycles in England prior to

By June 1965 Shelby American's growth caught the attention of the *L.A. Times*, which commented that the 42-year old Carroll Shelby's enterprise had gone from $0 to $12.5 million in just three years. But, ever the conservative, Shelby made sure to tell them he expected to hit $100 million in sales by 1967.
Road & Track/Hearst Magazines

COBRA CREATOR—Carroll Shelby, one-time international auto racing star who built dream car into multi-million dollar success, sits atop his "empire" at new facility near L.A. Airport. Shelby American plant produces both the Cobra sports car and a special version of Ford's popular Mustang.
Times photo by Frank Q. Brown

When It Comes to Cobras, Call Shelby---a Real Charmer

BY BOB THOMAS, Times Auto Editor

HAS SUCCESS changed Carroll Shelby?

It is true that he doesn't wear the bib-type, farmer-style overalls that were his trademark as a racing driver anymore.

And he goes to a hair stylist now instead of a barber.

Otherwise, though, he's still the same affable, always grinning Texan who turned a dream car into a big business.

In fact, the Shelby story can be traced in the footprints left by the typical "overnight" business success that always seems to happen to the "other guy."

It began in Shelby's case with a one-man operation in a garage in a Los Angeles suburb that—if three years can be considered overnight — has mushroomed into a multi-million dollar Southern California automotive operation with enormous international impact.

Label it Shelby American, Inc., and it is the largest independent producer of sports cars in the nation.

Brand it Ford and it is second only to Chevrolet's Corvette in sports car assembly in the United States.

Despite the all-important significance of Ford Motor Co. in the Shelby story, it is still primarily a business explosion by one man. Carroll Shelby made it happen.

Shelby owns all of the stock in a company that manufactures the Shelby Mustang GT 350 and Cobra sports car

in addition to a line of high-performance parts at a new facility that borders the Los Angeles International Airport on the south.

Although the plant has been in operation for two months, it was shown to the public for the first time last week. By November, its production capacity should reach its maximum output of 500 units per month.

That figure is not large by Detroit's high volume standards, but it is significant both to Southern California's auto economy and sports car production internationally.

It also marks a three-year sales growth from $0.00 to $7.5 million—or, $12.5 million if all Shelby enterprises are included. The total is going up.

"I fully expect by the end of 1967 this will grow into a $100 million business," said the tanned, 42-year-old executive. He spoke with a disarming Texas drawl. "The market is here."

Shelby isn't bragging.

The man who once won international sports car racing's most coveted event — the 24-hour Le Mans enduro in France in 1959—shortly before he had to give up competition due to a bad heart, is not surprised by the proportions taken by his dream project. "I always felt the potential was there."

Shelby says that it was his idea and energy — not his money — that got things rolling.

"I had depleted everything I had," he

Please Turn to Pg. 9, Col. 1

World War II, before graduating to four-wheeled conveyances. Prior to emigrating to the United States, he worked for various British auto manufacturers, both as a driver and in the development of the cars and engines themselves, giving him loads of experience that would prove invaluable to Shelby. He came to the United States on a one-year contract as a service manager for a company called Goff Industries and ended up staying for the rest of his too-short life. He clearly liked life in the United States, judging by the fact that he quickly became a US citizen. He started racing MGs almost as soon as he got here, though his driving style was not what US racers were used to; he was thrown out of his very first race for "dangerous driving." He said he'd toasted the brakes, and while he didn't actually hit anything on the track, his careening around without brakes "looked very bad." His career only got better, and he came up through the ranks of American drivers with contemporaries like Dan Gurney and, of course, Carroll Shelby. In the process Miles earned a reputation as the consummate driver, and when Shelby began manufacturing his Cobra, Miles was his first choice for a development driver.

Shelby was a firm believer in press releases, and he did create some spectacular ones. Who could blame him? Shelby American was growing by leaps and bounds.

Though he didn't take up Shelby's offer until about six months after Cobra production commenced, Miles had played a critical role in turning the Cobra into a world champion racer, and his immense driving talents would prove just as important in the development of the GT350. Ford sent chassis specialist Klaus Arning to assist Miles and his co-driver Bob Bondurant. The crew worked well together and soon had the Mustang's suspension sorted to proper racing form. Toward the end of development Ford sent out a couple of prototype independent rear suspension units, but by that time Shelby's team had the live-axle rear end dialed in, and they performed as well as cars equipped with the much more expensive independent rear suspension units. Unfortunately Ford's Competition Department had already released a press statement saying that it would be selling 100 competition Mustangs equipped with independent rear suspension based on the GT40 it raced at Le Mans, though virtually no one gave this faux pas much thought when the final product was ready for public consumption.

The decision to go with a live rear axle was fine with Ford's bean counters, since Arning estimated that developing the independent system would cost upwards of $85,000. Instead, the axle they used came from perhaps the most pedestrian offering in Ford's lineup: the Galaxie station wagon equipped with a towing package. This axle setup also had Ford's largest rear drum brakes—10 inches in diameter—which proved much more fade-resistant than the stock Mustang brakes, especially after they installed 2.5-inch-wide sintered metallic brake linings. Best of all, this axle bolted right into the Mustang chassis with very little modification.

SHELBY AMERICAN, INC.

Shelby American, Inc., is the personification of the old American success story.

In slightly more than three years Shelby American has evolved from a single room garage operation into a sprawling, thriving business. Located on the south side of the Los Angeles International Airport, Shelby American is now the largest independent producer of sports cars in the nation.

Current manufacturing in the 96,000 square foot plant at the 12 1/2 acre airport facility includes 150 1966 Shelby GT 350's and 20 427 Cobras per month, in addition to a wide line of Cobra Hi-Performance accessory equipment.

Wholly owned by Carroll Shelby, the company was incorporated in March, 1962. It was originally located in Santa Fe Springs, Calif., and was later moved to Venice, Calif., in late 1962.

Shelby American moved to its present location, which has a production capacity of 500 units per month, in March, 1965.

Shelby American's marketing operation includes the franchising of its own nation-wide system of Shelby American Hi-Performance dealers, in addition to a newly instituted expansion program to include foreign markets.

The world-famous Shelby American Competition Department, which developed and raced the World Champion 289 Cobra, prepares new 427 Cobras and Shelby GT 350's for international and domestic road racing and currently handles development and racing of the 7 litre Ford GT prototypes for Ford Motor Company.

Public Relations Department, Shelby American Inc.
6501 West Imperial Highway, Los Angeles, Calif. 90009

CAR LIFE ROAD TEST

(Year) 1965   (Make) Ford
(Model) Mustang   (Style) GT-350

JUNE CL
FILE

SPECIFICATIONS

List price ....
Price, as tested $4311
Curb weight, lb 4584
Test weight 2790
  distribution, % 31/40
Tire size 55/45
Tire capacity, lb.@24psi 7.75-15
Brake swept area 381
Engine type .... V-8, ohv
Bore & stroke .... 4.00 x 2.87
Displacement, cu. in 289
Compression ratio 11.5
Carburetion .... 1 x 4
Bhp @ rpm 28.5 @ 5000
  equivalent mph 102
Torque, lb-ft 325 @ 3000
  equivalent mph 61

EXTRA-COST OPTIONS

Cast magnesium wheels.

DIMENSIONS

Wheelbase, in 108.0
Tread, f & r 56.5/57.0
Overall length, in 181.6
  width 68.2
  height 51.2
  equivalent vol, cu. ft 366
Frontal area, sq. ft 19.3
Ground clearance, in 5.5
Steering ratio, o/a 19.1
  turns, lock to lock 3.75
  turning circle, ft 38.0
Hip room, front .... 2 x 22
Hip room, rear .... n.a.
Pedal to seat back, max 43.0
Floor to ground 10.0
Luggage vol, cu. ft 5.5
Fuel tank capacity, gal 16.0

GEAR RATIOS

4th (1.00) overall 3.89
3rd (1.20) 4.67
2nd (1.62) 6.30
1st (2.36) 9.18

PERFORMANCE

Top speed (6100), mph 124
Shifts, @ mph (manual, auto)
  3rd (6100) 110
  2nd (6500) 82
  1st (6500) 56

ACCELERATION

0-30 mph, sec ....
0-40 .... 2.4
0-50 .... 3.6
0-60 .... 5.2
0-70 .... 6.8
0-80 .... 8.7
0-100 .... 11.2
Standing 1/4 mile, sec 19.0
  speed at end, mph 14.7
   90

FUEL CONSUMPTION

Normal range, mpg 12-16

CALCULATED DATA

Lb/hp (test wt) 11.0
Cu. ft/ton mile 157
Mph/1000 rpm 20.3
Engine revs/mile 2950
Piston travel, ft/mile 1410
Car Life wear index 41.6

PULLING POWER

Max. gradient, %
70 mph
50
30
Total drag at 60 mph, lb 133

SPEEDOMETER ERROR

30 mph, actual 26.4
60 mph 50.4
90 mph 75.1

(from R&T test data)

LEFT: These notes from *R&T*'s road test of a 1965 GT350 street car show numbers that may not be impressive today but they certainly were in 1965: 0 to 60 in 6.8 seconds, the quarter mile in 14.7 seconds, and a top speed of 124 miles per hour. *Road & Track/Hearst Magazines*

BELOW: Back in the day before these were $300,000 cars, some people didn't think twice about naming their GT350s . . . and painting said name on the side as the "Asphalt Angel" demonstrates. *SAAC Archives*

You too will get the girl, if you get a GT350 first. *Road & Track/ Hearst Magazines*

With the suspension dialed in, Shelby turned to the car proper. He ordered three white fastbacks. One car became the first prototype of the street version, and the other two became the first two production racers.

This new Shelby Mustang needed a name. Carroll Shelby has told the story many times of how the GT350 name came to be. Shelby wasn't enamored of the name "Cobra-Mustang" that Ford had been tossing around. Nor was he impressed with any other names that his team kicked around, like "Mustang Gran Sport" and "Skunk." In fact, he wasn't really concerned with naming the car at all, but Ford needed a name for legal and marketing reasons. According to Shelby, nobody could agree on any of the many names

By the mid-1970s a 1965 GT350 was just a used performance car, and why own a performance car you won't use? 5S301 is shown here at one of the first SAAC conventions tearing up the autocross course. *Jeff Burgy*

thrown about, and in one of numerous meetings held on the subject, Shelby, no doubt frustrated with corporate politics, turned to Phil Remington and asked him what the distance between the race and production shops at Shelby American was. Remington's response was "about three hundred and fifty feet," to which Shelby said, "That's what we'll call it—GT350." Shelby's reasoning for such a hasty decision? The name wouldn't make the car. In his exact words, "If it is a good car, the name won't matter, and if it is a bad car, the name won't save it." A generic alphanumeric name that signified nothing also had practical applications: Shelby could upgrade and improve the car whenever it wanted without having to change the name and let the competition know what it was up to.

When Shelby was looking to set the GT350 apart visually from a regular Mustang, one of the ideas floated was the addition of Thunderbird taillights. 5S010 was sent to Bill Stroppe for the installation of a pair to gauge reaction. Thankfully nobody cared for them so the idea was nixed.

5S346 shows off its properly detailed—and dead stock— engine bay.

A Stud Hits the Street

Shelby ordered 100 Mustangs from Ford's San Jose, California, plant. He had Ford build these Mustangs to his specifications. These cars, called knockdown units to signify that they were incomplete cars, were white fastbacks with black interiors: no hoods were fitted, and the entire rear seat assembly was deleted. Radio delete plates replaced absent radios. Secretary's cars need radios, race cars don't. Each car left the San Jose factory fitted with K-code 289 engines, Borg-Warner T-10M close-ratio four-speed transmissions featuring lightweight aluminum cases, Ford's heavy-duty 9-inch rear axle with 3.89:1 gears, 11.3-inch four-piston Kelsey-Hayes front disc brakes with semi-metallic pads, huge Galaxie wagon 10x2.5-inch rear drum brakes with special sintered metallic segmented shoes, and 15x5.5-inch heavy-duty Kelsey-Hayes stamped-steel wheels, the same wheels fitted to Ford police cars and station wagons.

Peter Brock: Shelby Mustang Memories

There are several things I remember about the GT350 program. Most I'm sure you've heard before, but the one that remains strongest in my memory is the time Lee Iacocca called Shelby, saying that his minions had called the SCCA requesting official approval of their new fastback Mustang as a "sports car" and it had been rejected. So Lido calls Shelby and asks, "What can we do?"

Carroll says, "Hang on a minute, Lee," and immediately calls John Bishop, the president of the SCCA, in Westport on the other line. Shelby had been a good friend with Bishop for some time, so he flat out asks what the problem is.

"Well, to begin with, Shel', it has four seats . . . that isn't in our definition of a sports car."

"Ah kin fix that," Shel' replies.

"How?"

"Well, how 'bout I build 'em here in Venice with my name on 'em? I'll just take out the rear seats. Would that work?"

"Sure," Bishop replies.

"Thanks, John. . . . I'll call you tomorrow so we can take care of the details. 'Bye."

Shelby gets back on the line with Iacocca and tells him, "It's OK now. . . the SCCA has accepted the car, but you'll have to let me build 'em here in California. When do you want to start?" And that's the way the GT350 contract came to Shelby. It turned out to be the biggest deal he ever did with Ford, and it must have taken all of one minute. That was Shelby, one of the most charismatic smoke-and-mirrors promoters in the history of racing.

Our job was to make the Mustang into a sports car—without spending too much money. Klaus Arning, Ford's suspension guru, came up with the simple geometric change in the front-end A arms and specified the Koni shocks, traction bars, Detroit Locker, and wider wheels and tires. The SCCA's rule for production cars was that you could change the engine specification or the chassis, but not both. We advised Shelby of the SCCA's allowable internal changes for engines, so he wisely made the obvious decision to modify the chassis and then had Ford include their special 271-horsepower Hi-Po 289 as the new GT350's standard engine.

Shelby brought in Chuck Cantwell to set up the production line and be the chief engineer on the program. I was responsible for making Ford's vanilla-looking Mustang into something with a Shelby sporting image. My only limitations were that it couldn't cost too much (more Shelby!). I redesigned the easily removable components—such as the hood, which I made in fiberglass to save weight and to which I added a hood scoop. Initially, I wanted to make the opening at the rear next to the base of the windscreen, for more intake pressure, but that idea was rejected for marketing purposes because it was common knowledge that hood scoops should face forward! I also designed the wheels—two versions—and the instrument pod that mounted to the dash. Again, cost limitations prevented the use of good material and those early vacuum-formed pods turned into potato chips in the sun in short order.

The most important design element was the GT350's racing stripes. Those were a direct copy of my '46 Ford high school hot-rod. Being a great fan of Briggs Cunningham's efforts as the first contemporary American to try and win Le Mans with his own team of cars, I'd painted my high school ride to match his Cunningham cars that had run in France in 1951. Adding the stripes completely changed the character of the Mustang and it's now been copied by every manufacturer that wants their production cars to looks racy. I hadn't originally planned the side stripes on the rocker panel but the car had to be identifiable as a Shelby from every angle and I found that solution to be the least obtrusive. For the '66 model year, I designed the brake scoops on the sides, but cost limitations prevented me from doing the internal portion of the scoops, which would have flowed air right down onto the brakes. Instead, the decision was made to use a tiny hole in the side panel with flexible tubing, which was ineffective. In the end, the race cars had to use fiberglass scoops under the body, which were ripped off whenever the car went off course.

We took out more weight by removing the quarter window vents and converting those to Plexiglas windows. The 1966 GT350 was my favorite Shelby, but I have to say some of the later Ford-designed variants, and Steve McQueen's '68 390 Bullitt coupe, were pretty slick! Again, due to budget restraints, the side scoops for the brakes were never completed as I had designed. I wanted to make some smooth internal ducting after a portion of the body was cut away to make the exterior scoops functional rather than just something that looked cool.

I really enjoyed driving the GT350s on track. Ken Miles and I spent a lot of hours out at Willow Springs with Chuck Cantwell and his crew refining the R Models. The changes we made were pretty simple but very effective.

It was a great era. Today the Shelby name is most remembered in conjunction with the Mustang simply because of the number of cars built and how Ford has continued on with the Shelby name. I'm very happy to have been a part of it.

—Peter Brock

ABOVE: Shelby American, as a small manufacturer, was still feeling its way with the inaugural GT350. One area where a lot of change occurred was in the steering wheel. Originally it was the same 16-inch unit used in the Cobra, with a chrome hub, but later became a more legroom friendly 15-inch unit with a few different designs and hubs, dictated by supply issues.

BELOW: And 5S410 shows off its wild Weber carburetion setup and over the top detailing. *Drew Alcazar*

Mustang-Cobra project engineer Chuck Cantwell, who oversaw the project at Ford, arranged for a few other unusual pieces to be mounted on the Shelby cars. Cantwell, who was chosen as project engineer by Geddes, had previously been an engineer with Chevrolet and came highly recommended. He was also an accomplished sports car racer. At the time, Cantwell was working with Geddes in Ford's Special Vehicle Department, and he knew what parts the Mustang would need, what parts were available in-house, and what parts would have to be sourced elsewhere. By the time he started working on the project, he'd developed a comprehensive list that proved invaluable in getting the car ready in the short time available. He gave the cars what was called the "export brace," a one-piece, forged-steel brace that replaced the standard two-piece, stamped-steel brace that tied the cowl panel to the rear of the shock towers to add even more rigidity, effectively triangulating the chassis in this flex-prone area. This part had been previously used on all export Mustangs—hence the name "export brace." He also equipped the cars with a "Monte Carlo bar," a rod that strengthened the chassis by connecting to the shock towers in the engine compartment, effectively linking the right and left fenders together.

Early on, Cantwell went to the San Jose assembly line where the Shelby Mustangs would be built and studied the process to determine what could be deleted on the assembly line to speed production and conversion and, of course, to save money. At the end of this visit, Cantwell filled out a very specific and very unique order sheet for the first three cars to be delivered to Shelby's facilities. Cantwell's visit to the plant served an additional purpose—it fired up the staff in San Jose about building Shelby GT350s. Management and assembly workers alike took a personal interest in the Shelby project, and they took pride in building a car designed to beat Chevrolet's Corvette.

Once at Shelby American, the front suspension upper control arms were lowered one inch by drilling two new mounting holes per side. Although the change was labor intensive, it corrected the absurd camber gain of the stock Mustang setup, as well as preloading the springs, effectively raising the spring rate and lowering the car. A special quick-ratio pitman arm for the steering box and corresponding idler arm delivered racecar-like reflexes. A 1-inch-diameter front anti-roll bar replaced the 1.8-inch-diameter stock Mustang bar. Koni adjustable shock absorbers, the premium aftermarket shocks of choice for racers of the day, were installed on all four corners. Limiting rear axle downward travel was deemed necessary due to the shorter length of the Koni shocks, so a simple

arrangement of one aircraft cable per side, looped around the rear axle tube behind the brake backing plate and attached to the body above, did the trick. To control rear axle tramp and wind-up under hard acceleration or braking, Traction Master over-ride traction bars were installed. This was an involved process that required the rear axle to be removed, brackets welded on, and then holes cut into the floor of the car for the installation of another set of brackets for the forward mount of the traction bars. While the rear axles were out, Shelby also installed Detroit Locker "No-Spin" differentials. The battery was relocated from the engine compartment to the right side of the trunk to get weight off the nose and into the rear of the car, which improved balance.

Great stance is crucial on a GT350, and 5S476 has it figured out. *David Newhardt*

continued on page 47

There is no question this design has stood the test of time. And, if you squint just a little bit at 5S549 parked on the tarmac of a Kansas airfield, you can almost imagine it is LAX . . . and 1965.
Roger Morrison

Chuck Cantwell: Mr. GT350

Eric English

Anybody who has been around Shelby Mustangs for any length of time likely knows of Chuck Cantwell, Shelby's project engineer for the Mustang program. Besides being one of the nicest, most sincere people I have ever had the honor of calling a friend, Chuck is also one of the most intelligent people on the planet. He remembers people, facts, engineering details, race-car setups, and the minutest details of events from 50 years ago like they happened yesterday. Chuck's mind is the proverbial steel trap, and that, combined with his hand in creating the Shelby Mustang, meant I had to sit down with Chuck and pick his brain for this book—for without Chuck Cantwell, there may have not been a 50th anniversary to celebrate.

Q: *Chuck, most people don't know this, but you are an accomplished sports car racer. How did that start?*

A: I grew up in Speedway [Indiana] near the Indy track and developed a love for the race cars and the excitement that came there in May each year. After a couple of trips to Elkhart Lake [Road America] in the early days, I saw sports cars as a way that I might go racing with limited resources. So in 1959, I joined SCCA, bought a used MGA, and started racing. In 1961 I bought a used 1600 MGA, raced that for two years, and then bought a new MGB, which I raced in 1963–1964. I finished second in the Central Division in 1961 and was Divisional Champion in 1962, '63, and '64 in F and D Production, respectively. I set a lap record in the MGA at Road America due to acquiring a good set of tires, and raced an Elva-BMW there in the 500-mile race. I also raced a one-liter twin-cam Fiat Abarth Zagato several times.

When I was at GM, my friend, coworker, and garage-mate Jud Holcomb also raced and we got a lot of support from the people there, mainly because they were all car and race fans. My first race in the MGA 1600 was 100 miles at the Elkhart Lake June Sprints and I had a very competitive race with three Porsches and a Turner, which I was winning until my brakes wore out at the very end and I ended up second. Competition pads weren't available then. But when I returned to work, I was rewarded with a "Hero Driver" banner.

Q: *So you had this great job at GM Styling, where you worked alongside some of the greats: Bill Mitchell, Chuck Jordan, Wayne Cherry, Larry Shinoda. GM was king of the world back then, so close to a monopoly of the market the federal government feared they would have to step in. Why would you leave?*

A: My good friend Sam Smith, a Chevrolet engineer, went to work for Ray Geddes at Ford Special Vehicles and had the job of liaison between Ford and Shelby on "this new Mustang program." Sam invited me to dinner and explained the new program and asked if I might be interested in being the project engineer on that effort. I was a racer, so I knew of Carroll Shelby—I figured it was worth investigating and I saw it as a challenge. I flew out to California and met with Shelby and Peyton Cramer. They offered me the job. I saw it as a huge risk, a big move, but it sounded exciting. I was quite apprehensive about it, truthfully, but I was growing bored at GM and thought the Shelby job was worth a shot. I actually felt a little proud that I was willing to take that chance.

Q: *The phrase "culture shock" springs to mind. California versus Michigan. Shelby American versus GM. How did it hit you once you were there?*

A: When I got to Shelby I quickly felt comfortable. There were a few mutual friends there, and while I didn't work at GM Styling with Pete Brock, we quickly hit it off at Shelby. John Morton was there, and I knew John from the SCCA Divisional races when he raced his Lotus Super Seven and I raced my MGB. He has always been a good friend. Even though it was a full house at Shelby, and there were some questions about this group of new guys arriving with this new project, everyone was basically helpful, though there was some occasional annoyance, especially when Jerry Schwarz used an air hammer to flare out the first R Models rear fenders near the race shop. Ultimately the Cobra racers accepted the "Mustang crew" when they learned we were really good guys and especially when Ken Miles won the GT350's first race at Green Valley. A lot of fun. I will say California is a lot different than the Midwest—the climate and the people! When I returned from my honeymoon at the beginning of 1965, Shelby told us we'd be working six days a week and 10 hours a day. That was quite the understatement. I was working nonstop and living in a hotel room for a few weeks. Nothing was open on Sunday, so I had no time to find anything else, but finally the Ford bean counters made me get an apartment. Of course it was unheated.

Q: *You worked a lot with Ken Miles, unquestionably one of the all-time great drivers and a skilled race-car builder in his own right. How was that?*

A: We spent a lot of time together at Willow Springs working on GT350 setups, tire pressures, alignments, all that. I'd ride around with Miles; it taught me the track really fast, and there are not many people I'd ever

ride in a race car with, but I trusted Ken completely. One day he said, "Why don't you just test the cars?" This was already my dream job, as a racer—driving the cars was just icing on the cake. I sure wasn't going to turn it down! But driving was never in my job description. I just took every opportunity to test and did get a lot of laps at Willow and Riverside. So I drove and my times at Willow were right with Ken's. Ken was a great guy. We had a lot of adventures together.

Q: *That reminds me of one of your Ken Miles in the airplane stories. Care to share the one about the landing at Willow?*

A: Oh, yes. That is one I will never forget. Ken had just gotten his pilot's license. The first time we took out Shelby's Cessna, Ken hit the wing on the hangar door at LAX. He taped it up and we proceeded out to Willow to test. On the way back, the LAX tower lost radar contact and he flew right across the active jet runway at LAX. But the second flight was better. We flew to Willow to do some testing, and there was a horrible crosswind along the straight where we were going to land. Ken shot an approach and aborted it, decided to land on a dirt strip we saw at the track. We touched down and somehow the plane got off into soft dirt and flipped up on its nose, and damaged the right wing. Ken went and tested the cars, blew both motors almost instantly—I think intentionally because he wanted to get back to the plane. He wanted to patch it up and fly it out of there. I said no way, not with me! So we decided to drive the plane down the highway, bent wing and all, a couple of miles to the nearest airport. Usually there was nobody on this particular road, but that day there were cars all over. Ken had the thing going about 35 or 40 miles per hour, and cars were diving for the ditch and scattering every which way. It was quite the adventure. I don't think Shelby ever did anything about it, other than cashing the insurance check.

Q: *How was Ford to work with? Did they care about Shelby as such a small-volume manufacturer, and were they willing to incorporate your ideas without a fight?*

A: Well, it was Iacocca's wish for this project to take place, and I don't think that Shelby particularly wanted to do it. But he owed Iacocca one for the support he provided for the Cobras. So Ford was supportive of the Shelby Mustang project. My first job at Shelby was to spend three weeks at Ford Special Vehicles with Sam Smith and Ray Geddes; I had to learn it all, the processes and how they needed to build the cars, what equipment we did or did not want on them, that sort of thing. We also had to be very mindful of honoring Carroll's deal with John Bishop of the SCCA and what Carroll told him we were building for B Production competition. As I mentioned, my good friend Sam Smith was there and we were always on the same page. Plus, everybody at Ford's San Jose plant was just great to work with. They really cared about what we were doing. Some R Models actually came through with notes from the workers encouraging us to beat those Corvettes.

Q: *You raced a lot of sports cars prior to coming to Shelby, and you were obviously a very accomplished driver by the time you drove that first GT350. What did you think of it as a race car?*

A: Before I tested with Ken Miles, the fastest car I had ever driven was that 2L Elva. The Shelby was a lot faster than that! I thought it drove really well, very well balanced. I was really surprised by the brakes; they were really good. I was shocked that a GT350 could out-brake a lot of lighter sports cars. Overall the GT350 was very confidence inspiring; they just didn't do anything silly if you knew how to drive.

Q: *So you tested a lot of competition cars at Shelby. Did you ever get to race one?*

A: I only got to race a few times while at Shelby. But the first time was a divisional race at Willow in July 1965, in a 5R002, which I won. As a result of that, I also got to practice at Daytona for the runoffs as an alternate and in the process provided a backup car for Jerry Titus in case it was needed. I also drove with Ray Wolfe in the Riverside Trans-Am race in 1966, where we DNF'd. But also in 1966, Don Pike, Dick Smith, and I won the Riverside six-hour race overall, each driving two-hour shifts and beating 427 Cobras, Corvettes, et cetera. The cars were very reliable and we ran trouble free.

Of course, I also tested most of the R Models and all of the Trans-Am cars we built for customers at Willow Springs prior to shipping them out to the customers.

Q: *Obviously you were the go-to guy for all the GT350 racers. I'm sure you have some stories about that.*

A: One story that jumps to mind is Mark Donohue at the ARRC race at Riverside in 1966 [racing 5R105]. He was running big rear tires and they told him he couldn't run because his rear wheel well openings were too large. Mark called me at Shelby in a panic. I told him to get me some measurements from his wheel wells. He sent them over, and I sketched up a drawing on blueprint paper with the Shelby letterhead that had dimensions to cover what Mark's car had. I put a Shelby engineering number on it, stamped it, roughed them up by rubbing my hands over the blueprints, and had somebody run over a copy to Mark at Riverside. The race officials accepted it and Mark was able to race. Of course, this was the famous race he was later disqualified from when his crew used a shot of ether on the grid [obtained from Rick Kopec] to restart the car before they were sent back out after a mid-race accident.

Q: *After 45 years of being "Mr. GT350," in November of 2009, you bought your first one, a Sapphire Blue 1966 GT350 (SFM6S796). Had you always wanted one, or after all this time did you just feel compelled to own one so you could finally tell your fans you, too, were a GT350 owner?*

A: I never needed to own one at Shelby; I could drive as many as I wanted! When I left there I was raising a family, working—it just never crossed my mind. But as the years went on and I started going to all the Shelby events, yes, I really started thinking about owning one of my own. My friend Stan had owned this one for many years and kept telling me I should buy it. We went back and forth for about a year and a half; he was a friend but a tough negotiator! I didn't really get excited about it, but once it was mine then yes, I got really excited, and all of my friends in the club were excited as well. When we went to pick the car up, everybody wanted to play with the car and finally I had to speak up and say, "Hey, can I get a look at it?"

Q: *796 had been in storage for many years, and you wanted to do as much of the renovation as you could yourself. After all these years, did it feel good to be playing with a GT350 again?*

A: I really enjoyed fixing it up. And I was shocked at how many people came out of the woodwork to help me do stuff and donate parts and their time. It brought back a lot of memories, but it was also very educational. I enjoyed the process, and learning how much work it takes to restore even the most basic parts, like the rocker covers. Plus, there is nothing better than working on your own car.

Q: *Now that your car is done, do you use it a lot?*

A: I try to. It is tough living where there is winter, but I drive it as much as I can. I've probably put a few thousand miles on it since it has been done. I drove it 800 miles to Virginia International Raceway and back. I run all the Northeast Cobra Club tours, drive it to all the local shows. Joanne [my wife] rides with me to almost everything. She really likes it as well and we are both very happy to have it. And my kids—D.C. and Carol—and their kids really like it, too. I guess I waited long enough.

Q: *You have done so much in your career—GM Styling, Shelby, Penske, Chilton, GE Aerospace, and Lockheed Martin, where you retired. The Shelby years were such a small slice of all of it, but looking back. how would you rate them?*

A: Working at Shelby was great; going from GM to this small company was something I really enjoyed. We all had a real sense of accomplishment. They were really fun years—great guys, all the racing. We all felt a part of the team and Shelby was really on top of the world back then. The Cobras, the Ford GT project, and of course the Mustang program. But by the end, I knew Shelby only had a year left on his Ford contract, and when the racing program with Ford wound down, the writing was on the wall, so I accepted a job at another small race team [Penske Racing]. But I wouldn't trade those years for anything; it was really exciting stuff and a tough act to follow.

continued from page 41

Another weight-saving measure was fitting a fiberglass hood, which featured a small scoop to get fresh air into the engine. Quick-release hood pins replaced the Ford hood latch mechanism, and the Mustang's grille "corral" went as well.

A fiberglass rear parcel shelf took the place of the Mustang's rear seat, and provisions were made to mount the spare tire on this shelf to center the weight and locate it directly above the rear axle. Further interior changes included a Peter Brock–designed gauge pod mounted to the center of the dashboard that contained a "CS"-labeled tachometer built by Delco for Shelby, with a matching CS mechanical oil pressure gauge next to it. This placed the gauges more directly in the driver's line of sight than if the gauges had been in the dash, behind the steering wheel. Besides, it would have taken Ford three years to design and produce a new instrument panel, and Shelby had just three months to procure 100 of them. Mounting the needed instruments in a pod that nestled in the center of the dash was a much more efficient solution.

Another angle that shows 5S549 doesn't look any part of her 50 years. *Roger Morrison*

5S003, the first Street GT350 prototype built, is shown here at the Quail Motorsports Gathering in 2010, sporting an older restoration to R Model specs . . . and then . . .

A flat, three-spoke, polished aluminum unit with a wood rim replaced the stock Mustang steering wheel. At first Shelby used the same 16-inch wheel fitted to the Cobra, but he later changed to a 15-inch version for more legroom. A nonfunctional "Cobra" center cap was fitted, necessitating the replacement of the horn button with a simple toggle switch installed in the dash to the right of the instrument cluster. Speed-rated 7.75x15-inch tires were specially engineered exclusively for the GT350 by Goodyear, based on their Power Cushion HP. The GT350 tires were identified by a 7⁄8-inch raised blue dot molded into the sidewall of the tire and were aptly named Blue Dot tires. They were mounted either on the standard Kelsey-Hayes steel wheels, painted silver, with no hubcaps or trim rings, only chrome acorn-style lug nuts adding an all-business look, or on optional 15x6-inch Shelby five-spoke alloy wheels, manufactured exclusively for the GT350 by Cragar.

Under the hood, Shelby did minimal upgrades to Ford's already potent Hi-Po 289 K-code engine. Out went the Ford cast-iron intake and Autolite 4100 four-barrel carburetor,

In 2014 5S003 emerged from a meticulous three-year restoration back to its 1965 prototype street trim at the 2014 Amelia Island Concours. *Jeff Burgy*

replaced by an aluminum "Shelby" high-rise dual-plane intake with a Holley 715-cfm vacuum secondary carburetor fitted with center-pivot "Le Mans" float bowls on top. Holley employee Harold Droste assisted Shelby in selecting the best carburetor for the car's intended purpose. In addition to adding power, the Holley carburetor solved the fuel-feed problem the stock unit experienced under heavy cornering forces because the center-pivot float bowls didn't hang up. Custom "tri-Y" design tubular exhaust headers replaced factory cast-iron exhaust manifolds, and a special free-flow exhaust incorporating glass-pack bullet mufflers, along with side-exiting tailpipes, took the place of Ford's traditional rear-exiting exhaust. A 6.5-quart, finned aluminum "Cobra" lettered oil pan, 30 percent larger than the 5-quart unit on the standard Mustang, featured deep baffles to keep oil from flowing away from the oil pump under hard cornering. Sand-cast ribbed aluminum valve covers that read "Cobra Powered by Ford" made the top end of the engine visually match the bottom end. Shelby advertised the horsepower of this hot-rodded version of Ford's 271-horsepower engine to

ABOVE: Faithfully restored with many prototype features duplicated after years of research by owner Mark Hovander, 5S003 is a significant car we are all happy to see in such good hands. *Jeff Burgy*

RIGHT: When new, Peter Brock drove 5S003 extensively during the six months it was at Shelby American. And in 2014 he got to drive it again . . . over the podium at Ameila Island. Chuck Cantwell, behind the wheel of 5R002, follows Brock. *Jeff Burgy*

The immaculate interior of 5S410.
Drew Alcazar

be 306 horsepower. Whether or not there was any accuracy to that claim, with the barely legal side exhaust bellowing below the passenger's ears it certainly seemed to have all of 306 horsepower, or even more, and you could damn sure hear every one of them.

Don "Sully" Sullivan, an engine engineer at Ford, designed the Shelby intake manifold, a free-breathing, dual-plane aluminum piece. Sullivan developed the manifold and sent the specifications to the Buddy Bar Casting Company, which also produced the sand-cast, Shelby-logoed aluminum valve covers and the aluminum deep-sump oil pan.

Shelby and Geddes tasked Peter Brock with designing the look of the car. Brock, a former General Motors designer and jack-of-all-trades, was by that time Shelby's manager of special projects and had proven his chops as a designer with the stunning Daytona Cobra Coupes. Alex "Skeet" Kerr assisted Brock in designing the GT350. The team decided that all GT350s would be Ford Wimbledon White. Brock decided that Shelby's new white cars needed blue stripes. A thick blue center stripe, flanked by two thin blue stripes, ran along the rocker panel between both wheel openings, with the center stripe abbreviated on the lower front fenders for the callout of "G.T. 350." Brock also designed perhaps the most popular Mustang visual cue of all time: the bold "Le Mans" stripes—two blue stripes that ran up and over the entire length of the car. These Le Mans stripes later became optional, and an almost exclusively dealer-installed option at that, while the rocker panel stripes remained standard. The only other visual adornment was a small GT350 emblem placed to the right of the gas cap after the first few batches of cars were produced.

Brock's design may have been a hat-tip to America's famed "Gentleman Racer," Briggs Swift Cunningham, whose magnificent creations featured similar livery; but really, these were traditional American racing colors. In the post–World War II years, when cars weren't covered with sponsor stickers and painted in sponsor colors, the custom was to paint

British cars green, Italian cars red, German cars silver, and French cars blue. American race cars were painted white with blue stripes, which is why Cunningham used these colors. But the traditional American white with blue stripes served Shelby's purposes well. Brock needed a color scheme that was distinctly a Shelby exclusive, but also clearly emphasized the Mustang underneath the Shelby. After all, Ford's goal for the entire project was to raise the profile of the Mustang as a performance car and elevate the general gearhead opinion of the vehicle, to make it a ballsy performance car instead of a meek secretary's car. And, as with everything else, to do so while spending the least amount of money possible. The Wimbledon White base color emphasized the basic Mustang shape and also enhanced the GT350's image as a purposeful, stripped-down race car. The blue stripes were simply a way to make the overall design more striking and racy.

At the SCCA, Bishop fully expected Shelby to fail in his task to build 100 cars; when SCCA inspectors arrived at Shelby's facilities in the fall of 1964, they were shocked to find 100 Shelby Mustang GT350s parked in rows in Shelby's parking lot. The SCCA had no choice but to homologate the Shelby American Mustang GT for SCCA B/Production racing. When the homologation for what was called the "Mustang-Cobra" was announced in the November 7, 1964, issue of *Competition Press & Autoweek* magazine, there was no accompanying photo, so Corvette drivers could only imagine what sort of chicanery Ol' Shel was up to.

SFM5S003

The very first street version of the GT350 completed bore the serial number SFM5S003. Why not SFM5S001? Communications mix-up at the shop. Not that it mattered, since 003 wasn't part of regular production. It was one of the first three prototype cars that Ford shipped to Shelby, rather than the one of the cars Shelby American purchased from Ford. In fact, Shelby charged Ford for the development work it did on these three cars. Development work took place in a piecemeal fashion on all three cars, and 003 just happened to be the first car finished.

These three cars had started life as standard production Mustang fastbacks. According to the Ford door data plate, 003 rolled off the San Jose assembly line on October 26, 1964. Once GT350 production began in earnest, Shelby removed these data plates and replaced them with Shelby data plates, but the three prototype cars retained the Ford data plates with which they were born.

Ford delivered 003 to Shelby's facilities soon after it was built, which could have been any time within a three-week window of the October 26 door data date. Most likely it arrived at Shelby American in early November. Its siblings, 001 and 002, served as development mules for the racing R version of the GT350, while 003 became a test bed for the production street version. The hood used on 003 was the actual prototype provided by the Fiberglas supplier and didn't feature the final version of the scoop used on production cars. Peter Brock had to cobble 003 together with whatever he had lying around because Shelby needed the car for photo shoots for brochures, advertising, and other promotional material. Because of this, it was one of the few GT350s that actually left the Shelby shops with the Le Mans stripes—virtually all the rest got theirs either at dealerships or from owners themselves. Likewise, the passenger side of the car wore prototypes of the mag wheels designed for it by Brock and built by Cragar, while the Kelsey-Hayes wheels were mounted on the driver's side. This allowed the car to be photographed with both standard and optional wheels without having to do a tire change. Most 1965 GT350s left Shelby wearing the silver-painted steel Kelsey-Hayes wheels. Because the CS-logoed center caps weren't ready in time for its photo shoot, 003 featured plain Cragar caps with no emblems.

Brock began photographing the car almost the moment it was finished, which was sometime in December. Brock staged shoots for the car, driven by a Shelby employee named Eric Hoopingarner, in Coldwater Canyon, north of Hollywood, and later at the Shelby facility itself. The photos from these two shoots provided most people with their initial introduction to the Shelby version of the Mustang. But that was far from the end of 003's interesting life. In March 1965, Shelby loaned the car to Cragar. In May it was ordered converted to the same specs as the actual production versions and sold as a production car. At this point Shelby production plates were added to the car, and thus the first production GT350 street car received serial number 003. Cantwell had intended to give this car serial number 001, saving 003 for the car destined for racer Jerry Titus. Once it was ready to hit the street, 003 made its way to Leslie Motors in Monterey, California, and then to its first owner—Bill Moir.

One of the best things about 1965 GT350s is how usable they are. Fast, tough, and comfortable, they make idea tour and rally cars. I've owned 5S249, a Paxton Supercharged car, for a decade and in that time have added over 20,000 miles to its odometer. This photo was snapped on the 2011 Copperstate 1000 road rally. Clearly my wife hates riding in it. *Will Brewster*

5S249 was delivered without Le Mans stripes, and remains that way today. This leads to a lot of interesting conversations with people unfamiliar with the fact the stripes were optional. *Will Brewster*

While 003 is unquestionably a very historic GT350, every 1965 GT350 is a truly special, hand-built sports car whose capabilities belied its humble beginnings as a gussied-up Ford Falcon. The street version is a mildly disguised competition car—raw, elemental, loud—exactly what you'd expect, in other words. So good was the base GT350 that all Shelby had to do for the competition version was to gut the interior, remove some more weight, and properly prepare the engines for competition use with about 350 reliable horsepower. On the street there isn't another car like the original GT350. They ride rough, require demanding steering effort, and have traction bars that clunk and creak and locking differentials that pop and bang loud enough to make you think you broke something every time you turn a corner. The combination of loud side exhaust and a 3.89 rear axle ratio guarantees you will not hear for hours after spending any amount of time driving one of these at highway speeds. The manual brakes with competition linings are, shall we say, eye opening when cold and relentlessly stiff when warm. If it sounds like I am complaining, rest assured, I am not. It is these things that make driving a 1965 GT350 such an enjoyable endeavor. No other car as remotely pure and focused has ever left Detroit. The GT350 is a true dual-purpose car, along the lines of great European exotics like the Ferrari 250 SWB, but for those whose tastes dictate the Champagne of Beers rather than actual champagne. Although Shelby went on to produce many more Mustang variants over the next 40-plus years, to most the original GT350 is by far the best version, and most true to the original purpose. Shelbys were meant to be race cars; the street versions were simply afterthoughts. Such is the case with the 1965 GT350 and the reason why it remains the most coveted of all Shelby Mustangs.

Shelby sold the street version of the GT350 for $4,547 in 1965, almost double the price of a pedestrian Mustang, but everyone knew the Shelby version was something special. Though he far exceeded his intended 100-car output, in the end, just 562 of the 1965 GT350s, in all variations, were produced. In spite of this miniscule production number, there is arguably not a more historically significant model for either Shelby American or the Mustang. While Shelby had certainly made a name for himself building Cobras, keep in mind that the entire production of every Cobra ever built was just over 1,000 cars. But, through his involvement in creating the GT350, Shelby gave the Mustang an identity as a world-class performance machine, quite possibly keeping Ford's cute secretary's car from fading into obscurity. The 1965 GT350 is more than just a great car; it is the car that cemented Shelby American's place as one of the most iconic manufacturers of all time. As great as the Cobra was it was the 1965 GT350 that really cemented Shelby American as a true manufacturer of competition cars. Without the Shelby Mustang project, would Shelby be a household name today? I doubt it.

Not much can keep Chuck Cantwell away from racing or Shelby Mustangs, even 50 years later. So when you combine a car like 5R106 with a track like Road America, you better believe Chuck will be there with bells on.

Chapter 2

Shelby Builds a Racehorse

ABOVE: 5R002, the first competition GT350, outside Shelby American after a test session. The competition front valance, reworked rear wheel openings, and hood were all in their final development stages, while the side window supports are unique to 5R002. *Carroll Hall Shelby Trust/Carroll Shelby Licensing, Inc.*

OPPOSITE TOP: 5R002 during the filming of "Shelby Goes Racing with Ford" at Willow Springs Raceway. Shelby and Ford were eager to showcase their winning new Competition GT350 for obvious reasons. *Carroll Hall Shelby Trust/Carroll Shelby Licensing, Inc.*

OPPOSITE BOTTOM: Jerry Titus piloting 5R002 at Pomona Fair Grounds March 6 and 7, 1965, where he won both B/Production races. *Carroll Hall Shelby Trust/ Carroll Shelby Licensing, Inc.*

There may be no better example of the old saw that "racing improves the breed" than the original Shelby GT350. With relatively simple modifications to the basic 1965 GT350 street car by Shelby's skilled engineers and mechanics, the 1965 GT350 competition models, or "R Models," as they have come to be known, became nearly unbeatable in B/Production competition. Shelby ordered fifteen cars for the R version and stripped them even more than the original 100-car run, leaving them with no side or rear window glass, interiors (including insulation and headliners), heaters, defrosters, or gas tanks, creating the lightest possible Mustang for the track. Basic weight-cutting procedures, per SCCA rules, such as eliminating bumpers, the use of Plexiglas windows, a Fiberglas front apron and hood, and other such measures made the competition GT350 a fit and trim race car.

In place of the front bumper, lower valance, and gravel pan, Peter Brock designed a one-piece Fiberglas unit with a large opening that directed airflow through an oil cooler and the radiator. A pair of holes, one on each side of this opening, fed cooling air to the front disc brakes. The vents in the rear quarter windows of the stock cars looked wicked cool, but their effects on laminar airflow around the car at speed were just plain wicked, so Brock simply covered them up on the R Model by riveting on panels, saving a great deal of weight in the process. The Plexiglas rear window also saved quite a bit of weight, but it wasn't strong enough to withstand the air pressure generated inside the cab at speed, a problem solved by including a vent that ran across the entire top of the window.

It has been claimed this vent even creates down force at speed, but that might be pure speculation. Of course, you could ask some Corvette drivers. It wasn't particularly pretty when compared to the street version, but the resulting weight loss more than compensated

continued on page 62

TOP: Another shot of Titus sliding around 5R002 at Pomona while dominating B/Production. *Carroll Hall Shelby Trust/Carroll Shelby Licensing, Inc.*

ABOVE: At Tucson SCCA Nationals Titus again swept the B/Production class in 5R002, winning both races. *Carroll Hall Shelby Trust/Carroll Shelby Licensing, Inc.*

RIGHT: In April, 1965 at the Riverside SCCA Nationals, Titus leads the A&B Production field including a Lotus Elan, three 904 Porsches, and the lone Jaguar E-Type, the defending B/Production National Champion. Shelby's big, brutish R Model crashed the party for a lot of purebred sports cars in SCCA. *Peter Luongo*

RIGHT: Jerry Titus wasn't the only pilot of 5R002. As the engineering test mule for of Shelby's competition parts, 002 was Chuck Cantwell's rolling test bed. An accomplished racer himself, Chuck is seen here on his way to a B/Production win at Willow Springs in 5R002 in the summer of 1965. Shelby should have had a bumper sticker that read: "Our engineer can beat your race drivers." *Carroll Hall Shelby Trust/ Carroll Shelby Licensing, Inc.*

ABOVE: No matter how good the beauty shot, it is hard to make tires and wheels sexy, but these R Model magnesium American Racing wheels with "chicken foot" Goodyear Blue Streak racing tires as fitted to all original R Models sure comes close. *Carroll Hall Shelby Trust/Carroll Shelby Licensing, Inc.*

OPPOSITE: This spec sheet, from January 1966, spells out exactly what you'd get if you bought a $5,950 Competition GT350.

continued from page 58

for any aesthetic shortcomings. The rear bumper was simply removed and the mounting holes left unfilled, again, another aesthetic shortfall, but a big win in the weight loss column.

This, combined with 289-cid K-code engines that took advantage of Shelby's three years of experience with the same motor in the Cobra competition cars, resulted in a formula still in use by countless vintage racers today. Shelby's team knew how to coax 385 horsepower out of the 289; when tuned to a more modest 350 horsepower, the engine was both fast and reliable. For the R Models, they tore the engines down, sent the heads out to have the ports enlarged and polished, balanced all pistons, connecting rods, crankshafts, and other reciprocating parts, and reassembled the engines to extremely close tolerances. They mounted a Holley 715 CFM carburetor, which featured a center-pivot float that prevented the float from getting stuck against the float bowl and flooding the engine under hard cornering, and a set of tubular steel headers that dumped spent gases into a pair of glass-pack mufflers that exited under the door sills for maximum aural impact. All of this bumped output from the 306 horsepower of the stock K-code engine to 350 to 360 horsepower on Shelby's dyno. Combined with a chassis weighing 250 pounds less than the street version, this was enough horsepower to give the R version supercar levels of performance.

Shelby had the first two GT350 R Models ready in time to debut at Daytona in February 1965, and the rest of the cars were ready by the time racing got underway in earnest that spring. The first two R Models became Shelby's factory racers; the other cars went to customer race teams. Shelby's customer cars were identical to his factory racers—he wanted his customers to know that the only thing separating them from his factory team

shelby american, inc.   **6501 w. imperial hwy.**   **los angeles, calif. 90009**

COBRA   **SHELBY G.T. 350**   **FORD G.T.**

telephone: 213-674-1961   **twx no.: 910-328-6137**   **cable address: shelcobra**

SHELBY GT-350 MUSTANG RACE CAR

S.C.C.A. Approved for Class "B" Production. F.I.A. Homologated, Group 3, Grand Touring. Winner of 1965 "B" Production title at Daytona.

The GT-350 is fully prepared, within the SCCA regulations, for production car racing and includes the following as standard:

Engine: 289 CID, race prepared, dyno tested, balanced, ported and polished, degreed damper, Hi-Riser intake manifold, Holley 715 CFM carburetor with plenum chamber, reground camshaft, tubular headers with straight pipes, reground camshaft, high lift valve springs, additional breathers, gated and baffled aluminum pan.

Transmission: Close ratio, aluminum case, Borg Warner T10M

Differential: "No Spin" with 3.89 ratio

Suspension: Rear torque reaction arms, Koni adjustable shocks, upper arm pivot points relocated, 1" front sway bar fitted.

Brakes: Front discs fitted with racing pads. Rear drums, 10 x 2-1/2" fitted metallic linings. Front and rear fitted with brake cooling scoops.

Wheels: 7" magnesium racing wheels fitted Goodyear Blue Dot 7.75 x 15 tires. (Goodyear Stock Car Specials or Speedway Specials recommended for competition)

Cooling: Radiator 18 quart capacity, oil cooler fitted

Body: Fiberglass hood with air scoop and racing positive-type tie-downs, lightweight side windows, lightweight rear window with extractor vent.

Gas Tank: 34 gallon with large filler cap and electrical fuel pump.

Interior: Roll bar, seat belt and shoulder harness, fireproof interior trim, special racing instruments.

Finish: White with blue racing stripes and black interior.

Each car is track tested under race conditions at Willow Springs Raceway for compliance with Shelby American specifications. This "extra" service assures you of a properly prepared winning race car.

Price: $5,950.00

Price F.O.B. Los Angeles, California
Price and specifications subject to change without notice.

Our race vans cover the entire United States and can deliver a car to you for under $350.00. Quotation on request.

Further detailed specifications, photo and information available, contact the Competition Sales Department, Shelby American, Inc..

This photo shows the early version R Model valance with its round brake cooling duct holes. *Carroll Hall Shelby Trust/Carroll Shelby Licensing, Inc.*

While even rank amateur racers today sport impressive enclosed race trailers, Shelby American was one of the first professional teams to use such technology. They took full advantage of this for their "Cobra Caravan" tour, which showcased their impressive stable of winners, and the trailer let everybody know just what was inside. *Carroll Hall Shelby Trust/ Carroll Shelby Licensing, Inc.*

was driver skill and not equipment. Besides, for both Ford and Shelby, it wasn't important *who* won in a GT350; the important thing was that a GT350 won.

Stud Farm

Jerry Titus, an old acquaintance of Shelby's who had helped design a chassis for one of Shelby's Maserati race cars in the 1950s, tested an R Model for the March 1965 issue of *Sports Car Graphic*. Titus gave the car a rave review, and soon orders began pouring in. A total of 36 R Model cars were built in three batches. Two cars were considered prototypes, and 34 were production models built for customers. The production versions were priced at $5,950, about $1,500 more than a street-version GT350. A quick lesson in identifying 1965 R Model serial numbers: The fifth character in the VIN was *S* for street cars but was changed to *R* for "race car" on just the R Models. The *R* was followed by the sequential production number.

R Models remained competitive for many years, a quality not many race cars possess. However, no matter how competitive, some became a lot less pretty as the years went on. Compare this photo of Dick Jordan in 5R106 in the early 1970s to the earlier photo from 1965. Modifications to stay competitive were the norm, as were battle scars.

There were 562 cars of all varieties built, so the sequential production numbers range from 001 to 562.

The first of the initial 15 customer R Models was SFM5R094, delivered on April 10, 1965, to Tom Yeager of Marion, Ohio. The last first-batch car, SFM5R108, was delivered on September 22, 1965, to Gene Hammond Ford in Texas and sold to its first owner, Bill Steele. After the first batch was completed, the chassis numbers for the second batch of R Models produced went from 5R209 to 5R213, for a total of five cars.

The third and final batch of R Models consisted of 14 cars, all but one of them delivered after January 1966. Since they were built so late in the 1965 model year, the third-batch cars actually had 1966 GT350 grilles and tape rocker panel stripes. By this point, R Model buyers were

Few old racing adages ring more true than: "To finish first, one must first finish." And to do that takes a perfectly prepared car. Dick Jordan, the original owner of 5R106, is seen here doing his best to make sure he would finish.

drying up, because $6,000 would get you your choice of any number of new race cars. Evidence of this is the fact that the last R Model to be sold from Shelby American, 5R533, shipped on March 31, 1967—that's a nearly two-year-old "leftover" new race car!

It is reasonable to attribute a great deal of Shelby's success to the 1965 R Models. Although there were a mere 36 cars, with most campaigned by private race teams, the cars were so good, were so reliable, and had such phenomenal support from Shelby that they made an impact that few cars have or will ever be able to duplicate.

Rick Kopec:
Shelby Mustangs Changed My Life

When the Cobra came out, I was in high school and considered myself lucky to actually see one. Own one? Even pretending was unimaginable. Three years later, when the GT350 was introduced, it was still way beyond my reach. I crossed paths with a guy, not much older than I was, who owned a real Cobra and was actually racing it. He invited me to come to a race with him at Bridgehampton and it was too good to be true. As a member of the crew, that pit pass was beyond description. When I had previously attended sports car races, I was part of the sea of faces behind the fence—like extras in a crowd scene in the background of a movie. The drivers and crew members on the other side of the fence, moving around the cars purposefully and seriously, were the stars of the movie. The spectators could only watch from a distance. The fence separating us might just as well have been a bottomless abyss.

At Bridgehampton, my pit pass made me an insider and I recall everything that happened that spring 1966 weekend, although none of the individual details, on their own, seemed very important as time passed. Except for one thing: one of the cars we raced against was a GT350 competition car. It was bright white, but instead of the well-known twin blue stripes, this car had one wide black stripe bordered by thin orange stripes at the outer edges. It said *ESSEX WIRE* on the door.

The GT350 was an even match for the 289 Cobra and they swapped the lead several times during the 30-minute A-B-C-D Production race. In the closing laps, the GT350 was running second and finally made its move, pressing the Cobra on the uphill that led to the front straight. It got a good run and when the Cobra ran out of steam, the GT350 still had some oomph left and ran up on the Cobra, tapping it in the rear. Not hard, but enough to put a grapefruit-sized dent below the trunk lid. Then it carried some momentum and got past the Cobra. It was one of those things you don't forget when it happens right in front of you. I didn't see that particular GT350 the rest of the season. In fact, I never saw the Essex Wire GT350 race car again until 15 years later when it arrived at my house on a roll-back truck from Quebec, Canada.

The Cobras were off-the-scale cool, but they were as far out of reach for me in 1981 as they had been in 1963. This GT350 race car was a true barn find. A friend from Canada told me about the car and I prevailed on him to make a call to his brother-in-law. He visited the car the next day and called me with the serial number. I confirmed that it was a GT350 R Model and asked him to immediately put a $100 deposit on the car. The owner wanted $5,000 and I was afraid to negotiate because I thought he might realize what I was willing to pay. I wired him the money and asked a friend of a friend to deliver the car, which had no interior and was in several shades of primer. He agreed on $500 to make the round trip from Quebec to Connecticut. He crossed the border into Vermont and at the US Customs checkpoint was able to sweet-talk the car into the country with only a handwritten bill of sale for $100. Customs duty was $22.

By the 1980s, most Shelby enthusiasts knew what R Models were and retired cars were slowly beginning to surface. Vintage racing was taking off, providing the cars with a purpose instead of being display relics from past history. I made the decision to restore the car to original 1965 specifications. After looking at hundreds of factory-period photos, I knew what it was supposed to look like. I started gathering the necessary parts and was determined to vintage race it as a period piece.

By 1989, the car was completed, I had been through the Skip Barber School, had acquired a proper Nomex suit and an enclosed trailer carrying tools and spare parts. I was ready to go, once again, behind the fence—this time to drive the car I had seen race in 1966. With a minimum of effort I imagined I was racing against Jerry Titus and Ken Miles. Looking at a race car sitting on a show field is one thing; driving it on a track—hearing, smelling, and feeling it as it performs—is like being in another world. It is very seductive.

About a half dozen guys in Shelbys, a couple of them real R Models and the rest street cars made to resemble the factory competition models, raced together that season on tracks in the northeast. We were pretty evenly matched, limited by cars with nearly stock specifications, a lack of driving experience, and general naïveté. By the end of the third season, most of my racing buddies were ahead of me on the grid, put there not by superior driving skill but by more horsepower, bigger brakes, wider wheels and tires, and any number of go-faster modifications to their cars. It would have been easy to join them. But something held me back.

That something was the desire to race 5R098 the way it was in 1965, no matter what everyone else was doing. Looking back in history, the GT350 was a steppingstone for the drivers who raced it. After a season or two, guys like Jerry Titus and Mark Donohue moved up to the Trans-Am, and they didn't stop there: USRRC, Can-Am, and, in Donohue's case, USAC and Formula 1. The point is that few R Model drivers stayed with the car more than a couple of seasons and [so they] never had an opportunity to learn the cars' nuances. In vintage racing, drivers tend to stick with the same car for more than a few seasons.

Vintage racing can be something of a revolving door, with new drivers joining the fray, competing for a few seasons, and then either choosing to stay or to "retire." The costs are usually beyond the beginner's imagination because the price of being competitive [i.e., running up front] continually rises. Ten years is a long time for most drivers. 5R098 stayed essentially the same, as "new" old Shelbys appeared, gridded behind me, and within a few seasons were upgraded to the point where they were faster. Sometimes not by much.

I continued to compete for 19 consecutive years in about 120 events, give or take. While I never won a race, I only had one DNF and never put a dent or wrinkle in the car. The value of R Models continually escalated during those years, and at one point I realized I was the only one still racing a genuine GT350 factory competition car. When the risks exceeded the rewards, I knew it was time to stop. It was a great few decades racing with my memories of Jerry Titus and Mark Donohue. There are many who contend cars are appliances and can't change your life. That's probably true of most cars, but not Shelby Mustangs and certainly not my time with 5R098.

—Rick Kopec

Rick Kopec in 5R098, the Essex Wire R Model, became as predictable as daylight at vintage races for two decades. Here he negotiates Laguna Seca.

Rick Kopec demonstrates, in 5R098, the calm demeanor a race car driver only gains after so much seat time that they become one with their car.

TOP: As time went on, Shelbys were viewed less as race cars and more as collectibles. Witness this R Model on display at a Shelby Club meet in 1978. *Jeff Burgy*

ABOVE: One concession to street use appears to be the addition of a rear bumper and bumper guards. *Jeff Burgy*

Collectors realized the significance of the R Models very early. Just as the cars became moderately competitive "old race cars" in the early 1970s, people realized they were special and started collecting them. Today, 30 of the 36 original R Models are accounted for—over 88 percent of the original production run. Of course, today there are good R Models and bad ones; as with any race car, history and originality are paramount. Not many R Models escaped without serious on-track incidents, and finding one with a great race history and most of its original DNA intact is a challenge. Re-bodies and substantial repairs were not frowned on when these were old race cars, but when R Models are viewed as collectible items, potential buyers need to do their homework. Good R Models have sold for impressive amounts, but, in my opinion, they have earned the price tag. R Models possess unquestionable historical significance and double-digit production numbers, and they appeal not only to muscle car buyers, but also to sports car buyers. Just like famous prewar Grand Prix cars, Shelby GT350R Models have the credentials to be among the most sought-after collectible performance cars for decades to come.

1965–1966 GT350 Factory Drag Cars

With just eight built, the rarest factory-built competition Shelby Mustangs are the little-known 1965 and 1966 Shelby GT350 Drag Units. They are so rare, in fact, that hardly anybody knows about them!

TOP: 5R107 was delivered to Ford Advanced Vehicles in England and sold to its first owner, Jochen Neerpasch, a former Shelby team driver, who started his own race team with R107 in Germany. After an illustrious European racing career it was parked when it was "used up" and no longer competitive. Discovered behind a gas station in Germany in the 1980s, it was returned to the United States and restored to 1965 specifications. I was lucky enough to own it for five years. It now resides in Switzerland, where it is licensed for road use!

ABOVE: Not an R Model, and not a street GT350, this is 5S207, one of the four original 1965 Drag Unit cars sold by Shelby American. *Sam Murtaugh*

ABOVE: In all of his years of racing 5R098, Rick Kopec strived for period-correct preparation at all times, as evidenced by this engine compartment photo.

BELOW: 5R101 was originally sponsored by Harr Ford and possesses a fantastic race history. By the 1990s it was owned and raced by Tommy Thompson, who not only faithfully restored R101 but also built a replica of the original Cobra Caravan transporter. It was always a crowd pleaser at vintage races. *Jeff Burgy*

Much like the Shelby Cobra "Dragonsnake" drag cars that preceded them, the GT350 drag cars were the product of Shelby American employees who wanted to go drag racing. Remember, in 1965 Shelby American was still just a small manufacturer, and most of Carroll's talented crew were Southern California hot-rodders. These guys grew up building hot rods and drag cars, not road racing or traveling to Europe to hang out in the pits during Formula One races. Don McCain, a drag racer who also happened to be Shelby's sales representative, thought the GT350 would make a competitive National Hot Rod Association B/Sports drag race car. McCain presented the idea to Max Muhleman, Shelby's public relations director, who agreed that having a new GT350 drag racing was not bad publicity. McCain was to receive one GT350 with the stipulation that he would prepare the car and race it on his own time. Two other Shelby American employees joined McCain in this drag team effort, sponsors were secured, and plans were made to turn the first GT350 into a "Drag Unit."

Although Shelby was a master marketer and always quick to come up with a catchy name for his special projects, the GT350 drag cars were never given a name.

ABOVE: A lone R Model motors past a staggering array of 1965 GT350 street cars roasting in the sun on the tarmac at LAX.

BELOW: Not every GT350 racecar started out as an R Model. This is 5S419, an original street specification GT350 that was converted to a vintage racecar in 1997. Current owner Chuck Wegner, who goes by the name of Ram Rod on race weekends, is seen here putting the power down during a race at the Coronado Naval Air Station in 2010.

The Cobra drag cars were "Dragonsnakes," and the later 1967 GT500 with a GT40 engine was the "Super Snake." Other notables were the "Slalom Snake" and "King Cobra." One can only guess that, because the Drag Units were McCain's idea and not Shelby's, they were deemed an after-school program for the Shelby kids and not an official Shelby project, and therefore a no-name affair.

To keep the price down, the basic Drag Unit package used the standard GT350 engine. Of course, the options sheet offered any level of full race engine, but drag racers tend to be hands-on people and usually like to build their own engines. Plus, building their own engines ensures that any hot tricks they use to gain the advantage remain secret from their competitors. A further cost-cutting measure involved delivering the Cobra blow-proof bell housing and drag racing clutch and flywheel in the trunk, on the assumption that before any car went racing, its owner would pull the engine to hop it up. No sense wasting money on installing parts that were coming out anyway.

NHRA rules mandated specific safety modifications and approved the upgrades desired by McCain and his crew to make the GT350

ABOVE: The prototype R Model rear window of 5R002, showing the aluminum trim used at its upper corners, which differs from the production version. *Jeff Burgy*

TOP: The "office" of 5R002, restored in exacting detail right down to the Lucas tachometer. *Jeff Burgy*

OPPOSITE TOP: By 2011 5R002's new owner John Atzbach commissioned an impressive restoration to bring this piece of history back to its 1965 Green Valley Raceway debut condition. This is where Ken Miles famously gave it flying lessons. Atzbach debuted the car at the 2014 Amelia Island Concours. *Jeff Burgy*

OPPOSITE BOTTOM: I bet nobody at Shelby American in 1965 could have dreamt of the day 5R002 would be the center of attention at a concours. *Jeff Burgy*

5R108, the last of the first batch of R Model GT350s, was delivered new to Mexico for original owner Freddy Van Buren.

competitive. Les Ritchey of Performance Associates, a well-known race car builder in Glendora, California, was chosen to develop the GT350 into what Ritchey later labeled the GT350 "Performer." His team made numerous tweaks, including yanking the motor to balance and blueprint it and installing custom exhaust headers and a Cobra cast-iron scattershield in place of the stock aluminum bell housing. The crew mounted 90/10 Cure-Ride drag shocks up front with 50/50 drag shocks in the rear and installed a 4.86:1 ring-and-pinion gear set. They modified the original Borg-Warner T-10 transmission by installing drag racing synchronizer rings for faster shifts and mounted a Hurst Competition Plus shifter to row the synchronizers. A set of 8x15x8-inch Casler Spraling rear slicks were given the task of transmitting the power to the pavement. Other modifications included an impressive welded-in rear crossmember with adjustable rear suspension lift bars and a custom-fabricated built-in driveshaft hoop. The outside featured a special lightweight fiberglass hood with a rural-route-mailbox-look hood scoop sourced from the Berry Plastic Glass Company. In total, Performance Associates charged roughly $1,500 for the conversion.

There was no rhyme or reason to the way street cars were selected for Drag Unit conversion. They were built to order, so when an order came in, a random completed street car was pulled from inventory and sent to Performance Associates for the conversion. There is no special designation in the serial numbers, nor were they built in specific batches. The only way all eight were identified was by an SAAC hunt through the original factory work orders and sales invoices.

TOP: 5R538 ran at Sebring and Daytona before being purchased by Charlie Kemp in 1967, who only added immensely to that resume. Out of 54 race starts in R538, Kemp won 32 races, once winning an unprecedented 17 in a row! Kemp eventually sold R538 in the early 1970s to concentrate on Can Am, but bought it back (for $850) roughly five years later. That proved to be a good investment; Kemp sold R538 for $984,500 at RM Auction's 2014 Amelia Island sale. *Jeff Burgy*

ABOVE: The unmistakable single fat black center stripe, flanked with orange, of the Essex Wire car.

TOP: After its time at Shelby as a development mule and factory team race car, 5R002 was sold in 1966 to Ford Engineer Bill Clawson, who raced it in 1967–1968. Clawson then sold it to Russ Fish, who won 18 out of 21 races in 1968–1969. In 1970 it went to Mexico and disappeared. Long thought to have been destroyed, it was found in 1989 sitting on a trailer in Mexico amazingly intact. It soon returned to the United States exactly as you see it here.

ABOVE LEFT: 5S360, the GT350 Drag Unit Don McCain's team used to set a B/Sports record in 1965. ABOVE RIGHT: The first of four 1966 Drag Unit cars, 6S011.

ABOVE: The as-found interior of 5R002. Note the original seat, roll bar, fuel tank, and override traction bars as well as the holes on top of the driver's door from the window hardware unique to this car. An incredible time capsule and one of the best finds in Shelby history!

LEFT: Other than the later Sun tachometer, 5R002's dash is just as it left Shelby.

TOP: After a rather short racing history, 5R095 remained basically untouched as it moved through the hands of a series of owners who each used it as a street/show car. It ultimately came to rest in the garage of early Shelby expert and SAAC's illustrious 1965 and 1966 Registrar Howard Pardee, who has maintained its incredible originality and dutifully brings it to every SAAC national convention so he can drive it on the track without risking damage in actual wheel-to-wheel competition. *SAAC Archives*

ABOVE: One of the few mandatory modifications needed to race an R Model today is a mandatory five-point harness and a window net for the driver, unless you want to wear arm restraints. Rick Kopec elected to use a window net to keep him inside 5R098 should the worst case scenario present itself. *SAAC Archives*

The first Drag Unit did not end up being the "factory" car. That honor went to the second unit because the first one sold immediately upon completion to George May Ford in Ohio. Seems that they threw the biggest temper tantrum and were quieted by getting the first car. The second car, 5S360, was campaigned by Don McCain and set a B/Sports record with a 12.93 at 107 miles per hour pass in September 1965.

Of the eight factory Drag Unit cars, only six examples are known or presumed to exist today. It's no secret that the 1965 and 1966 GT350 cars were much better road racing and sports cars than they were drag cars. While Shelby tried to promote his cars in every type of motorsport, drag racing was not one where the early GT350 could dominate.

Although a competent drag car, and a record-setting one at that, its success was short-lived. Even though it is considerably more rare than the 1965 R Model, the factory GT350 Drag Unit is a little-known and highly unique footnote to the early years of Shelby Mustangs.

Goal: Achieved

If the GT350 Drag Units were moderately successful footnotes, the R Models were monstrously successful domination units. Ford's goal with the Shelby Mustang project was to win races, and win the car did. Just like the original Cobra, the Shelby GT350R proved virtually unbeatable, earning the SCCA/B Production title in 1965 and again in 1966, although the cars raced in the latter year were 1965 versions. A list of all races won by GT350R Models would fill this entire book. Suffice it to say that I believe no other production-based car, built in such small numbers, has won so many races. The Shelby GT350R took the racing world by storm—just as Ford had hoped and intended. In 1965, GT350R Models won five out of six regional SCCA championships. At the 1965 ARRC National race, 10 out of the 14 B/Production cars entered were R Models. In the end, Jerry Titus won the 1965 B/Production National Championship in 5R001. The Mustang now had not just teeth, but fangs.

Shelby ran a factory Mustang race team in 1965 only; in 1966 Shelby American withdrew the Mustang from competition. The goal of the program had been to give the Mustang credibility through racing success, and toward that end Shelby had exceeded expectations by a margin that was almost impossible to measure. Shelby completed a handful of R Models in 1966, but these were 1965 cars with 1966-style grilles. However, even after closing down the factory race team, Shelby continued to foster the racing success of his overachieving GT350s, running a contingency program in which Shelby drivers would receive a check for $150 for every first-place finish and $75 for every second-place finish.

ABOVE: Under the hood more of the same: 1965 all over again for 5R002. *Jeff Burgy*

BELOW: Benjamin Warren Jr. was the original owner of 5R095, and is seen here on his way to a 4th overall and 2nd in B/Production finish at Virginia International Raceway in July 1965. *Howard Pardee Collection*

Chapter 3

Gelding the Pony

ABOVE: Some of the first 1966 GT350s (Carryover cars in fact, based on their 15-inch wheels and 7.75-15 Blue Dot tires) wait in line at Shelby American for installation of their new rear quarter windows, scoops, and rocker stripes. *Road & Track/ Hearst Magazines*

OPPOSITE: A 1966 GT350 specification sheet, a prized collectible today.

Both Ford and Shelby had a single-minded goal for the GT350: winning races. Toward that end, they kept the car basic to the point of being primitive. Options for 1965 GT350 street cars were nearly as limited as the color choice was. If you wanted to personalize your new rip-roaring Shelby, there were two options available: Le Mans stripes and Cragar mag wheels. The Le Mans stripes only came in blue. Although most people today believe they were standard on all cars, because rarely do you see a 1965 without them, that couldn't be further from the truth. Very few cars left Shelby's facilities with Le Mans stripes, and those that did were primarily demonstrator or magazine-use cars. Almost all Le Mans stripes were dealer installed in 1965. All cars were delivered from Ford with silver Kelsey-Hayes steel wheels, mounted with chrome lug nuts and nothing else. Cragar/ Shelby aluminum mag wheels were optional. Almost every 1965 GT350 today has Cragar wheels, but as with the Le Mans stripes, that sure wasn't how they left the factory or even the dealer when new. And, as one would suspect, those original Kelsey-Hayes steel wheels that came standard on the 1965 GT350 are perhaps the hardest original part to find today, since most were tossed and replaced with Cragars or aftermarket mag wheels.

Given that the point of the program was to build a race car, creature comforts were in short supply. Ford and Shelby worried about selling the 100 units they had to build to homologate the GT350 for racing and never gave much thought to the commercial viability of the car as street transportation. But a funny thing happened on the way to the racetrack: Ford dealers sold a bunch of Shelby GT350s. When the dust settled, they'd sold 521 street versions of the car, and total 1965 production amounted to 562 units. Much to the surprise of everyone involved, there was a market for Shelby Mustangs.

SHELBY G.T. 350

SHELBY AMERICAN, INC., 6501 W. IMPERIAL HWY., LOS ANGELES, CALIF. 90009

G.T. 350 SPORTS CAR

Two-place fastback coupe; Shelby American prepared 289 cubic inch OHV Cobra V-8 engine equipped with special high riser manifold, center pivot float four barrel carburetor, specially designed hand built tubular "tuned" exhaust system featuring straight through glass packed mufflers, finned Cobra aluminum valve covers, extra capacity finned and baffled aluminum oil pan; fully synchronized Borg Warner special Sebring close ratio four speed transmission; computer designed competition suspension geometry; one inch diameter front anti-roll bar; fully stabilized, torque controlled rear axle; wide base steel wheels mounted with 130 m.p.h. rated, low profile nylon tires; Kelsey Hayes front disc brakes with ventilated disc and special full competition pads; wide drum rear brakes with metallic linings; adjustable shock absorbers; integrally-designed functional hood air scoop; all black interior with bucket type seats and Shelby approved competition "quick release" seat belts; cowl mounted tachometer; two speed electric windshield wipers and washers; competition type wheel; 19:1 quick ratio steering; rear brake air scoops; rear quarter panel windows; rocker panel identification stripes; heater. Complete With Above Standard

Equipment $4428.00*

Factory Installed Options:

Cast Alloy Wheels $267.00
Rear Seat . . . . $ 50.00
Rallye Stripes . . . . $ 64.00

Dealer Installed Option:

No Spin Rear Axle Unit (Not Available on Automatic Transmission Models) $189.00

The G.T. 350 is available in White, Sapphire Blue, Candy Apple Red & Ivy Green.
*plus license, taxes and freight, FOB St. Louis, Mo.

DIMENSIONS

Wheelbase, In.	
Tread Front and Rear, In. (std. wheels)	108
Length, Overall, In.	57
Width, In.	181.6
Height, In.	68.2
	55

SPECIFICATIONS

Curb Weight, Lbs.	2800
Tire Size	7.75 x 15 or 6.95 x 14
Brakes	Disc front, Special drum rear
Engine Type	289 cu. in. OHV V-8
Compression Ratio	10:1
BHP 6000 RPM	306
Torque 4200 RPM	329 ft/lbs
Weight Distribution %	53/47
Construction	Steel, monocoque

ENGINE

Type	V-8 High Performance (Special)
Fuel	premium only
Capacity	289 C.I.D.
Firing Order	1,5,4,2,6,3,7,8
Bore	4.00 inches
Stroke	2.87 inches
H.P.	306 @ 6000
Torque	329 @ 4200
Oil Sump	Aluminum
Cylinder Block	Cast Iron
Cylinder Heads	Cast Iron
Intake manifold	Aluminum
Crankshaft	Cast Iron, supported in five main bearings with external counter balances
Bearings	Copper-lead
Main bearings diameter	2.25 inches
Rod bearing diameter	2.125 inches
Valve operation	Push rod, from cam in block
Valve diameter	Inlet 1.68 inches
	Exhaust 1.46 inches
Special Order	Inlet 1.88 inches
	Exhaust 1.63 inches
Valve Springs	1, & 1 damper spring per valve
Valve lift	0.450 inches
Carburetor	Holley, four barrel, 715CFM

IGNITION

Dual breaker-point distributor centrifugal advance	
Voltage	12V
Coil	Ford
Alternator	Ford

GEARBOX

Borg Warner T10M—Close ratio 4 speed.
Ratios

High	1:1
3rd	1:1
2nd	1.20:1
1st	1.62:1
	2.36:1

CLUTCH

Ford, heavy duty, diameter 10.5 inches

OPTIONAL AUTOMATIC TRANSMISSION **

Make and model	Ford 289 Cruise-O-Matic high performance
Type	Vacuum controlled shifting with torque converter multiplication
Number of speeds	Three and one reverse

REAR AXLE

Ford—heavy duty	
Ratio standard	3.89
Limited slip differential optional equipment	

SUSPENSION

Front, coil spring above upper "A" frame with strut type hydraulic shock absorber heavy duty adjustable. Extra heavy duty springs and sway bar standard equipment. Rear, heavy duty leaf springs with additional radius rods to control axle wind up, strut type hydraulic shock absorbers heavy duty adjustable.

BRAKES

Kelsey Hayes . caliper disc front with special racing pads, drum rear with metallic linings

Front discs	11.3 inches diameter, ventilated
Rear drums	10 inch x 2.5 inches

TIRES

7.75 inches x 15.0 inches or 6.95 inches x 14 inches. High speed, low profile, nylon tires.

WHEELS

Steel—15 inches—6 inch rim
Steel—14 inches—6 inch rim
(optional alloy) 14 inches—6½ inch rim

CAPACITIES

Radiator	
Engine	15 quarts
Fuel	7.5 quarts (with filter)
	17 gallons

BODY STYLE

Fastback, two passenger coupe. Hood with functional air scoop and racing type positive locking devices, rear brake air scoops, rear quarter panel windows.

*Prices and specifications subject to change without notice.

**Ford 4V carburetor standard with automatic transmission.

The difference between the Shelby G.T. 350 and the Mustang…plenty!

1 The cast aluminum high-rise manifold increases the engine's ability to breathe at high speeds and extends its useful power range. Matched to the manifold is a Holley low-restriction four-barrel carburetor with center pivot floats which prevent flooding or fuel starvation under the most severe driving conditions.

2 Custom aluminum Cobra rocker covers have excellent sound deadening qualities.

3 The Cobra cast and finned oil pan increases oil capacity, aids cooling and prevents oil surge during hard cornering, acceleration or braking.

4 The Borg Warner special Sebring close ratio four speed transmission is fully synchronized.

5 The breathing ability of the engine is improved further by the use of hand-made steel tube exhaust headers and low restriction, straight-through mufflers.

6 Inner pivots of the front wheel upper control arms are moved down one inch improving cornering power and bite.

7 Full one inch diameter anti-roll bar further increases roll stiffness and cornering ability.

8 Monte Carlo reinforcing bar plus extra heavy reinforcing yoke add body stability and strength under severe driving conditions.

9 A pair of torque reaction arms are added to take the burden of acceleration and braking forces and allow the springs to handle the weight of the car effectively.

10 At the front, Kelsey Hayes disc brakes are added with ventilated discs and special full competition pads. At the rear, the G.T. 350 has 10" drums with metallic linings. This combination is practically fade-free. Special wheels are mounted with 130 mph-rated Goodyear "Blue Dot" high performance tires.

11 Heavy duty shock absorbers are adjustable.

12 Overall steering ratio is reduced from 21:1 to 19:1 for quicker, more precise steering.

13 Competition type locking studs and safety pins eliminate the danger of the hood ever flying open at high speeds.

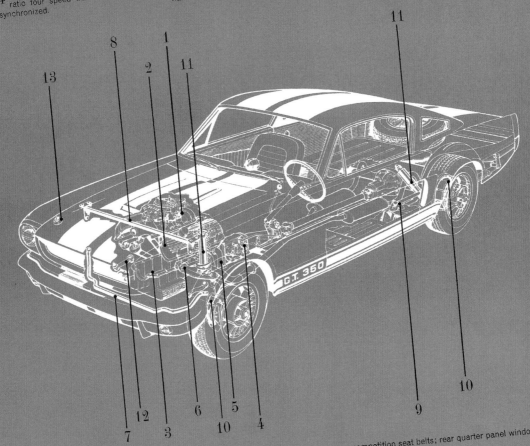

PLUS: special instrumentation including cowl-mounted illuminated tachometer; competition seat belts; rear quarter panel windows; rear brake air scoops; true two-seater; interior luggage shelf.

SHELBY G.T. 350

Refining the Clapped-Out Race Car

Magazine editors had, for the most part, fallen in love with the GT350's raw data, publishing Shelby's claimed performance numbers of 0 to 60 miles per hour in 5.7 seconds and a top speed of 133 miles per hour. Which may have been accurate. For the R Model. With Ken Miles at the wheel. But when *Sports Car Graphic* tested a street version for its May 1965 road test, the editors complained about the GT350's loud exhaust, which "felt as though the pipes came in at each window and plugged in, stethoscope-style, at each ear." That same month *Car and Driver*'s Steve Smith called the Shelby "a brand-new, clapped-out race car."

Fueled in large part by the success of the GT350, Shelby American was rapidly evolving from a boutique builder of sports racing cars into a full-scale, big-time manufacturer. Both Ford and Shelby realized that the project had serious potential and planned big things for the GT350 for the 1966 model year. But to achieve that potential, Shelby would have to compromise the car and make it more palatable for mass consumption, because customers had been complaining about the very same issues that *Sports Car Graphic* and *Car and Driver* nailed in their road tests.

At Iacocca's insistence, Shelby had built a raw, rough-edged racing car. The racetrack was its intended habitat, and use a transportation device was barely a consideration in

ABOVE: The front of Shelby's promotional post card for the 1966 GT350.

OPPOSITE: For those who wanted to know the difference between a Mustang and a Shelby Mustang, well, here it was all spelled out.

ABOVE: New for 1966—colors, and rental cars! *David Newhardt*

LEFT: And the back of the postcard for "the most going car around."

OPPOSITE: *Motor Trend*'s November 1965 review of the new 1966 GT350 points out the details of this new softer, gentler Shelby.

See the difference. Drive the difference.

SHELBY G.T. 350

America's only race-bred sports car.

She's a Mustang Fastback on the outside... a powerhouse of performance inside. Internationally-known Carroll Shelby has reworked the going Ford 289 engine to produce 306 horses...the suspension, exhaust system, brakes and detailing make the G.T. 350 the most going car around. Except for the striping, rear windows and air scoops, you'd swear it was a Mustang. Until you drive it. Do.

the development of the original car. What worked on the track not only compromised street use, but in some cases was actually illegal. For example, exhaust pipes exiting ahead of the rear wheels were illegal in both New Jersey and California, making every GT350 customer in those states a cop magnet and earning owners drawers full of equipment citations. Again, no big deal for a race car, but the GT350 quickly and accidentally evolved into a street car.

The fact that street versions outsold the race models took both Shelby and Ford by surprise. Likewise, the uncompromising race car they had brought home took many customers by surprise, and they complained to the Ford dealers who sold them the cars. The suspension was too stiff, the exhaust and differential too loud, the overall car too rough around the edges. Buyers wanted a back seat, more creature comforts, and color options that were less boring than Wimbledon White. They

Mustang 350-GT

SHELBY-AMERICAN'S "prodified" street version of Ford's popular 2+2 Mustang has come in for a few changes for 1966. For starters, a stamped steel hood replaces the fiberglass hood formerly used. A new bar grille has been added, and rear quarter windows now replace the grilled louvers in the fastback body (the only style available). There's a new side scoop for added cooling air, ducted to the rear-wheel drums; also a straight-through exhaust system that gives exhaust gases a straight path out the rear through twin fiberglass mufflers. A new steering wheel graces the dash, and now the tachometer mounts up high along with the oil-pressure gauge.

Big news comes in the form of a special "289" Cruise-O-Matic automatic transmission, a high-performance version, available for the first time in 1966

models. Another new feature family men will appreciate is the availability of a rear jump seat with a straight-through door to the trunk. That's where the spare will be, in the trunk where it belongs, at least on the street version. Optional fancy aluminum-alloy wheels will be available, but wide-base steel wheels mounting Goodyear high-performance Blue Dot tires are standard.

Basically it's the same Mustang Ford makes, but when Shelby-American works it over, it gains a lot in the transformation — like 306 hp, H-D suspension, and a 133-mph top speed. /MT

Mustang 350-GT's hood latches with lock rings. And this is one scoop that works.

Much-criticized Mustang 2+2 louvers have been replaced with stationary glass window in 350-GT. This is only body offered.

Wooden steering wheel, dash-mounted tach complement fully instrumented panel. Folding rear seats are an optional extra.

REAR SCOOP COOLS BRAKES. ALL SUSPENSION AND RUNNING GEAR ARE HEAVY-DUTY, WITH SPECIAL CAST WHEELS AND MEATY RACING TIRES.

ABOVE: One of Shelby's press release photos that read "The first consignment of 1966 Shelby GT350s on their way to a franchised dealer." As opposed to a guy on a street corner I assume? *Road & Track/Hearst Magazines*

BELOW: Another Shelby PR photos of an early 1966 GT350 showing 10-spoke wheels with painted centers. *Road & Track/Hearst Magazines*

wanted automatic transmissions and power steering. In short, they had bought a race car to use on the street and then discovered that what they really wanted was a street car that looked like a race car. Was this the roots of the wussification of America?

Taming the Stud

Always a quick study, Shelby began making changes to improve the GT350 as a street car almost immediately. When some California and New Jersey owners were awarded with noise violation tickets for their stock 1965 GT350s side exhaust, Shelby American had to come up with a quieter solution for those customers who required it. Another problem that reared its head during street use was that because the battery was mounted in the trunk, and because the trunk was poorly sealed from the passenger compartment, battery fumes would seep into the interior. The first fix for this, around car number 114, was battery vent caps that directed fumes out through hoses that exited the bottom of the quarter panel, but by car number 325 Shelby just left the battery where Ford put it—in the engine compartment.

This side shot of 6S392 shows the new-for-1966 tach, side scoops, and 14-inch wheels with fatter, lower profile tires that Phil Remington, Shelby's chief engineer, insisted on and worked with Goodyear to develop. *Road & Track/Hearst Magazines*

ABOVE: The first factory supercharged car, 6S051, is shown here when new at Shelby American. It was originally white, but painted Ivy Green prior to delivery, making it the first non-white GT350 as well. Note the "GT350 S" rocker panel stripes. Purchased by Steve and Joyce Yates in 1976, it was gifted from their estate in 2013 to the Shelby American Collection museum in Boulder, Colorado. *SAAC Archives*

BELOW: Very few original window stickers survive, but here is the one belonging to 6S2329. *Roger Morrison*

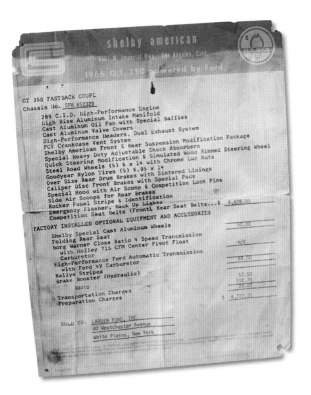

Still, demand for the Shelby GT350 remained high, its performance image driving sales, but this success created new challenges. In addition to making the car more comfortable and civilized, Shelby had a few other problems to contend with if he wanted to be able to build, and thereby sell, more cars. The 1965 GT350 was labor intensive to build. Modifications like the lowered front suspension A-arms, "override" rear axle traction bars, and the Detroit Locker differential were time consuming. The mechanical locking rear differential, which was perfect for racing, also had the disconcerting habit of operating with a loud *bang!* in tight maneuvering, scaring the bejeezus out of customers, who were convinced they had broken some expensive part—or perhaps the car—in two pieces. Returning to the dealership for warranty work and being told this terrifying characteristic was normal often didn't do much to alleviate customers' fears. Likewise the traction-bar rear suspension generated noises most street-car customers were not used to hearing.

Customer feedback showed that many buyers wanted a car with four seats and other traditional passenger-car luxuries—like a quieter exhaust and a differential that didn't sound like a wrecking ball trying to punch through the rear axle housing on turns—and they also wanted their expensive new sports car to, well, look more expensive than a plain white Mustang 2+2.

As a result, Shelby made major changes on the 1966 GT350. To make its external appearance unique—and also to improve rear visibility—clear Plexiglas side-quarter windows designed by Peter Brock replaced the standard

Mustang's fixed vent louvers. Functional brake cooling scoops were added to the rear quarter panels, funneling cool air through 3-inch ducting to the rear brakes. A new-for-1966 ribbed grille was used, again with the Mustang's center "corral" removed, and with the ribs polished instead of blacked out as they were on Mustangs. The gas cap lost its Mustang emblem and gained one that read "G.T. 350," behind which lurked a cobra spreading its hood. Thankfully a wire lanyard kept this pretty—and pretty pricey—cap permanently attached to the car.

Chimera Cars Enter

Given the relatively small scale of operation at Shelby American, the company didn't shut down assembly and completely retool for the new model year, as do giant auto corporations. The changes between the 1965 cars and the 1966 cars were more gradual, begging the question: when is a 1966 GT350 really a 1965? When it is one of the first 252 1966 GT350s built. Called "changeover" or "leftover" or "carryover" or "1965½" cars, depending on who you ask, the first batch of 1966 cars was unique. Just as nobody can quite agree on what to call these cars, which I personally refer to as carryover cars, not many agree on the reason they exist.

The official word is that late in 1965, Shelby American was concerned that they would run out of the Mustang donor cars needed to start the production of their new 1966 GT350 on time. Since the 1966 was similar to the 1965, Shelby is reported to have placed one last order for 250 K-code Mustang cars at the end of the 1965 model

ABOVE: Yamaha wasn't shy about jumping on the Shelby bandwagon, evidenced by their using a 1966 GT350 in their print ads.

BELOW: For their July 1966 issue, *Car Life* magazine road tested a supercharged GT350 (6S392) and compared its performance to an A Code Mustang, a K Code Mustang, and a non-S/C GT350. As the graph shows, they found the Paxton blower added 44.6 percent more horsepower and 28 percent better performance. *Road & Track/Hearst Magazines*

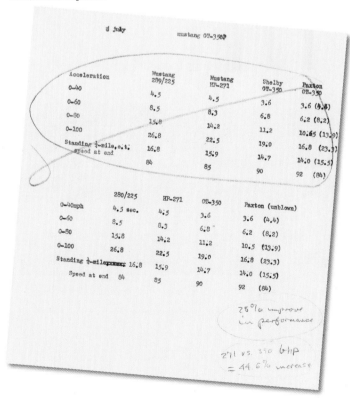

CALCULATED DATA

Lb./bhp (test weight)	8.6
Cu.ft./ton mile	165
Mph/1000 rpm (high gear)	18.1
Engine revs/mile (60 mph)	3320
Piston travel, ft./mile	1590
Car Life wear index	52.7
Frontal area, sq. ft.	19.3
Box volume, cu. ft.	366

SPEEDOMETER ERROR

30 mph, actual	29.8
40 mph	37.5
50 mph	44.6
60 mph	57.6
70 mph	63.4
80 mph	74.4
90 mph	81.7

MAINTENANCE INTERVALS

Oil change, engine, miles	6000
transmission/differential	as req.
Oil filter change	6000
Air cleaner service, mo.	12
Chassis lubrication	36,000
Wheelbearing re-packing	30,000
Universal joint service	30,000
Coolant change, mo.	24

TUNE-UP DATA

Spark plugs	Autolite BF-32
gap, in.	0.032-0.036
Spark setting, deg./idle rpm	12/1000
cent. max. advance, deg./rpm	21.5/5000
vac. max. adv., deg./in. Hg	22/17
Breaker gap, in.	0.018-0.022
cam dwell angle	32-35
arm tension, oz.	27-32
Tappet clearance, int./exh.	0.016/0.018
Fuel pump pressure, psi	4.5-5.5
Radiator cap relief press., psi	12-15

PERFORMANCE

Top speed (7000), mph	127
Shifts (rpm)@ mph	
3rd to 4th ( )	
2nd to 3rd (6200)	77
1st to 2nd (7100)	52

ACCELERATION

0-30 mph, sec.	2.6
0-40 mph	3.6
0-50 mph	4.8
0-60 mph	6.2
0-70 mph	8.0
0-80 mph	10.5
0-90 mph	13.4
0-100 mph	16.8
Standing 1/4-mile, sec.	14.0
speed at end, mph	92
Passing, 30-70 mph, sec.	5.4

BRAKING
(Maximum deceleration rate achieved from 80 mph)

1st stop, ft./sec./sec.	24
fade evident?	no
2nd stop, ft./sec./sec.	24
fade evident?	no

FUEL CONSUMPTION

Test conditions, mpg	9.3 cond.
Est. normal range, mpg	10-12
Cruising range, miles	160-192

GRADABILITY

4th, % grade @ mph	
3rd	22 @ 75
2nd	31 @ 60
1st	45 @ 40

DRAG FACTOR

Total drag @ 60 mph, lb.	134

RIGHT: Here are the results of *Car Life*'s instrumented performance testing. Pretty impressive stuff for 1966. *Road & Track/Hearst Magazines*

BELOW: To help demonstrate the performance of the GT350 to Hertz executives, Shelby brought Ken Miles out to Riverside Raceway, in a suit no less, to scare—whoops—I mean give rides to all who wanted. *SAAC Archives*

RIGHT: The plan must have worked, because soon Hertz had 1,000 GT350s for rent, as this ad explains.

year to convert into the first 1966 models. Others argue that the eventual 252 cars (not 250) were simply leftover 1965 models that Shelby couldn't sell or didn't finish building in time.

The facts of exactly how these cars were built and sold, however, are not subject to debate. Using 1965 Mustangs, complete with 5R09K Ford serial numbers, Shelby built 252 1966 GT350s that ended up featuring an interesting blend of 1965 and 1966 features. Some feel they represent the best of both the 1965- and 1966-model-year characteristics.

All carryover cars had the following 1965 GT350 equipment: suspension with lowered control arms, over-ride traction bars, 15x6-inch Kelsey-Hayes argent-colored steel wheels or optional 15x6-inch Shelby Cragar alloy wheels, Blue Dot tires, and all 1965 interior features, such as smooth vinyl seats rather than the 1966 basketweave material, '65 dash pad, '65 curved glove box door, and '65 door panels. Under the hood the engines were painted gloss black rather than the Ford Blue used on the engines of the "real" 1966 cars. And, like all other 1965 GT350s, you could have any color as long as it was Wimbledon White.

Under the hood of 6S392, the Paxton supercharged road test subject. Note the Monte Carlo bar modified to clear the blower plumbing. *Road & Track/Hearst Magazines*

continued on page 98

ABOVE: As unlikely as it may seem, Herb Tousely Ford in tiny White Bear Lake, Minnesota, sold a ton of Shelbys in the 1960s, far more than many dealers in towns that were a lot bigger than eight square miles, too. This was Tousley's very impressive display at the 1966 Minneapolis Auto Show featuring a red GT350 and just about every Shelby accessory part available, including a fully dressed 289 HiPo. *Vern Estes*

RIGHT: I know a lot of guys who would kill for just some of the displays and memorabilia here, not to mention the GT350. To sell so many performance cars in a place with a population of 20,000 and six months of winter was quite a feat. Tousley Ford is now an AutoNation Ford store; there are no more dual quad intakes in their parts department, White Bear Lake's population has swelled to 24,000, and the biggest company in town is Smarte Carte. Yes, the people that make the luggage carts you can rent at the airport. *Vern Estes*

ABOVE: Yes, it's real. Ken Young's 1966 GT350 convertible 6S2378 on display at a Shelby Owners Association meet in Knoxville, Tennessee, in 1974. *Jeff Burgy*

TOP: 6S1541 sports 15-inch Cragar mags, which never came on any Shelby that wasn't white but lend a particularly cool look. *Roger Morrison*

LEFT: One big reason more family men were allowed to buy a GT350 in 1966. *Roger Morrison*

ABOVE: Shelby converted 16 K-Code Mustang coupes to Group II racers, essentially four-seat GT350R models with steel hoods. This is car number 12, originally built for Ken Miles, who was tragically killed before he could race it. *Mecum Auction*

RIGHT: Unlike the more aerodynamic R Model with its vented rear window, the Group II cars needed extra help retaining their rear windows. *Mecum Auction*

OPPOSITE: Under the hood it is all standard Shelby competition-spec fare for the Group II cars. *Mecum Auction*

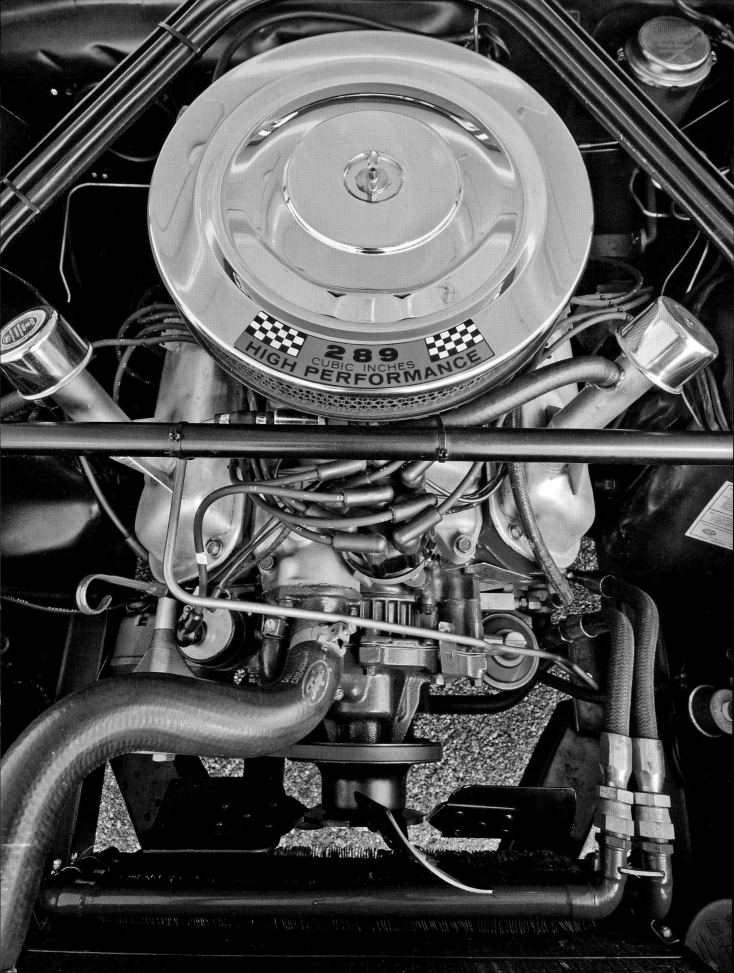

continued from page 93

Blended into these 1965 features were new-for-1966 features such as the Plexiglas quarter windows and quarter-panel brake cooling scoops mentioned above. For 1966 Shelby used the standard Mustang GT's gauge cluster, which came from the factory with a built-in oil pressure for 1966, in addition to the coolant temperature, amp, and fuel gauges used in 1965. This solution was much less expensive than the center dash gauge pod. Shelby replaced the center-mounted tachometer with a pedestal-mounted, 9,000-rpm Cobra tachometer, manufactured for Shelby by Faria, atop the dash. The hybrid 1965–1966 cars used the 1966 dash gauge clusters with the pedestal-mounted tachometers on the dashes. The hybrid models also featured other interior changes designed to streamline production and lower production costs. For example, in place of the old wooden three-spoke Shelby steering wheel was the Mustang GT's optional wood-grained plastic deep-dish three-spoke wheel, but with a GT350 emblem on the center cap, which now operated the horn.

Though the 1965–1966 hybrid cars retained the noisy Detroit Locker rear end, they did offer optional rear seats (although 78 of the 252 cars were fitted with the ribbed, '66-only package tray in place of a rear seat). Under the car, Shelby saved not only eardrums but also money by simply retaining Ford's factory-installed rear-exiting dual exhaust rather than installing the raucous side exhaust. And Shelby American simply installed its own 1966 SFM6S ID number tags over the 1965 Ford VIN, just as it did on 1966-model-year cars.

Whatever the reasons for their existence, and whatever you care to call them, there is no question that the first 252 1966 GT350s represent a very unique part of Shelby history. They show how a small company was quickly learning the ropes of being a big company, and adjusting to new challenges well.

And, standard-spec R Model 36-gallon fuel tank and S-W 240A fuel pump in the trunk. *Mecum Auction*

Like a Rainbow

After the first batch of 252 changeover cars were built, Shelby offered four optional colors: Sapphire Blue, Ivy Green, Candy Apple Red, and Raven Black. As with the 1965 models, side rocker panel stripes (now decals rather than painted on, saving Shelby $5 per car) were standard, although for 1966 they were slightly smaller. Optional topside Le Mans stripes remained available as a factory or dealer-installed option. One note: on Wimbledon White cars, the side and Le Mans stripes were blue, while on other colors they were bright white.

LEFT: Diane Burgy with 6S1206 at the Cleveland Autorama hot rod show in 1976. Diane made the dress with a pattern for a majorette's outfit. Carroll Shelby autographed it at SOA III in Wichita, Kansas, in 1975. *Jeff Burgy*

BELOW: Sapphire Blue with standard gray-painted Magnum wheels is just a stunning combination as 6S2329 demonstrates. *Roger Morrison*

The standard 1966 wheel was a 14x6-inch styled steel Magnum 500, painted gray, with an optional chrome version of the same wheel and new optional 14x6.5-inch Shelby alloy "10-spoke" wheels available.

The hybrid 1965–1966 cars had featured a number of other interior changes designed to streamline production and lower production costs. When production of 1966 cars commenced, all cars received numerous changes. One of the most obvious was the optional Mustang fold-down rear seat, although fewer than 100 of the 1966 GT350s sold without one. Basketweave seat covers replaced the smooth vinyl covers of 1965.

Under the skin, the changes for 1966 were far more significant. Some were done purely to save time and money in production, while others made the GT350 more user-friendly. The driveshaft safety hoop was gone, and the lowered front suspension A-arms were phased out early in the production run, so the Mustang's factory ride height and geometry remained. At about the same time, the over-ride traction bars were replaced with bolt-on "under-ride" Traction Master bars, which also saved a lot of time and expense in the production process, since it eliminated the complicated process of cutting holes in the floor pan and attempting to seal up the holes once the traction bars had been installed.

The Detroit Locker differential was now an option; a nice, quiet open differential came as standard equipment. The Shelby engine modifications remained the same as in 1965, but, as mentioned above, the Tri-Y exhaust headers now led to the standard Ford Mustang

ABOVE: Fine. I'm a sucker for painted Magnum wheels, and 6S1693 has a nice set.
Sam Murtaugh

OPPOSITE TOP: Delivered new as a white GT350 to Marv Tonkin Ford, 6S2134 was immediately transformed into a road racecar. It has never seen street use and is still racing today.
Bob Pengraph

OPPOSITE BOTTOM: One of the 252 famous carryover cars, 6S246 gives away that status with its 15-inch Cragar wheels, raked stance thanks to factory lowered upper control arms, and override traction bars.

ABOVE: Unlike 1965, the 1966 cars received GT350 gas caps in place of the standard Mustang units.

BELOW: Sapphire Blue works particularly well with gold Hertz stripes. *David Newhardt*

rear-exiting dual exhaust. The standard transmission remained a Borg-Warner T-10 four-speed, still with an aluminum main case on early cars, but changing to cast iron by late in the production run. And, to the joy of many who didn't like to row their own, Shelby offered Ford's C4 automatic transmission as an option. Cars equipped with the automatic were fitted with a 3.50:1 rear axle ratio from the factory.

Inside, the spare tire moved from the rear of the cabin to the trunk to make space for the optional rear seat, a change made possible by the shift from 15-inch to 14-inch wheels. This also moved more weight to the rear, compensating for moving the battery to the engine compartment. These changes were in large part designed to make the GT350 a more appealing street car, but by simplifying the production process and jettisoning many of the exotic and expensive parts, Shelby saved a lot of money on the process of converting a standard Mustang to a Shelby GT350. For example, the plastic-wood Mustang GT steering wheel cost less than the wooden Shelby unit, and use of the standard Mustang

TOP: A popular modification after the 1967 and newer Shelbys were out was to add a fiberglass rear deck lid and end cap with a built-in duck tail spoiler on 1965 and 1966 Mustangs. *David Newhardt*

ABOVE: Of course black and gold is the go-to color for Hertz car fans. *David Newhardt*

Hertz presents the G.T. 350-H

SHELBY DESIGNED, COBRA BRED, FORD POWERED AND RENTED EXCLUSIVELY BY HERTZ

ABOVE: A lot of the carryover cars desirability can be found in this small area.

LEFT: Hertz certainly used the Shelby and Cobra names to their advantage. *Vern Estes*

dash and the dash-mounted tachometer saved still more money. All of this tweaking and tuning of standard equipment and revised production operations translated into serious cost savings, which Shelby passed on to his customers—the 1966 GT350 had a base price of $4,428, which was $119 cheaper than the 1965 it replaced.

Blown Pony

A very rare factory performance option was the Shelby/Paxton supercharger. Featuring a Paxton compressor that fed about 5 psi of boost to a 460-cfm Autolite 4100 four-barrel (the standard carburetor on automatic-equipped K-code 289 V-8s) mounted in a Cobra-lettered pressure box, this setup claimed to add 46 percent more horsepower to the GT350. This centrifugal unit mounted to the engine with very little modification, making it an incredibly appealing way to get a massive power boost. Shelby had been experimenting with mounting a supercharger on the GT350 as early as midyear 1965. It took until the spring of 1966 for his crew to develop the prototype sufficiently to send it out to magazines for testing. He still hadn't committed to offering it as an option, but feedback from magazines would help to decide if the concept was viable.

Car Life magazine, an enthusiast publication based 30 miles from Shelby American's Los Angeles shop that featured Dean Bachelor as its editorial director, tested one of the first prototypes for its July 1966 issue. This unit featured the optional automatic transmission, which was a good choice for

continued on page 109

ABOVE: The completely untouched, unrestored engine compartment of 6S2371 offers many points of reference for restorers.

LEFT: Beyond the color scheme and stripes, all Hertz cars received chrome Magnum wheels with Hertz-specific decals on the center caps. *David Newhardt*

Jeff Burgy: Living the Shelby Dream

I have been a car nut all of my life. I fondly remember the days in the '50s and early '60s when I would ride my bicycle to the back lot of the local Ford dealer to check out the new models each fall. I was fifteen years old when the Shelby Cobra was introduced, and I was ecstatic that Ford now had a real sports car to compete against the Chevrolet Corvette.

I knew that someday I had to have a Shelby. Since I was still in high school at the time, I was not able to fulfill my dream immediately and be one of those lucky guys who bought one brand new. I was one of the second wave of Shelby owners, who bought their Shelbys used, when the cars were just old used cars and the prices had nearly bottomed out. I bought my first Shelby, a 1966 GT350, for $1,200 in 1971. It was Wimbledon White with Guardsman Blue racing stripes, and the first time I got behind the wheel and headed out on the road, looking out over that hood scoop with the racing stripes, I thought I was in heaven.

I really liked my GT350 but wanted it to be more aggressive than it was when I bought it, which was bone stock with chrome 14-inch Magnums. My infatuation with Shelbys and Cobras had already led me to modify the 1965 Comet Caliente hardtop that my parents had given me for graduation when I finished college, so I had a very good start swapping the Cobra dual quad setup and the Shelby 14-inch 10-spokes from the Comet onto the GT350 where they belonged. The timing was just right, and Bill Maier of Maier Racing had started a business reproducing hard-to-find Shelby parts. I was one of his earliest customers and ordered an R Model racing apron and fiberglass rear package shelf for my GT350. I added a roll bar and glass-pack mufflers to it, ran the pipes out in front of the rear wheels like a '65 GT350, and started to compete in autocross and open-track events with it.

I heard about the SOA [Shelby Owners Association] in *Competition Press* [now *Autoweek*] and joined up. I began seeking out other

Shelby and Cobra owners in the Detroit area and forming a group of friends who would eventually form a local regional chapter of the SOA. I worked at Ford in Dearborn, Michigan, as a technical illustrator and technical writer. I loved to tinker with my cars, and as I made modifications to my GT350, I started writing illustrated technical articles for the SOA newsletter. Most of my mods—lowering the upper control arms, fabricating a special air cleaner for small-block dual quads, beefing up the C4 tranny, and fitting oversize 15-inch wheels and tires—were covered in the old SOA newsletters. In 1973, I was thrilled to hear that the SOA was having a national convention in Reading, Pennsylvania; I packed up my GT350 with spare parts and literature to take along to sell. It was an exciting experience to see all of those Cobras, about a dozen or so, and a couple hundred Shelby Mustangs all in one place. I met many Shelby enthusiasts there who have become lifelong friends.

By 1975, the SOA had gotten large enough that Carroll Shelby recognized the group and attended the third National Convention, held in Wichita, Kansas. I was selected to drive out to the airport in my 1968 GT500 convertible to greet Carroll Shelby. I'll never forget that moment, seeing the tall, lanky Texan, carrying a Hertz Sports Car garment bag over his shoulder, walking through the airport. Shelby and his ex-wife, Jeanne, rode with Gerry Wagner in his 1969 GT500 convertible, and I got to carry their luggage in the trunk of my GT500. (I sure did want to keep that Hertz garment bag!)

Shortly after SOA III, the Shelby Owners Association imploded, the Cobra Club out of Michigan disbanded, SAAC was born, and Motor City SAAC replaced the Michigan SOA. The new club was bigger, stronger, and more organized than ever before, and SAAC National Conventions got bigger and better. Carroll Shelby attended SAAC I in Oakland, California, along with a large group of his former employees, a trend that grew and grew over the years. Eventually, SAAC would incorporate an open-track segment into their convention schedule along with the popular-vote car show and parts swap meet. Later conventions would add a judged concours car show that would become a standard for the marque. My obsession with the cars and their history steered me to collecting serial numbers, pictures, and owner information on early GT350s and original Cobras. Eventually I would share this information with Howard Pardee and Bill Kemper, forming the basis of what would one day become the SAAC World Registry of Shelbys and Cobras.

In the early '70s through mid-'80s, I had three 1966 GT350s and a 1968 GT500 convertible. I collected Shelby parts and literature with a passion. I had extra sets of wheels and tires and spare induction systems for nearly every one of my Shelbys. My Cobra dream was not happening, though, because the cars kept escalating in value. SAAC was like a two-edged sword in this regard, offering in-depth knowledge of the cars, access to Shelby and the people who designed and built them, and a venue to show them off or exercise them on the track. The flip side was that, as the club grew, the values of these old muscle cars started to escalate, and, in the case of the original Shelby Cobras, the prices shot right into the stratosphere.

Over the years, I've owned a number of Shelbys and other cars that Shelby was associated with. In addition to my Shelby Mustangs, I've had two Sunbeam Tigers, several early-model HiPo Mustangs, a Boss 351 Mustang, and a 1972 DeTomaso Pantera that I tricked out with a full roll cage, Boss 351 engine, and Weber carbs. I eventually gave up the quest for an original 289 Cobra and built myself an ERA 289 FIA replica. I kept the 351 engine from my Dad's '71 Boss that I had swapped into the Pantera, for the Cobra replica I knew I would one day build. I finished my ERA 289 FIA in 1997 and debuted it at SAAC XXII at Elkhart Lake. I've had it on the road now for over twenty years and have brought it to a number of SAAC conventions to blow the carbon out.

SOA had 3 national conventions, and SAAC has had 43 national conventions. I have been to every single one of them—only one other person shares this distinction with me, my friend Ken Young of Green Bay, Wisconsin. Being on the board of the SOA, and then SAAC, I was fortunate to get to spend time with Carroll Shelby at many of these conventions. A number of SAAC conventions included a private board of directors dinner with Carroll Shelby in attendance. I have loaned my rental car to him, driven him around on a golf cart, and even gotten a few hot laps on the track with him at Portland in 1992. The ride in CSX3056 at Portland International Raceway has to be one of the highlights of my association with the Shelby legend. Rides with Carroll in his newly completed continuation Cobra were offered in return for a donation to the fledgling Carroll Shelby Children's Heart Foundation. I was extremely lucky to be the first to go out with him right after lunch break, and I was delighted to hear him say in that famous Texas drawl, "We're gonna take a few extra laps to get these tires warmed up!" Sliding around the track with Carroll Shelby at the wheel in his personal Cobra was a thrill I'll never forget. And to think, it all started with that $1,200 GT350!

—Jeff Burgy

ABOVE: The Paxton blower is actually ideally suited to fitment on automatic GT350s such as this Hertz car. The C4 can bang off shifts faster than anybody this side of Ronnie Sox, and keeps the supercharger on full boost in the process. *David Newhardt*

BELOW: The interior of a carryover car is an interesting mix of 1965 and 1966 features. Can you spot them all?

It doesn't have to be a 1965 GT350 to be an ideal rally car. David Hidalgo and Kelly Whitton are seen here enjoying the Copperstate 1000 at speed in 6S1693.

continued from page 104

the supercharged engine. A slushbox tranny wasn't what the magazine expected, and the editors described the combination as "at best a chancy project," but they were impressed with the results. They were surprised to discover that the automatic transmission with its firm, quick shifts kept the supercharged engine under boost and made it a potent, yet docile street car. The end result, according to the magazine, was a 289-cubic-inch engine that felt like it put out more power than most 400-cubic-inch engines.

Though the engine felt strong, performance numbers weren't particularly impressive. The standard GT350 accelerated from 0 to 60 in 6.8 seconds; the supercharged version did it in 6.2 seconds. The standard GT350 covered the quarter mile in 14.7 seconds; the supercharged version did it in 14.0 seconds. If the supercharging option had been cheap, it might have proven popular . . . but it wasn't cheap. An expensive option at almost $700, only 11 factory Paxton-equipped GT350s ever left Shelby American. This kit was also available as a dealer-installed or over-the-counter item. Many owners soon retrofitted the Shelby/Paxton kit to their cars because it made the already potent Hi-Po 289 thoroughly impressive, adding a huge amount of low-end torque.

TOP: White with gold, another classic Hertz color combo. *David Newhardt*

ABOVE: One of just four original GT350 convertibles, 6S2377 is simply stunning. *Jeff Burgy*

ABOVE: Not only is it one of four, 2377 is also a four-speed car with factory air conditioning. But usually it is just better like this, with the top down. *David Newhardt*

LEFT: Do you think 2377s original owner, Bob Shane of the Kingston Trio, was drawn to the "music" from the tailpipes? Perhaps. *David Newhardt*

ABOVE: 6S001 showed up with its clothes off at SAAC-1 in Oakland, California, in 1975. On a trailer. Being pulled by a 1965 Mustang. Now that is making an entrance! *Jeff Burgy*

BELOW: I've raced 6S151, a carryover car converted to vintage race car, for 10 years. They are just as much fun to race now as they were then, and thanks to the amazing popularity of 65/66 Shelby Mustangs there are always plenty to race with.

Further dealer-installed options included a radio, any number of optional rear axle gear ratios, a real-wood steering wheel similar to the 1965 item (and later 1967 item as well), and, one can assume, just about any Mustang accessory a Shelby buyer might have wanted.

Rent-a-Shelby

One of the most significant developments for Shelby in 1966 was the beginning of its relationship with Hertz, culminating in 1,001 GT350 Hertz or "GT350H" cars. For years Hertz operated the Hertz Sports Car Club, which offered executive and business travelers with good credit and clean driving records who were at least 25 years old the opportunity to rent a variety of high-performance cars. Members had a special Hertz membership card and had to pass a driving test. Hertz's leading competitor at the time, Avis, had been taking an increasingly large share of the rental car market, thanks in part to its brilliant advertising campaign: "We're number two; we try harder." The advertisements were so effective that Avis was dangerously

ABOVE: This super-sanitary Ivy Green Hertz car, without Le Mans stripes, just looks so right. *Roger Morrison*

RIGHT: I'm sure a lot of Shelby guys would have preferred Hagerty Insurance using a Chevy for this ad.

close to becoming number one, a situation Hertz was not about to allow. Offering popular models, such as Chevrolet's Corvette, in the hot-car program was part of Hertz's efforts to keep the number-one title.

Shelby's GT350 seemed an obvious choice for the program, so Shelby tasked Peyton Cramer, whom he had poached from Ford, with getting the GT350 into the Hertz rent-a-racer program. Cramer researched Hertz' history and learned that John Hertz started his automobile rental business in 1925 by acquiring a Chicago-based livery service that built its own cars. Hertz' plan was to sell cars, and he conceived of the rental service originally as a means of exposing his cars to potential customers. To distinguish his cars, he gave them a striking black paint job with gold stripes.

Research completed, Shelby developed a prototype Hertz GT350, properly adorned in black-and-gold livery, to be sent to Hertz' New York headquarters for testing. Like most GT350s, this example was equipped with a four-speed transmission. Shortly thereafter, at Hertz' request, an automatic GT350 was also sent for evaluation. Although Hertz found a few issues with the cars, namely the metallic brakes that were ineffective when cold and required a very strong leg to operate, they decided the GT350 was a good addition to the Hertz fleet, provided Shelby would accommodate a specific Hertz request: placing an *H* after "GT350" in the rocker panel tape logo. On November 23, Hertz placed an

ABOVE: 6S476 is a very interesting car. It is one of just a few original Hertz cars that were delivered in white with standard blue rocker panel stripes; no "H" in sight.

RIGHT: If not for the gas cap and GT350 tail panel badge, one could mistake 6S476 for a plain-jane Mustang Fastback. But that would be a mistake.

OPPOSITE TOP: On the inside you can just make out the Hertz-only brake warning sticker on the dash, below the tachometer, and the Hertz-only emergency brake warning lamp on the left side of the dash.

OPPOSITE BOTTOM: The Magnum wheel still looks great today, especially in a world filled with some hideous (and hideously large) wheels.

order for 200 cars, letting Shelby know that if customer response was strong enough, the company might order more. Customer response was more than strong enough. In late December 1965, Hertz placed an order with Shelby American for an astounding 800 GT350 Hertz cars. This was nearly double Shelby's entire GT350 production for 1965. Because of a mixup regarding initial specifications, the first 85 Hertz cars were delivered with four-speed transmissions, but the remainder all had automatics. All cars had a standard AM radio and chrome 14-inch Magnum 500 wheels. They were not all Raven Black, because Hertz mixed up the colors and received Candy Apple Red, Ivy Green, Wimbledon White, and Sapphire Blue cars as well, all with gold rocker panel and Le Mans stripes.

Throughout this run of Hertz cars Shelby dealt with issues as Hertz reported them. The main issue continued to be brake problems, since most drivers unfamiliar with competition brakes had difficulty adjusting (i.e., they ran into stuff). Eventually Phil Remington, a.k.a "Mr. Fixit,"

found a master cylinder that acted as a brake booster by virtue of its dual piston design. This "MICO" master, as Rem said, was "designed for tractors," with its additional line pressure combined with softer, non-metallic brake linings, but seemed to keep most rental car drivers from hitting stuff. Lest they forget that's bad, warning labels were applied to the dashboards that cautioned them to be aware of the high brake pedal effort and poor performance when cold. It wasn't cheap to rent a GT350H from Hertz, with rates of $17 a day plus 17 cents a mile. But, in spite of the abuse one would expect a rental GT350 to take, in addition to sometimes substandard maintenance from Hertz agencies, the 1966 GT350 Hertz cars held up remarkably well. At the end of the 1966 model year, all were retired from service, and most were returned to Shelby American and Ford for reconditioning and eventual sale as used cars.

Topless Snakes

Perhaps the most interesting 1966 Shelby GT350s were the final four the company built: serial numbers 2375, 2376, 2377, and 2378.

A factory memo, dated June 7, 1966, answers the question of just why these four drop-top GT350s were built. It states: "Four experimental convertibles are being run through the shop at the present time. One of these units is sold and the other three will be used for test purposes in anticipation of a 1967 1/2 GT350 convertible."

As we now know, a factory production GT350 convertible didn't actually happen until the 1968 model year. But these four 1966 experimental cars have since become among the most desirable Shelby Mustangs of all, and amazingly all four survive today.

All told, the 1966 model year was a very successful one for Shelby American. It produced 2,378 GT350s, a major jump from 1965. Production was getting streamlined, and more cars on the road led to more visibility for Shelby. The Shelby/Hertz association was huge, giving many drivers a taste of what the Shelby Mustang was all about. Ford was thrilled with the upscale image the GT350 provided for their Mustang and stood ready to help Shelby any way it could. The year 1966 signified that Shelby American had arrived.

TOP: A rare factory red-with-white Le Mans stripe car, 6S744 also sports factory 10-spoke mag wheels. No denying it has "eyeball."

ABOVE: A closeup of the 1966 tach, manufactured by Farina for Shelby.

OPPOSITE TOP: If the GT350 didn't make such a fantastic vintage race car, I doubt we'd see so many still out there. *Bob Pengraph*

OPPOSITE BOTTOM: And they certainly do dress up just about any track for the spectators. *Bob Pengraph*

Turn your Mustang into a snake.

Let's say you have a groovy Mustang with a 289 engine. Notch back, fastback, convertible. Makes no difference. Your Ford high performance dealer can't exactly turn it into a Cobra, but he can get mighty close.

Your barrel carburetion and a high-rise aluminum manifold will tack on about 35 more horsepower. The G.T. 350 street exhaust system from the headers right on back will not only give you that sound of might and main, but will also give you a bundle of power. For that real sports car feel, have him add a front stabilizer bar and a steering kit. Real cornering loss ahead. And don't forget the dress-ups. Chrome large diameter air cleaner, valve covers and dipstick will really make that engine sparkle. Add a rear quarter panel window if you have a fastback and rear brake air scoops for cooling. Just a word of caution. When it's all done and you drive it easy, get a good grip on yourself.

FREE GUIDE TO THE FUNDAMENTALS OF HIGH PERFORMANCE. This forty-page book gets right down to the ABC's of the engine, clutch, transmission, traction, roadability, carburetion, compression, camshafts, exhaust, ignition and gearing. And all in a language you can understand. Just send your request for this free informative book to: Shelby American, Inc., 6501 W. Imperial Highway, Los Angeles, Calif. 90009.

COBRA KITS

CAR and DRIVER

TOP: The more you look at a 1966 GT350, the more you understand why the design is timeless.

ABOVE: Not all Shelby competition cars run on road race courses. Randy Gillis has drag raced 6S477 since buying it in 1974, with a best time of 10.75 seconds at 126 miles per hour. That's one hell of a rental car! *SAAC Archives*

LEFT: Shelby saw opportunity in every Mustang that wasn't a Shelby. As such, Shelby American advertised "Cobra Kits" to help you get your lowly Mustang "mighty close" to the real thing.

OPPOSITE: Nothing looks better than a properly setup race car in action, when the tires fill the wheel wells and you can hear and feel the speed. No race car should be a static display.

6S319 is a unique 1966 GT350. An early production "override" traction-bar car, it was also delivered new with the standard 14"x6" steel wheels. In 1965 Shelby used 15" x6" Ford Kelsey-Hayes wheels, but for 1966 the Mustang was changed to 14" wheels and Ford had no suitable 6"-wide wheel for Shelby's GT350 conversion. To address this issue, Shelby American sourced and installed these heavy-duty Chrysler station wagon wheels for the roughly 50 GT350s that were ordered with this "base"-specification wheel. Today these cars are so rare that 6S319 is the only known 1966 GT350 to retain its original set of these Chrysler wheels—delivered just as you see here with chrome lug nuts and no hubcaps, just like the 1965 K-H steel wheel cars. 6S319 was also delivered with no Le Mans stripes, and it is one of a few cars built with no "GT350" tail panel emblem. After more than four decades in storage, it remains in 100% original condition including its factory-applied paint, making it a great reference-level GT350.

Chapter 4

Go Big or Go Home

ABOVE: Shelby continued the use of promotional postcards for the 1967 model year.

OPPOSITE: Shelby American was growing by leaps and bounds in late 1966 and they hit the ground running with an aggressive campaign for their all-new 1967 GT350 and big block GT500 "true GT" cars.

By the end of Shelby American's second year of building Mustangs, one thing was clear—very few buyers existed for race cars thinly disguised for street use, but plenty of buyers existed for street cars heavily disguised as race cars. As proof of this, almost all of the 562 buyers of the 1965 GT350 model had some form of racing or performance use in mind and were willing to sacrifice comfort to do so. For 1966, when the kinder, gentler GT350 was offered, sales took off. People liked having a quieter exhaust, a back seat, and bright colors with Shelby-specific styling. So, for 1967, Shelby decided to cater to the demographic that was writing the checks—people who wanted flashy road cars with sporting intentions, not race cars with license plates that shook out their fillings over bumps.

For 1967 the Mustang was all new. Bigger in every dimension, and unfortunately heavier, it was moving more toward a personal luxury car than a sporty compact car as the 1965 and 1966 cars had been. Shelby took this opportunity to do more than just add a few stripes and details to an otherwise standard Mustang fastback and designed a distinctive version all his own.

A Ford stylist named Charles "Chuck" McHose played a huge role in the styling of the 1967 Shelby Mustangs. Ford loaned McHose to Shelby to assist with the redesigned car, resulting in four frenzied months of activity and what many enthusiasts consider the most handsome American automobile of the classic muscle car era. McHose's first love was airplanes, but like any American male who came of age after World War II, he developed a love of cars as a young man. While in the navy he bought a Porsche 356, which led him to the world of sports car racing. After leaving the navy, he graduated with honors from

continued on page 128

Carroll Shelby Presents The Road Cars...
G.T. 350 and G.T. 500 for 1967

Do you agree with Carroll Shelby that good driving is a fine art? Then these all new 1967 Shelby GT cars are custom-crafted for you. By incorporating his competition-proved design and engineering features in the Mustang, Carroll Shelby has created two unique road performers that carry the *lowest* price tags of *any* true GT cars.

The GT 500 features a brand-new Cobra LeMans dual 4-barrel engine, developed from the V-8 that powered the 1966 LeMans winners. GT 350 power comes from the high performance Cobra 289 with free-breathing Shelby induction and exhaust. All-synchro four-speed box or heavy-duty Cruise-O-Matic are optional on both cars.

These goodies make your Shelby GT one of the *safest* cars you can drive: Massive disc front and air-cooled drum rear brakes. Shelby-modified suspension for 30% less cornering roll. Crisp 16-to-1 power steering*. LeMans-proved wide tread nylon super-safety tires. Integral roll bar*, double shoulder harness*, quick-release seat belts and eye level brake and turn indicator lights.

Naturally, you'll find true GT features. Unique Shelby styling. Luxury interior with bucket seats, complete instrumentation, wood-rim steering wheel, folding rear seat*.

You should expect a lot from a car built by America's first F.I.A. World's Champion. You'll get all you expect when you drive a Shelby GT 350 or GT 500. One is waiting at your Shelby dealer's now.

SHELBY G.T.
350 and 500
The Road Cars
Powered by *Ford*

Shelby American, Inc., 6501 West Imperial Highway, Los Angeles, Calif. 90009. Builders of the Cobra, Manufacturers of Cobra high performance parts and kits.   *optional at extra cost

IS _THIS_ ANY WAY TO SELL AN AUTOMOBILE?

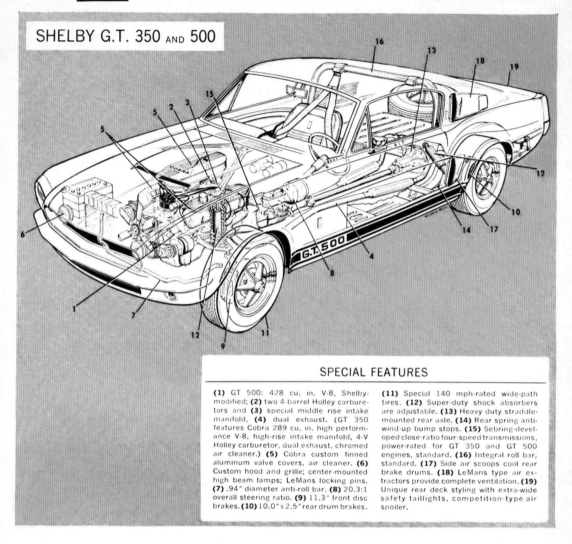

SHELBY G.T. 350 AND 500

SPECIAL FEATURES

(1) GT 500: 428 cu. in. V-8, Shelby-modified; **(2)** two 4-barrel Holley carburetors and **(3)** special middle rise intake manifold, **(4)** dual exhaust. (GT 350 features Cobra 289 cu. in. high performance V-8, high-rise intake manifold, 4-V Holley carburetor, dual exhaust, chromed air cleaner.) **(5)** Cobra custom finned aluminum valve covers, air cleaner. **(6)** Custom hood and grille; center-mounted high beam lamps; LeMans locking pins. **(7)** .94" diameter anti-roll bar. **(8)** 20.3:1 overall steering ratio. **(9)** 11.3" front disc brakes. **(10)** 10.0" x 2.5" rear drum brakes.

(11) Special 140 mph-rated wide-path tires. **(12)** Super-duty shock absorbers are adjustable. **(13)** Heavy duty straddle-mounted rear axle. **(14)** Rear spring anti-wind-up bump stops. **(15)** Sebring-developed close-ratio four-speed transmissions, power-rated for GT 350 and GT 500 engines, standard. **(16)** Integral roll bar, standard. **(17)** Side air scoops cool rear brake drums. **(18)** LeMans type air extractors provide complete ventilation. **(19)** Unique rear deck styling with extra-wide safety taillights, competition-type air spoiler.

Maybe not . . . but the Shelby GT 350 and GT 500 aren't just _any_ automobiles.

Carroll Shelby's aim was to build _road_ cars with enough comfort and convenience for anyone's taste—but cars in which even a _racing_ driver would feel at home. The 1967 Shelby GT 350 and GT 500 are the result. If you'll read the features listed above, you'll see why these cars are unique.

They're all yours for just $3995 (GT 350) or $4195 (GT 500).*

Did you read every word? Then you deserve a touch of _traditional_ auto advertising. So there!

SHELBY G.T. _350 and 500_ **The Road Cars** Powered by Ford

Shelby American, Inc., 6501 W. Imperial Highway, Los Angeles 90009

*Manufacturer's suggested retail prices. Options, accessories, delivery, dealer preparation, state and local taxes additional.

LEFT: Brittany Blue without any added accouterments creates a subtle yet striking look, as this GT350 shows. *SAAC Archives*

OPPOSITE: The GT350 and GT500 aren't just any automobiles.

BELOW: This early GT350 shows two very rare features: Running lights in the upper rear scoops, a feature only on the first 200 cars, and factory black paint, a very rare choice. *David Newhardt*

1967 SHELBY G.T. 350/500
The Road Cars

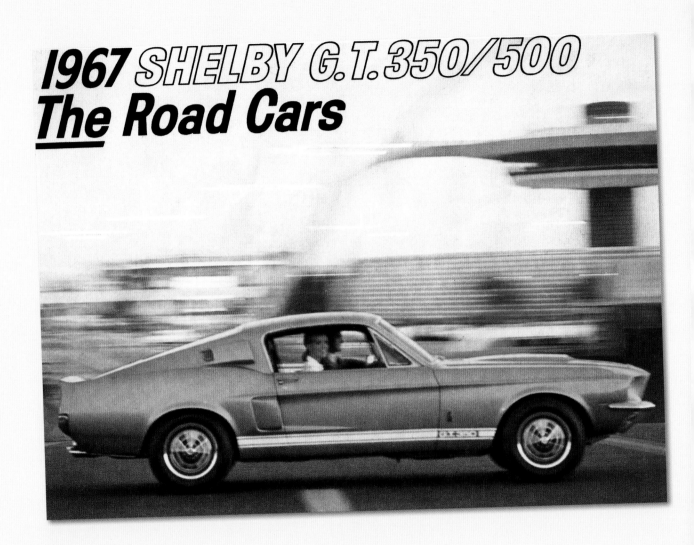

ABOVE: A sign of the times: the 1967 brochure car was Lime Gold. But look how much fun these folks are having sailing past LAX.

OPPOSITE TOP: It appears as if they made it to the beach in the brochure car as well.

OPPOSITE BOTTOM: Lime Gold may be an acquired taste for some, but with a Parchment interior it is one of my favorite combinations.

continued from page 124

the Art Center College of Design in Los Angeles. The typical career route for anyone who wanted to design cars was to head straight to Detroit upon graduation, but McHose took a different route and went to work for Ford of England. He intended to stay only a year, but he enjoyed the British racing scene so much that he remained there from 1961 until 1965, designing grilles, instrument panels, and interiors for vehicles such as the Cortina Mark II.

He then transferred to Detroit, where he worked on some unglamorous jobs, such as designing refrigerators for a company that Ford owned, but on some fun jobs, too, one of which was working on Ford's popular Mustang. In May 1966 he was assigned to go to California to help design Shelby's 1967 models. He arrived on May 21, but the first cars weren't due from Ford until June 10, so McHose spent the intervening weeks designing aluminum wheels for Shelby. On June 10, two Fiberglas bodies assembled by Dearborn Tubing arrived at Shelby's facilities to be used as design mules. Shelby also received a metal body to be used for the clay modeling; it had been used for crash testing and was pretty beat up and bent from the 40-miles-per-hour impact crash testing. Shelby's crew did their

best to straighten the body and mostly got it aligned, but one result of the damage the car sustained is still visible on 1967 Shelby Mustangs to this day: the left sides of the hoods ride higher than the right sides. The vendor built the Fiberglas hoods to Shelby's specifications, which were based on a car with a bent chassis. Shelby's employees did their best to align the hoods during the assembly process, but perfect alignment just was not possible.

Divine Inspiration

McHose took a lot of his inspiration from Ford's magnificent GT40, which was dominating the 24 Hours of Le Mans in historic fashion just as design work got underway for the 1967 Shelby Mustangs. The abovementioned scoop

continued on page 135

SHELBY MUSTANG GT350 & GT500

By Jerry Titus

THE PRE-1967 GT350, A SHELBY-AMERICAN RE-WORKED MUSTANG, WAS A PERFORMING CAR but, in many respects, it was more of a hot rod than a Grand Touring car, With a stripped-out interior, the optional suspension, a rock-crusher limited slip, the mechanical-lifter 289 high-performance V-8, and quick steering, it made a Mexican Road Race Ferrari look like an LTD when compared for noise, comfort, and driving ease. But there were plenty of buyers excited by this kind of "furry-ness," and the prime requisites of roadability and performance were certainly satisfied, so the cars sold. However, the people within Shelby-American were well aware of the shortcomings and the market limitations that they imposed. The '67 production Ford Mustang is a more sophisticated machine, and the GT350 takes maximum advantage of its attributes to improve not only the ride, comfort, driving ease, and noise level, but the handling as well! It is a substantially better and more practical machine, without sacrifice in the performance area.

Jerry Titus again did Shelby a solid with an in-depth and glowing review of the new 1967 Shelby Mustangs in *Sports Car Graphic magazine*.

SHELBY MUSTANG GT 350 & 500

BASE PRICE
$4195 (GT 350)
$4395 (GT 500)

ENGINE
Type....V-8, iron, water-cooled
Head.....Cast iron, removable
Valves....Ohv, pushrod/rocker
   actuated

GT 350
Max bhp.....306 @ 6000 rpm
Max. Torque.....329 lbs. ft. @
   4200 rpm
Bore....4.005 in. (101.73 mm)
Stroke.....2.87 in. (72.9 mm)
Displacement......289 cu. in.
   4737 cc
Compression Ratio....10.5 to 1
Induction System..Single Holly
   4 bbl.—750 cfm
Exhaust System.Standard, dual
Electrical System.........12 V
   distributor ignition

GT 500
Max. bhp....355 @ 5400 rpm
Max. Torque.....420 lbs. ft. @
   3200 rpm
Bore....4.13 in. (104.9 mm)
Stroke....3.984 in. (91.19 mm)
Displacement......428 cu. in.
   7015 cc.
Compression Ratio...10.5 to 1
Induction System....Dual Holly
   4 bbl. – 600 cfm
Exhaust System Standard, dual
Electrical System.........12 V
   distributor ignition

CHASSIS
Frame ....Unit, welded
Body.....Steel and fiberglass
Front Suspension .....Unequal
   arms, coil springs, adjusta-
   ble tube shocks, anti-sway
   bar.
Rear Suspension.....Live axle,
   multi-leaf springs, tube
   shocks
Tire Size & Type......Goodyear
   E70-15

WEIGHTS AND MEASURES
Wheelbase ....108 in.
Front Track ....58 in.
Rear Track ....58 in.
Overall Weight ....51.6 in.
Overall Width ....70.9 in.
Overall Length ....51.6 in.
Ground Clearance ......6.5 in.
Crankcase ....6 qts.
Cooling System.........20 qts.
Gas Tank..............18 gals.

GT 350
Curb Weight ....2723 lbs.
Test Weight ....3048 lbs.

GT 500
Curb Weight ....3286 lbs.
Test Weight ....3576 lbs.

CLUTCH
Type.........Single disc, dry
Diameter ....10.5 in.
Actuation ....Mechanical

TRANSMISSION
Type..Four-speed, full synchro
Ratios: 1st ....2.32 to 1
   2nd ....1.69 to 1
   3rd ....1.29 to 1
   4th ....1.00 to 1

BRAKES
Disc Diameter front ....11.3 in.
   rear .....10. in.
Swept Area ....n.a.

DIFFERENTIAL
GT 350
Ratio.................3.89 to 1
Drive Axles (type)....Enclosed,
   semi-floating
GT 500
Ratio.................3.25 to 1
Drive Axles (type)....Enclosed,
   semi-floating

STEERING
Type..Recirculating, ball sector
Turns Lock to Lock.........3.5
Turn Circle..............37 ft.

PERFORMANCE RESULTS

ACCELERATION
GT 350

0-30	2.8 sec.	0-70	9.0 sec.
0-40	4.1 sec.	0-80	11.8 sec.
0-50	5.6 sec.	0-90	15.0 sec.
0-60	7.1 sec.	0-100	
			19.3 sec.

Standing ¼ mile......15.3 sec.
   @ 91 mph
Top Speed (avg. two-way run)..
   129 mph

GT 500

0-30	2.8 sec.	0-70	8.1 sec.
0-40	4.0 sec.	0-80	11.8 sec.
0-50	4.9 sec.	0-90	15.0 sec.
0-60	6.7 sec.	0-100	
			16.9 sec.

Standing ¼ mile......14.3 sec.
   @ 92 mph
Top Speed (av. two-way run)..
   132 mph

FUEL CONSUMPTION
GT350
Test ....13 mpg
Average ....15 mpg

FUEL CONSUMPTION
GT500
Test ....9.4 mpg
Average ....11 mpg

RECOMMENDED SHIFT POINTS
GT 350
Max. 1st ....55 mph
   2nd ....78 mph
   3rd ....104 mph
RPM Red-line ....6200 rpm

SPEED RANGES IN GEARS:
1st .... 0 to 55 mph
2nd ....15 to 78 mph
3rd ....25 to 104 mph
4th ....35 to 129 mph

BRAKE TEST
74 Average % G, over 10 stops.
Fade encountered on 8th stop.

REFERENCE FACTORS
GT 350
Bhp. per Cubic Inch.......1.06
Lbs. per bhp. 8.8
Piston Speed @ Peak rpm.....
   2870 ft./min.
Swept Brake area per lb. ..n.a.
GT 500
Bhp. per Cubic Inch.....0.829
Lbs. per bhp. 10.0
Piston Speed @ Peak rpm.....
   3586 ft./min.
Swept Brake area per lb. ..n.a.

SPEEDOMETER ERROR
GT350

Indicated	30	40	50	60	70	80	90
Actual	30	40	51	61	70	79	88

GT500

Indicated	30	40	50	60	70	80	90
Actual	30	39	49	58	69	80	92

that mounts to the top of the bar. Its angle is wrong for any real crash protection, but a transverse bar at shoulder height (needed for correct mounting) would also bar access to the 'optional-but-you-can't-get-one-without-it' fold-down rear seat. Yet a lot of care has been exercised to make the bar both effective in an inverted emergency and to blend it into the interior as unobtrusively as possible. Most of the interior is regular-production Mustang. A wood-rimmed steering wheel bears a Cobra insignia, and the right side of the dash has an emblem that designates the model. The large speedo and tach, mounted directly forward of the wheel, are quite legible, but a small, twin nacelle below the dash houses the oil pressure and ammeter

(Continued on page 74)

The powerful GT500 (instrumentation and engine compartment shown at right) uses two four-barrel carburetors atop the 428-inch engine. Our test unit was equipped with air conditioning and automatic transmission. The sparkling GT350 shown in photos below makes good use of the wider track for improved ride and superior handling in tighter corners.

Photos: Bob D'Olivo

An added model for '67 is the GT500. It features a 428-inch engine. We frankly laughed out loud some 18 months ago when we heard such a prototype was planned. A huge hunk of cast iron sitting that high and that far forward? Lots of luck! Paying us no mind, they did it anyhow, and wound up with a very practical automobile. Combined with a three-speed automatic, the 427 is far more docile and more quiet than the 289, and outperforms it in every respect except gas mileage. You can feel some of the compensations made for the extra weight of the engine, but the end result is surprisingly good.

There were three major goals that Shelby's design/engineering team set out to accomplish with the '67 model: improve its quality, make it more distinctive, and *reduce* its cost. The latter requirement certainly isn't compatible with the first two. The goals were achieved only through months of intensive effort and several weeks' delay in getting the production line rolling. The result has been more than worth the effort and the wait, however.

In striving to make the GT look distinctive, redesign of the front and rear ends has been accomplished with the use of fiberglass components. Last year there were some problems with warpage of the fiberglass hoods, and it was expected that this year's model would have to absorb the extra weight of a steel hood in order to be assured of a decent fit. The problems were cured, however, and the '67s sport 'glass hoods with a split scoop in the center. The complete front grille surround-ing is also fiberglass and combines with the extended hood to make a very tasteful and effective change from the standard Mustang grille. The rear deck has a small spoiler lip molded in, and the rear fender caps or extensions (normally die-cast bolt-ons) are also of glass and flare up to match the deck contour, giving the entire rear a 'spoiler' configuration. Wide, special tail lights and a Cobra gas cap complete the distinctive appearance of the rear, but extractor type scoops cover the quarter sections of the roof and a small red 'safety' light is included in the aft opening of each, readily visible from behind and wired to actuate with the brake and turn-indicator lights. Lower in the rear quarter section is a functional air scoop for the rear drum-type brakes. This year you can buy the Shelby products in a wide range of colors and the bold, cop-attracting stripes have been left off. Shelby employees have found their 'ticket ratio' substantially reduced in the unstriped version.

Chassis changes are many. Power steering and power brakes are standard for both GT350 and GT500. The track, as on the production Mustang, is two inches wider. There is still good roll-stiffness, but the ride is quite a bit softer. Brake-pedal pressure is light, as is steering pressure, the latter a result of both the power assist AND a reduction of caster angle. This makes it a little bit too sensitive when you enter a fast corner, but this is a matter of driver adaptation. Also standard in both models is a roll-over bar. Optional — fortunately — is shoulder harness of the reel type,

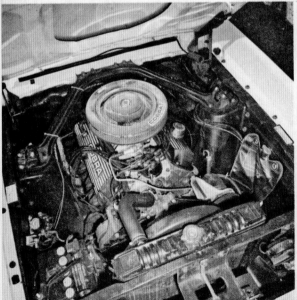

To enhance distinctive styling, high beams are moved to the grille center, rear fenders and deck are restyled to include a spoiler, and scoops are installed in quarter-panels for functional ventilation and brake-cooling. The 289 engine, lower left, is noisy, but light and very responsive. GT500 interior is shown below with auto-trans quadrant on the floor. Insert shows reel-type shoulder harness mounted to roll bar.

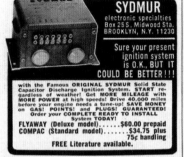
Next month in SCG
DAYTONA

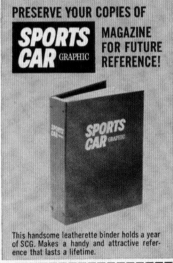
SHELBY MUSTANGS

Continued from Page 35

gauges. You can't read them without leaning hard to the right in the driver's seat.

The GT500, with its very efficient automatic transmission (at this writing it still hasn't been decided if this model will be offered with manual four-speed or not) doesn't perform much better than the GT350 in a straight line, but it does it with comparative ease and with a great reduction in noise level. Since the basic chassis in both models is a lot quieter, the solid lifters in the 350 are especially noticeable. This is further magnified at cruising speed because of the low (3.89) final drive ratio. The top speed of both models is nearly identical. The 500 got to 132 mph with a slow-reading speedo. Only the last ten mph came hard. The 350 worked fairly hard from the century mark up, but, even with ignition break-up on the top end, it still indicated 129 mph on a slightly fast speedo. With two Holleys, the 325-hp rating of the 500's power plant is probably conservative. There's nothing conservative about the amount of torque it puts out, however. It is a *very* docile engine and a very responsive one. The carburetion works well in both hard corners and hard stops — the severest tests. We didn't have a chance to check the hot-weather starting, but there certainly weren't any problems in a moderate ambient temperature. The 289 is, of course, in a higher state of tune with its hi-riser manifold and hot cam, so it idles rougher and noisier, but is otherwise quite easy to handle.

On the road, the 500 has a heavier 'feel' to it than the 350, but the only major difference is noticed when you come to dips in the road that really work the front springs and shocks. Then it wants to 'porpoise' a bit. The 350 is exceptional in this respect. It really flies over rough, dippy roads at high speed. Its comparatively better balance and an excellent choice of spring and shock rates are readily apparent. In corners, the 500 demands a considerably tighter 'hand on the reins', but it gets around surprisingly well, with less understeer than we expected. The 350 will go through the same corner appreciably faster, and is less demanding from a control standpoint.

The brakes on both models worked exceptionally well, but a softer-than-previous friction material made itself known by slight fade, squeak, and dive after continued hard use. Recovery was rapid and complete, however.

There is only two hundred dollars difference between the 350 and 500, so the major choice seems to be in the type of car you want. The 500 is a bit hotter in performance (with the automatic), considerably quieter, and more comfortable for normal use. It sacrifices overall handling and cornering power, however, and under-10-mpg fuel consumption is noteworthy in this de-partment. Factory installed air-conditioning is also available this year, and would be far more logical with the big engine. The 350, on the other hand, is really a highly roadable GT, and a long way from uncomfortable or unmanageable in traffic. Our congratulations, to the guys who built it, were shrugged off with, "Wait until you see what we have on the market in a couple of years if you think *this* one is more sophisticated!" Meanwhile, the present model will more than do. It only takes a ride around the block to see what we mean.

continued from page 129

festoonery, for example, mimicked the side scoops found on the GT40 race car, as did the tasteful rear spoiler—both of them McHose's work.

The air extractor scoops on the rear caused some controversy within Shelby American, mostly because Carroll Shelby himself had his heart set on retaining the clear rear quarter windows of the 1966 GT350s. The clear windows really were a more functional design, especially now that the cars had rear seats—they kept rear-seat passengers from becoming claustrophobic—but the redesign of the body shell didn't allow for as clean and fluid a design as that of the original. Available space only allowed for a chunky, trapezoidal, and extremely inelegant-looking window. After seeing this, Shelby agreed that McHose's air-extraction scoops were far better looking and relented, allowing the team to move ahead with McHose's design.

McHose intended the extractor scoop to be functional, and in accomplishing this, he put his childhood experience designing model airplanes to use. To test the function of the

ABOVE: The 1967 GT350 069 is finished in Acapulco Blue. Amazing how in just two years the Shelby Mustang could go from having a single color option to 10. *SAAC Archives*

OPPOSITE TOP: I found this car, 1318, in original paint deep in the slums of Phoenix many years ago. This is what it looked like after a proper restoration.

OPPOSITE MIDDLE: Inboard headlights, Magstar wheels, and just as it left the factory, with no stripes. A clean, sharp look if you ask me.

OPPOSITE BOTTOM: Parchment interiors are a desirable feature today and you can see why. It really brightens up an otherwise dark space.

LEFT: The new-for-1967 428-cubic-inch engine, with two Holley four-barrel carbs, really stuffed the engine compartment. Maintenance takes a lot longer to perform than it does on a GT350!

ABOVE: Bob Colby was a 21-year-old student who was also tending bar at Charley Brown's Steak and Lobster in Woodland Hills, California, in 1968 when a waitress said her husband needed to sell his 1967 GT350 because she was divorcing him. Some $2,600 later the young Mr. Colby was the Shelby's new owner. He remembers it was fast, good for attracting women, and bad for attracting driving awards, the latter which eventually forced its sale. *Tom Colby*

BELOW: This PR photo shows a very early 1967 Shelby GT, with its one-piece nose, parked on the tarmac at Shelby's LAX facility. *Road & Track/Hearst Magazines*

extractor scoop, he had someone race the car back and forth on a quarter-mile stretch of pavement outside the converted airplane hangar that served as Shelby American's manufacturing facility. As the driver floored it on this de facto drag strip, McHose sat in the back seat and smoked a cigarette. Observers alongside the pavement watched to see if smoke came out the extractor vents. Smoke came out, so apparently they worked to some degree.

Shelby did get his way when it came to the front end of the car. It was his idea to increase the length of the car, a change to be accomplished with redesigned Fiberglas front and rear fascias. However, making his idea reality was a huge job, requiring extensive additional work in designing an entirely new front end for the car, including a new hood. Originally the plan had been just to add a scoop to the existing hood. The rear was less problematic, given that the rear taillights were lifted from Mercury's Cougar, which shared the basic Mustang platform, but it still was no simple bolt-on operation. McHose had initially estimated the project would take four weeks. It took him four months, during which McHose worked virtually seven days per week.

LEFT: According to Rick Kopec of SAAC, this is one of the 1967 Mustangs that were used for the clay molds that mocked up the 1967 Shelby fiberglass. *SAAC Archives*

BELOW: The one and only 1967 Super Snake. *David Newhardt*

LEFT: Just in case the whitewalls didn't do it, the triple stripe across the top should make for a positive ID. *David Newhardt*

OPPOSITE TOP: Maybe I am just getting old, but don't the whitewall tires look great on the Super Snake? The stance is also perfect. *David Newhardt*

OPPOSITE BOTTOM: I don't know about you, but as cool looking as they are, I don't think I'd want to go 170 miles per hour on those skinny Goodyears, even when they were brand new. *David Newhardt*

McHose worked with Peter Brock and his assistant Pete Stacey at Shelby, and he also hired Joe Farrer, his former clay-modeling instructor at the Art Center, who assisted in interpreting the design sketches. In addition to lengthening the hood by 3 inches, they recessed the grille to make a dramatic tunnel. Stacey suggested using four headlights plus separate high-beam headlights. To simplify installation, he suggested mounting the high-beam headlights together in the center of the grille, creating a dramatic and unique face to present to the world.

The hood scoop was moved forward, even though the optimal position was in the more rearward position used on the 1965–1966 cars. This was done on the orders of Carroll Shelby, who felt that the forward position looked more balanced. Brock and McHose molded the scoop into the hood instead of tacking it on, as was done on the earlier car, creating an integrated whole.

In another nod toward the GT40 race car, the 1967 Shelbys featured red-bullet side-marker lights on the inside trailing edges of the extractor scoops. These were used on the GT40 to enable Ford's timing crew to better keep tabs on the racer at night on the track.

Just as in 1965 and 1966, the 1967 Ford Mustangs were built at Ford's San Jose plant as knockdown units and sent to Shelby American's plant at the Los Angeles International Airport for conversion into finished GT350 and GT500 cars.

Richard Morrison:
You Can Go Back—My GT350 Story

When it comes to American automobiles, it seems I've always been attracted to Fords. A family friend gave me a 1925 Model T Coupe—which I still have—52 years ago in 1962, when I was 14. My father, Milton Morrison, was born in 1917 and drove Ts in his youth. He taught me how to drive mine. Our family business had enough trucks to warrant a dedicated two-man shop to keep them in repair. That is where I rebuilt the T's engine and got it in good enough condition to drive to school for two years.

Since I'd drive it flat out down the hill at 40 miles per hour or so, my safety-conscious parents thought I should have a car that at least had good brakes. The front-wheel-drive-with-transverse-engine configuration was a new innovation at the time and seemed a sound safety idea for good traction in slick conditions. A used Safety-Fast-

Floats-on-Fluid-Most-Advanced-MG-Ever 1100 Sports Sedan with hydrolastic suspension became my transportation through high school. My first week at the University of Kansas, I loaned the MG to two fraternity pledge brothers who had a double date with girls from my home town of Salina. Ted must have been too infatuated with his date, because he ran a stop sign and caught a Monte Carlo near the rear wheel. The MG's body, from the doors forward, took an angle to the right. There was $400 damage to a $500 car, so it was totaled.

My brother, Roger, had convinced Dad that the roll bar built into the Studebaker Avanti made it a good safe car for him. "Hmmmm," I thought. "Shelby Mustangs have built-in roll bars!" The safety ploy worked, and soon I was ordering a new 1967 GT350 from my roommate Tim North's family's Ford dealership in Emporia. (Tim employed NASCAR driver Clint Boyer in his body shop.) The car was delivered to Broadway Ford in Kansas City, Missouri, where I picked it up. I had ordered a blue car with gold stripes like the Hertz GT350H had. Options were Mag Star wheels, four-speed transmission, air conditioning, power steering, power brakes, and AM/FM radio. I received a call that delivery would be delayed a couple months, but they had one, identically optioned, ready to ship. It was Medium Metallic Gray, though, and had no Le Mans stripes over the top. I asked how I would know how that combination would look; they told me to go to my Ford dealer and look at the exclusive Thunderbird color, Charcoal Gray. I did and decided I'd like that better than blue. I was soon cruising Mount Oread, the hill KU is built on, in No. 1242. My mother made a cushion that fit between the front seats on the driveshaft tunnel, so my girlfriend could sit close to me or so we could fit three across in the front seats.

The next summer, on my way to work on our farm in Arkansas, as I approached West Plains, Missouri, the car suddenly would barely run. I was able to limp into the Ford dealer. A couple days later, I learned the camshaft had broken, explaining why it was running on four cylinders. The car had just over 4,000 miles, the limit of the warranty. My protestation that the odometer ran 10 percent faster than actual distance, so it really was under warranty, got nowhere. Four thousand miles later, Ted—yes, the guy who wrecked the MG—and I were going to the KU–Oklahoma University football game when the cam broke again. Ted's uncle worked for the Oklahoma City Ford dealer and we were well taken care of there. The culprit turned out to be a missing bearing for the cam. We still were unable to collect on the warranty, even with such a gross error by Ford. I kept the car for nearly four years until I had an opportunity to purchase a Ferrari 250 GT/L Lusso, which

I still have. I sold the Shelby to a Salina hot-rodder and custom painter who painted it with sparkling glass beads in the clear coat and squiggly rounded corner rectangles down the sides. The last I saw it was on a local used car lot.

I always missed my 1967 GT350 and some 25 years ago, when I heard that Jim Nance was restoring a '67 (No. 2282) and it was for sale, I bought it from him. Jim had restored other Shelbys and has served as a SAAC judge, so I knew he would do a great job finishing it. It was in primer and ready for the color. I had to decide whether to keep it its original white or make it Medium Metallic Gray like my first one. The gray was so striking that that is what I chose, and I'm glad I did. Both cars had four-speed transmissions, air conditioning, power steering, power brakes, and Mag Star wheels. The only differences were the exterior colors and AM versus AM/FM radios. Number 2282 now has the proper AM/FM. I actually have the Sony under-dash cassette player that I had in No. 1242, but haven't installed it. I enjoy my "new" GT350 immensely. Driving one leaves no doubt that they are performance cars, yet civilized just enough that you don't feel beaten up when you finish. That is my definition of the perfect Gran Tourismo.

—Richard Morrison

Then . . . and now. Same people, and almost the same car!
Morrison Family

Without question all of the fuss over the Super Snake stems from this, the 427 GT40 Mk II engine stuffed under its hood. *David Newhardt*

Equine Growth Hormone

The big news for 1967 was big-block power. The GT350 model continued as the base vehicle, still using the 289/271-horsepower K-code Mustang, but to take full advantage of the much larger 1967 engine compartment, in place of Ford's available 390-cid engine Shelby stuffed in Ford's 428-cid Police Interceptor engine to create the GT500. This was, of course, the production engine used in the cars Ford sold to police fleets. Experience with the original GT350s had shown Ford and Shelby that people wanted the appearance of performance more than actual performance, and they believed that money would be better spent on developing the appearance of the Shelby Mustangs than on developing a race engine for the street.

Unlike the earlier Shelby Mustangs, the focus for 1967 was to create, as Shelby's literature of the day touted, "The Road Cars." Under the skin, no major reworking or racy engineering was put into play; the basic Mustang package got only mild tweaks, and all modifications were installed at Ford. The standard Mustang GT heavy-duty suspension was used, but with Shelby-specified stiffer springs and Gabriel adjustable shocks, a lower-cost substitution for the Konis used in prior years. A larger front sway bar was fitted as well. Power steering and power front disc brakes were standard. On the ground were special E70x15-inch Goodyear Speedway 350 tires on standard 15x6-inch Ford steel wheels with five-spoke hubcaps (lifted from the 1967 Thunderbird), optional 15x7-inch Kelsey-Hayes Magstar five-spoke aluminum wheels, or optional 15x7-inch Shelby aluminum 10-spoke wheels.

And, proving just how far they had come since 1965, 10 exterior colors were available, along with 3 different interior colors. The ever-popular Le Mans stripes that you see on almost every Shelby these days were never a factory option on 1967 and later cars. Owners have added almost all of them after the fact.

ABOVE: Even with a GT40 427 and a chromed grille, at the $7,500 or so a production Super Snake would have cost, Shelby clearly understood they wouldn't have sold any. *David Newhardt*

LEFT: This Dark Moss Green GT500 shows off its inboard headlights, with the later version chrome trim rings, and dealer- or owner-added Le Mans stripes. *SAAC Archives*

Transmission choices for 1967 saw changes as well. Gone was the Borg-Warner T-10 four-speed of 1965 and 1966, replaced by a standard Ford Toploader four-speed, used for both GT350s and GT500s. Automatic-equipped GT350s were fitted with the Ford C4, while automatic GT500s had the heavy-duty Ford C6 unit. Rear axle gear ratios for the GT350 remained unchanged at 3.89:1 for four-speed cars and 3.50:1 for automatics. The new GT500, with its torque monster 428, came with 3.50:1 gears in four-speed cars and 3.25:1 gears for automatics. All had an available factory-installed Ford Traction-Lok limited-slip differential or an optional dealer-installed Detroit Locker differential. As in the past, you could get just about any rear axle ratio you wanted installed at the dealer level.

On the inside, Shelby's touch was quite evident. All cars had Ford's Deluxe interior trim, and Shelby upgraded from there. A racy, if not at all functional, roll bar was fitted behind the front seats, with aircraft-style retractable shoulder harnesses mounted to it. A wood-rimmed, three-spoke, aluminum steering wheel with a Shelby snake center cap was the tiller, and under the center of the dashboard were two Stewart-Warner Green Line gauges for oil pressure and amps mounted in a modified 1965–1966 Mustang "Rally Pac" housing. Ford fitted a 140-mile-per-hour speedometer and an 8,000-rpm tach in the Mustang's gauge cluster, which also had the requisite

ABOVE: Shelby Mustangs landed right in the demographic of young, stylish people, a fact not lost on the Hathaway clothing company. This photo is an outtake from their print ad shoot. *Vern Estes*

BELOW: This is 483, a relatively early GT500 four-speed car in white with the optional Magstar wheels, and of course, the added-on Le Mans stripes that people can't get enough of!

temperature and fuel gauges. No longer was a rear seat optional; all cars came with fold-down rear seats. A factory-installed AM radio was available, with an AM/FM available as a dealer-installed option. For the first time, factory-installed air conditioning was available. After all, to look cool you need to be cool.

In the engine compartment, Ford's solid-lifter K-code 289 received only minor upgrades for use in the GT350. A Shelby dual-plane, high-rise aluminum intake manifold, essentially the same one used in 1966, was bolted on—again with a Holley 715-cfm four-barrel carburetor. Gone were the exhaust headers fitted in 1965 and 1966; for 1967 Shelby simply used Ford's stock cast-iron exhaust manifolds that led to the completely stock and highly restrictive Ford dual exhaust, which

for 1967 had dual resonators and a single transverse muffler. For a little flash, the familiar finned aluminum "Cobra Powered by Ford" valve covers were fitted, but for 1967 they were finished in black crackle paint with polished ribs and letters, the same treatment the late-1966 GT350s received. Horsepower remained rated at 306, but I wouldn't place any bets on the actual output getting close to that. For those who wanted a truly muscular GT350, 1967 was the second and last year that a factory-installed Paxton supercharger was available. This option promised a 46 percent bump in horsepower but lightened your wallet by almost $800—about $500 more than the GT500 option. As a result, just 28 cars left the factory with Paxton blowers under the hood.

The GT500's 428 Police Interceptor engine featured a mild hydraulic performance camshaft and was fed by two 600-cfm Holley carburetors on a Ford aluminum intake, with the whole works topped by an oval finned aluminum air cleaner. A measurement of 1,200

ABOVE: From the July 20 1967 press release: "NEW SHELBY MANIFOLD – Shelby American, Inc., racing engineer Chuck Cantwell examines details of new manifold for 289 CID Ford engine that was developed out of the Trans-American racing program to increase horsepower. Price, including two four-barrel carburetors, ranges up to $249.50, is less without carbs." An engineer AND a model? There is no can't in Cantwell. *Road & Track/Hearst Magazines*

BELOW LEFT: Ed Casey, Field Sales Manager from 1967–1970, loaned this 1967 GT500 to the Bridgehampton Race Circuit as a press car for their USRRC race in May, 1967. *Vern Estes*

BELOW: What makes this tag worth about a million bucks more than the one on any other 1967 GT500? Hint: Three stripes. *David Newhardt*

If you bought a new GT500 in California, it was delivered with Ford's "Thermactor" smog system as seen here. Most were quickly removed and, umm, "recycled," so a complete smog system is tough to come by these days.

cfm may have been serious overkill for this engine, but it sure did look the part. The engine was also dressed with matching finned aluminum valve covers that read "Cobra Le Mans." Heady stuff for a Mustang in 1967! The GT500's 428 was rated at 355 horsepower, all of which exhaled through stock Ford exhaust manifolds and the same restrictive exhaust used on the GT350, but with a slightly bigger transverse muffler. The ultimate option listed for the GT500 was the 427-cid medium-riser engine. At around $2,000, it is no shock that only two were ever built. A third 427 GT500 was built, this one with a 427 engine from a GT40, and named the Super Snake.

1967 Shelby GT500 Super Snake

Without question, the most famous 1967 GT500 of all is an engineering study car they call the Super Snake, or serial number 544. In February 1967, Carroll Shelby asked his chief engineer, Fred Goodell, to build a high-performance GT500 to be used for Goodyear Tire's high-speed testing. Goodell took the words *high speed* to heart and stuffed a white GT500 (serial number 544) full of the good stuff: a GT40 Mk II medium-riser 427 engine with a solid-lifter cam, lightweight aluminum cylinder heads, an aluminum water pump, wild GT40-style "bundle of snakes" exhaust headers, a big 780-cfm single Holley four-barrel, and a host of other GT40-style improvements for durability. The standard GT500 Toploader four-speed was retained, but a special Detroit Locker 4.11:1 rear end was fitted to get the 427 in the fat part of its power curve. To set the Super Snake apart from standard GT500s

visually, a unique three-band variation of Guardsman Blue Le Mans stripes—one fat stripe flanked by two skinny ones—was installed. The Super Snake is the only GT500 ever to leave Shelby with this stripe treatment. Upon completion, the Super Snake was ready for high-speed duty at Goodyear.

On March 17, 1967, Shelby American's principal engineer sent out a memo regarding Goodyear test vehicles. The memo outlined specific procedures for testing the Super Snake at Goodyear's San Angelo, Texas, test track from March 23 through March 27. Shelby employees were instructed to bring a "Spare lightweight 427 engine; Five (5) Shelby American Aluminum wheels (stowed in car); and a Mechanics tool box (stowed in car)."

At the San Angelo test track, Goodyear had arranged to film a promotional movie of the 500-mile high-speed tire test. The goal was to demonstrate the durability and safety of Goodyear's tires at high speeds. Carroll Shelby did his part by warming up the Super Snake and giving some easy 150-plus-mile-per-hour rides to the journalists on hand. After Shelby was done, Fred Goodell took over for the actual testing. During the 500-mile session, the Super Snake was clocked at 170 miles per hour and set a record

TOP: Compared to the 1965 and 1966 Shelby Mustangs, the 1967 version had it all over the earlier cars in comfort and trim level. Brushed aluminum trim, an exotic wood wheel, retractable shoulder harness belts, and numerous other creature comforts did indeed transform the B/Production champion into a grand touring car.

ABOVE: The rare Parchment interior color, one that the aftermarket has never seemed to be able to reproduce with any accuracy. *SAAC Archives*

ABOVE: With the addition of an automatic transmission, the 1967 interior becomes accommodating for even more drivers seeking ease of operation in their performance cars. *David Newhardt*

OPPOSITE TOP: From above you can really see the aircraft influence in Chuck McHose's design. *David Newhardt*

OPPOSITE BOTTOM: Dark Moss Green and no stripes: 3168 is all business. I wonder where Frank Bullitt got the idea for his Mustang? *SAAC Archives*

142-mile-per-hour average for the entire 500 miles. Obviously, the large engine oil cooler did its job keeping the carefully built GT40-spec engine alive!

Once the Super Snake was done testing tires, it was shipped home to Shelby American in Los Angeles. As was procedure with demo cars that were no longer needed, Shelby American went looking for a buyer for this well-broken-in GT500 with the funny stripes. Goodell contacted Don McCain, the former Shelby American sales representative who was also responsible for Shelby's GT350 Drag Units. McCain had stepped in as the high-performance sales manager for Mel Burns Ford in Long Beach, California, one of Shelby's best performance dealers. McCain loved the idea of this 427 GT500, with its potential to be a real Hemi killer. His idea was to have Shelby American build a limited run of 50 427-powered GT500s like the Super Snake, to be sold exclusively through Mel Burns Ford. The problem with this idea lay in the expense of the 427 engines. Even using a standard 427, these special GT500s would have cost more than $7,500. In 1967, that was 427 Cobra money. There was no way McCain could sell 50 Super Snakes. Only two other 1967 GT500s were fitted with a 427 from Shelby American, serial numbers 289 and 1947, but they were not Super Snakes.

The Super Snake was eventually sold to its first owners, James Hadden and James Gorman, both commercial airline pilots from Texas. Amazingly, the Super Snake has survived and remains a true piece of Shelby American history. The building of this car wasn't surrounded by the red tape usually imposed on manufacturers, and the only limit was how much they wanted to spend to make the ideal car. Just think how many Goodyear dealers showed the Super Snake movie and mentioned that their tires could go 500 miles at an average of 142 miles per hour safely. While every Shelby Mustang is

As you can see, it wasn't always sunshine and lollipops when Shelby went to the track, as evidenced here by the Shelby-prepared 1967 Trans-Am car of Jerry Titus after a particularly tough day at the track. *Road & Track/Hearst Magazines*

The Green Hornet after its recent, dead-nuts historically accurate restoration under Craig Jackson and his team at Billups Classic Cars. Note its correct retina-searing candy green paint, precisely matched to remnants of the Hornet's original finish discovered during restoration under the incorrect hue it had worn for years. Trust me, the photo doesn't do it justice! And while that may look like a vinyl top it actually is a textured satin black paint, another unique and correct aspect returned to this national treasure during restoration by the Billups crew. *Craig Jackson*

special, the Super Snake is certainly in a league of its own. As proof of that, in January 2019 the Super Snake sold at auction for $2,200,000, making it the highest priced Shelby Mustang ever sold up to that time—and a record that just might hold well into the future.

Junk in the Trunk

Although the new chassis' slick styling and newfound comfort was well received, it came at a price: added weight. The original 1964½ Mustang had weighed a mere 2,500 pounds. By 1966, the more luxurious and softer Shelby GT350 had grown to 2,800 pounds. For 1967, the Shelby, in GT500 form, had bloated to a porcine 3,370 pounds.

Even worse, most of that weight resided in the front of the car. Shelby had gone to great lengths to give the original GT350 even weight distribution, going so far as to mount the battery in the trunk in an attempt to get as close to 50/50 weight distribution as possible. The 1967 GT500 had a front-to-rear weight bias of 57/43. The problem was less pronounced in the GT350, which featured a 53/47 front-to-rear weight distribution, but even with the solid-lifter K-code 289, the small-engine version had too much weight to haul around. The GT500 had more snort, but even that was strained when hauling around an additional 500 pounds of flab.

In addition to sapping performance, the extra weight took a toll on fuel economy. *Sports Car Graphic* only managed to squeeze 9.4 miles out of every gallon of gasoline. Still, magazines loved the new GT500, which *Car and Driver* called "a grown up sports car for smooth touring. No more wham-bam, thank-you-ma'am."

Flexing Ford's Muscle

Ford had loaned Shelby another key figure in the development of the 1967 Shelby Mustangs: Fred Goodell, Shelby's chief engineer for the project. Ford had big plans for Shelby, hoping to nearly double 1966's output. Ford's goal for 1967 was 4,000 units, and Don Frey believed that output would be a lot easier to achieve with another Ford employee in a key position. Frey was correct to worry; upon joining Shelby, Goodell discovered that he'd stepped into a steaming mess. Goodell arrived at Shelby American in September 1966, three months after production was supposed to have begun, and of the hoped-for 4,000 cars, Shelby had completed just 40.

Part of the problem was that much of the development had taken place on the abovementioned bent body, and installation of parts was taking far too much hand labor and hence far too much time. Mechanics were spending hours hand-sanding and finishing parts that should have taken just minutes to bolt on. But another part of the problem was that suppliers were having a hard time mass-producing Fiberglas parts to the required tolerances. In the end, fiberglass panels were sourced from a number of suppliers, with a number of construction and fabrication differences throughout the 1967 production run.

With Goodell's assistance, the pace of production improved. In its third year of building Mustangs, Shelby American again upped production considerably, selling a total of 3,225 cars for the 1967

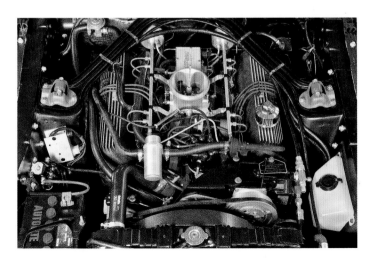

TOP: A vintage 1968 factory photograph of the Green Hornet's original independent rear suspension. This, like the EFI, was really high-tech stuff back in 1968. Note the coil-over shocks that look very much like GT40/Cobra Daytona Coupe units. This IRS setup was later removed and replaced with a conventional live axle.

ABOVE: From a Shelby press release dated November 24, 1967: "Carroll Shelby (second from right) accepts Trans-American Sedan Championship trophy from John Bishop, executive director of the Sports Car Club of America. Shelby-prepared Mustangs won the over two-liter championship for the second straight year. At left is Jerry Titus, who drove the No. 17 Mustang to victory in 4 of the 12 events. Jacque H. Passino (right), *Ford Motor Company* special vehicles manager, announced that Ford would seek to maintain the Mustang championship in the 1968 Trans-American series."

LEFT: Paint color and cosmetic details aside, by far the coolest aspect of the recent restoration of the Green Hornet is the reinstallation of its complete, functioning original Conolec EFI system. Cooler still, it was fitted by Chris Long, son of Conolec creator David E. Long. I can bear witness that it works better than any carburetor after watching Craig Jackson smoke the Green Hornet's tires for roughly a city block on his first drive! Another fantastic technical detail of the restoration was returning the independent rear suspension to its exact original specification, as shown in the vintage photo above, including the correct adjustable Armstrong shocks—the same as were used in the 427 Cobras. *Craig Jackson*

model year. In a complete about-face, what started out as an endeavor to sell just enough cars to get SCCA homologation for racing was now a full-fledged effort to build street cars for people to buy. It was a sign of things to come at Shelby American.

Inboard-Outboard

Like earlier cars produced at Shelby American, the 1967 models were not immune to running production changes. However, by 1967 most of the bugs were being worked out with suppliers and production techniques, so most new changes were minor in nature. The biggest and most visible change was to the location of the grille-mounted high-beam headlamp. Soon after production began it was discovered that the center-mounted headlamps were illegal in some states and had to be moved. Shelby had been so overwhelmed by building the early cars with the misaligned and poorly manufactured Fiberglas parts that it hadn't cleared the grille-mounted high beams with any state's department of motor vehicles, including California's omnipotent DMV. After Shelby had built nearly 200 GTs, Goodell met with representatives of California's DMV in Sacramento and learned that the state had strict requirements regarding the distance between headlights. This necessitated a new grille design, which moved these lights far apart—hence they are called "outboard"-light cars. Because meetings with the DMV folks in Sacramento had been especially contentious, Shelby made certain that the inboard cars left the state of California.

The DMV also took issue with the red side-marker lights Shelby used, and this was a nationwide issue rather than just a California issue. No state allowed the use of red side-marker lights on anything other than emergency vehicles like ambulances and fire trucks. But before Shelby had a chance to make this change the first 200 cars or so left the factory with the now highly sought-after factory side marker lamps. Of course, as we all know Shelby American was a small manufacturer that was continually juggling production issues, compliance with laws and regulations, and a tight budget, so by no means was the side marker light debacle the last running production change for the 1967 model year by a long shot!

1967 Shelby Little Red Prototype

One of the coolest prototypes built at Shelby American was the 1967 Mustang notchback coupe (serial number 0131), which became known as Little Red. Its purpose was to

ABOVE: The one and only "Little Red" as photographed by Marty Schorr at Shelby's 1968 model-year press preview at Riverside Raceway. It is one of just a few photos known to exist of "Little Red" when new, so thankfully Marty decided to go to Riverside that day as photographs like this are invaluable references to one-off prototypes like this, especially when the goal is to restore them precisely as they were when new. Rest assured Craig Jackson and his team at Billups Classic Cars will be spending many hours looking at these old photos with magnifying glasses in hand! *Martyn L. Schorr*

OPPOSITE TOP: The 1967 Shelby Trans-Am Mustangs line up on the grid at Bridgehampton, 1967. Lew Spencer marks the grid position of number one directly in front of the car while Chuck Cantwell marks the position at the front left tire.

OPPOSITE MIDDLE: A 1967 Shelby team car in action at Sebring.

OPPOSITE BOTTOM: In the pits at Marlboro, August 1967, Carroll Shelby kneels down for a closer look at his crew hard at work keeping one of their dogs in the hunt. Yet more evidence that everybody involved took racing seriously and wanted to do nothing more than win.

evaluate the concept of offering a notchback body style Shelby. Starting life as one of three 428-cubic-inch powered Candy Apple Red Mustangs all ordered on August 9, 1966, the unassuming red coupe soon was subjected to numerous modifications. It was a real-world test bed for lots of ideas that never saw production, but we all certainly wish they had. For example, the 428-cubic-inch Police Interceptor engine with dual Holley four-barrels was fitted with not one but two Paxton superchargers while at Shelby. Add in 10-spoke alloy wheels, a black-painted top, full GT500 bodywork (scoops and all), and luxury items like a full leather interior, and it made for one wild ride.

Little Red was used at various press previews and promotional shows and was loaned out to select automotive journalists and even celebrities like Bill Cosby. When Little Red wasn't "working," Carroll Shelby and Fred Goodell were no strangers to its driver's seat, and could you blame them? Little Red was also the inspiration for the styling of the 1968 Mustang GT California Special.

But the best part? For 50 years, Little Red was believed to have been crushed when its experimental duties were complete. However, in 2018, through an amazing series of events, Little Red was found hiding in plain sight in Texas. Having sat outside for decades, Little Red was weathered and missing its drivetrain, but it was unmistakably the long-lost

Both 1968 styling prototype cars, the convertible 0139 and the fastback 0100, act natural for the camera.

Shelby that even the most dedicated car hunters had written off decades prior. The Green Hornet's owner, Barrett-Jackson CEO Craig Jackson, soon heard of this discovery and immediately seized the opportunity to purchase this hugely historic Shelby. The reuniting of these two cars in one garage makes what is unquestionably one of the most significant pairings of Shelby prototypes of all time. Under Jackson's stewardship, Little Red will be comprehensively restored to its exact 1967 specification, and I know I'm not alone in anxiously awaiting the end result.

1967 Shelby GT500 Convertible

In late 1966, Shelby American ordered two other 428-powered Mustangs to accompany #0131 that became "Little Red." They consisted of a convertible (#0139), along with an identically equipped Fastback (#0100). While Little Red was a well-known prototype at Shelby, the convertible has always been more of a mystery until recent years.

When Ford took control of Shelby in October 1966, the plan to offer a convertible Shelby Mustang simply moved to the 1968 model year. As such, #0139 was turned into a "1968 design" GT500 Convertible styling prototype for photographic (advertising) use with help from A. O. Smith Plastics. Artist renderings were used to fabricate a redesigned fiberglass hood, front end, tail light panel, and center console. These components would be the most visible differences over the 1967 styling and would offer great improvements to the build quality and performance of the Shelby GT models.

Between April and July 1967, the restyled convertible (#0139) and Fastback (#0100) were photographed at Malibu Beach, the San Jacinto Mountains, Hollywood Park Horse

Here's Little Red, as found March 3, 2018, in north Texas. This amazing find had the entire Shelby world rejoicing. I was privileged to see Little Red shortly after its discovery, and I was amazed by its condition and how well its original features had survived. Seeing this car in the flesh immediately answered many questions and laid to rest many inaccurate assumptions long held as fact. I know I'm not alone in anxiously awaiting the day when Little Red emerges from the exacting restoration now underway, not to mention the awesome fact that it will live next to the Green Hornet prototype. *Craig Jackson*

ABOVE: Here is 0100 in one of the better-known early 1968 Shelby PR photos.

OPPOSITE: It is interesting to see where Ford placed their PR cars for various ads, and what cars they would pair up. Here 0139 is joined by a Torino Sportsroof at a school administration building. Maybe they thought students were an emerging market?

Track, Shelby's L.A. airport facility, and Idyllwild. Initial photos captured the convertible wearing its original Candy Apple Red paint, with subsequent shoots revealing the car had been repainted Wimbledon White.

Select dealers and members of the press were first introduced to the two "new" 1968 Shelbys at Ford's Long-Lead Technical Conference (LLTC) held at Riverside International Raceway, on July 6–7, 1967.

In August 1967, the 1968 dealer marketing materials were sent to the printer, the Shelby American operation facility in Los Angeles closed, and a small staff was relocated to Ionia, Michigan. Some company cars were sold off. Others, including the '67 convertible, were shipped to Dearborn for "disposal." Because the Shelby GT convertible was a regular production car that had retained all its original driveline and federally mandated safety equipment, Ford most likely made the decision to sell the car through its employee purchase and auction resale lot (commonly referred to as the "B-lot"). It appears that #0139 may have been sold to a Chicago-area dealer and is known to have remained in the Chicagoland area for many years after that. In August 1978, James Ventrella acquired the car. Like the owners before him, Ventrella purchased the car thinking it was a 1968 Shelby

An exclusive Los Angeles members-only club, a prototype GT500 Fastback with crazy emblems, and a model relaxing on your trunk. Life is good in a 1968 Ford ad.

GT500 convertible, because, well, that is what it had always looked like. Despite its exterior appearance, Ventrella discovered several anomalies and was the first to propose that the convertible was actually something more than "just another Shelby."

#0139 was purchased by its current caretakers in 2009 who exhaustively researched its history, making much of its shrouded past known. In 2013, based on this research, the convertible was restored to its December 1966 "earliest point as a Shelby" configuration. While we may never know all of the details of its early years, we know a lot more than was known decades ago—and for Shelby history buffs everywhere, that is a good thing.

1967–1968 Shelby Trans-Am Mustang Race Cars

By 1967, SCCA professional racing and the Trans-Am series were serious business. After winning the series and the Manufacturer's Championship in 1966 with Shelby-prepared Mustang notchback coupes, Ford was foaming at the mouth to do the same in 1967. However, rather than just have Shelby American prepare Mustang race cars for SCCA Trans-Am, Ford employed lessons learned about relying on privateers to win the series. Doing so in 1966 would have cost them the series, had it not been for Shelby's last-minute intervention, so company execs were convinced that they needed a factory effort. And who better to field the factory team than Shelby? So, for 1967, Shelby American not only built Ford's Group II SCCA race Mustangs, it also ran the factory two-car effort. Additional cars would be built and sold to privateers as well to ensure a strong Ford presence in this ultimate SCCA series, which had fans lining the fences (and piling into showrooms as a result of Ford's win).

Both Shelby and Ford knew that 1967 would not be like shooting fish in a barrel. Nobody likes to lose, especially GM and Chrysler, both of whom would be hot on Ford's heels. The competition would be tough; Chevrolet's new Camaro was a serious threat, as was Ford's own Mercury division, which would be entering the series with Bud Moore–prepared Mercury Cougars. Nothing like a little sibling rivalry. Ford wasn't about to race without a backup plan to win the SCCA title, should Shelby fail.

The car prep rules for 1967 were essentially the same as in 1966: four-seat "sedans," full interiors, factory glass windows, steel body panels, no hood scoops, and so on. The result was a 1967 Trans-Am Mustang that was just an evolution of the 1966 version, which under the skin was essentially a 1965 Shelby GT350 R Model. After all, if it ain't broke, don't fix it, right? Under the hood for 1967, the full-race 289-cid Shelby engine remained, but with a new dual-quad, high-rise, aluminum intake manifold topped by a pair of Holley 600-cfm carburetors, as well as other detail changes.

The transmission remained a close-ratio aluminum T-10M, just like that in the GT350. In the trunk was a modified 32-gallon R Model fuel tank, essential for the long-distance races in Trans-Am. After racing this same basic package for two years, Shelby knew it worked. It had won the SCCA B/Production National Championship in the GT350 and the A/Sedan Trans-Am National Championship in the Mustang notchback.

In the end, the 1967 Mustang Group II race cars did indeed win the fiercely competitive 1967 Trans-Am Series Manufacturer's Championship, narrowly defeating the Cougars from corporate cousin Mercury. Chevrolet

ABOVE: This one shows the wonders of photo editing in these pre-Photoshop days. Can you spot the differences?

BELOW: Ford (and Shelby) were always economical with their prototype cars. Here 0139, now painted red, is parked with 0100 and Carroll Shelby for a PR shot.

The faithful reproduction of the original prototype GT500 badges on 0139. *Samantha and Brian Styles*

You can only change so many engines in a weekend, and Shelby's team found the limit in a hurry.

ran a distant third with the new Camaro Z/28. All told, Shelby built 26 Group II Mustang race cars for 1967, 4 of which he used in his factory effort in the series and 22 of which were sold to other teams.

Unfortunately, and unbeknownst to Shelby at the time, it was the last year he would have a dominant car in the Trans-Am series.

After winning the 1966 and 1967 Trans-Am series, Ford was hoping for a three-peat in 1968. Shelby was again seen as the right man for the job, although the logistics and corporate landscape at Shelby American had recently changed greatly. Shelby American had split into new companies. The Shelby Racing Company remained in California, with headquarters in Torrance. As the name implies, this division handled anything to do with the many racing projects in which Shelby had a hand. It was Shelby Racing that would take charge of building the 1968 Trans-Am Mustangs. Ford shipped Mustang coupes from Dearborn, Michigan, to Torrance for the conversion.

Although the cars look very similar to the 1967 Group II racers, 1968 was a year of big changes under the skin in SCCA Trans-Am car preparation. Arguably to keep things interesting on the track and the competition fierce, the SCCA loosened up the rules for 1968. As long as the minimum weight of 2,800 pounds was achieved (it usually wasn't), and the cars looked reasonably stock on the outside, certain liberties were allowed. No longer did the SCCA require full interiors; roll cages were now allowed, as were 8-inch-wide wheels and fender flares. Four-wheel disc brakes were now acceptable, and other rule changes made the field much faster than before.

The 1968 Shelby Group II cars were suitably upgraded and featured huge Lincoln front disc brakes, with 1965–1967 Mustang Kelsey-Hayes four-piston front disc brakes fitted to the rear. Stopping was not an issue. The roll-cage rule was used to full advantage with the addition of a carefully designed roll cage that stiffened the chassis considerably. Numerous suspension modifications were implemented and, in what Shelby and Ford deemed the equivalent of bringing a gun to a knife fight, Ford's new Tunnel Port 302-cid engine was to be used. The Tunnel Port name came from a port design based on the NASCAR 427 engine, with nearly straight intake ports on the heads. The engines also featured huge valves and a high-rise dual-quad intake with Holley carburetors, as well as four-bolt main bearing caps in the short block. This was a true racing engine, not a modified street engine. Power was reported to be in the 450-horsepower range. However, in perhaps one of the most detrimental decisions made by Ford in the 1968 season, the company mandated that all of the Trans-Am engines would be built at Ford in Michigan and shipped to Shelby for installation, and they were to be returned to Ford for post-race teardown and inspection. It was a classic case of a manufacturer making change for the sake of change itself, and it proved to be a huge mistake.

The Ford engines were notoriously unreliable, with massive oiling-system problems that caused engines to blow left and right. It was not uncommon for a single car to blow two engines in practice and one during the race. It was a disaster. You can only change so many engines in a weekend, and Shelby's team found the limit in a hurry.

As a result of Ford's micromanagement of the Shelby Racing Company team, 1968 was a disaster. The competition that had nipped at their heels in 1967 was better than ever in 1968, and Chevrolet's Penske/Sunoco Camaro Z/28s soundly trounced Ford, ending its chances of winning the 1968 championship. Chevrolet walked away with the series, with 105 points to Ford's 63 points in the final SCCA standings. Five 1968 Shelby Mustang Trans-Am cars were built and raced, along with two of the 1967 cars that had been updated and brought along as backup cars. Who knows what would have happened, had Shelby Racing been allowed to build its own engines? The fact remains that 1968 was a disappointing year in Trans-Am for both Ford and Shelby.

TOP: Now fully restored to its red 1968 bodywork configuration, 0139 has enjoyed a nationwide tour over the past few years. *Samantha and Brian Styles*

ABOVE: As complex of an engine compartment you'll ever see in a Shelby. 0139 has power everything, A/C, and the Thermactor system. *Samantha and Brian Styles*

Chapter 5

The Beginning of the End

ABOVE: 1968 was a year of major change for the Shelby Mustang. Now built in Michigan at A. O. Smith, and not in California at Shelby American, the writing was on the wall. The Ford GT program had spoiled Shelby and he lost interest in being a manufacturer of sporting Mustangs. But nobody can deny they were still striking machines, especially in a loud color such as this GT350, 03218, that is one of just three cars finished in WT5185 Special Orange paint. If the color looks familiar it should: WT5185 was previously called Poppy Red.

RIGHT: Speaking of A. O. Smith, here is a press photo showing the first Shelby GTs to roll down the line at what was technically the Smith Plastics division in Ionia, Michigan. Smith Plastics produced the special hoods, noses, and deck lids for Shelby. *Road & Track/ Hearst Magazines*

The introduction of the GT500 fueled a huge boost in sales. While not quite achieving Ford's targeted 4,000 units, Shelby did have a record year. Sales of the GT350 were down slightly, at 1,175 units, but that was only because most buyers were stepping up to the GT500, which sold almost twice as many units: 2,048 GT500s for the 1967 model year. Including the convertible and the Little Red notchback prototypes, Shelby produced a total of 3,225 Mustangs that year.

The 1968 model year marked the beginning of a new chapter for Shelby. For once, the cars changed little while the way they were made—and the company that made them—changed drastically. By the end of 1967, Shelby American was building far more cars than the company ever expected and had simply outgrown its production plant at Los Angeles

Carroll Shelby
designed his COBRA GT
to go like it looks

A brand-new Ford 302 cubic inch V-8 delivers for the GT 350. On the GT 500, a Ford 428 cubic inch V-8 is standard, with a new 427 V-8 powerhouse as a super-performance option. □ Four-speed transmissions are standard, close-coupled automatics are low-cost options. □ Great handling comes from competition engineered suspension, 16-to-1 ratio power steering, adjustable shocks, heavy duty driveline and rear axle, and special high performance 130-MPH rated nylon tires. Front disc brakes, of course. □ And with this superb performance, Cobra GTs deliver head-turning styling and luxury, too. □ Interiors gleam with unique simulated wood grain trim on instrument panel, steering wheel, console and door panels. □ The exterior styling features work for you. □ Hood scoops supply extra carburetor air, fastback louvers are air extractors. □ Safety has not been overlooked— wide-rim wheels, integral overhead bar and shoulder harnesses are included. □ Carroll Shelby's unique fastbacks and new-for-'68 convertibles, are design-based on the Mustang, winner of two consecutive Trans-Am road racing championships. □ And that means real economy, a surprisingly low price for you. □ All four Cobra GTs say "Let's go!" □ See your Shelby Cobra dealer—and get going!

(S) Shelby COBRA GT 350/500   POWER BY Ford

TOP Photos such as this one of a 1968 GT350 engine taken during R&T's road test are worth their weight in gold for today's authenticity police and restorers alike. *Road & Track/Hearst Magazines*

ABOVE: Even a kinder, gentler GT350 could still light 'em up. *Road & Track/Hearst Magazines*

LEFT: This early 1968 ad mentions that a 427-cubic-inch engine would be available, but that was not to be. Wishful thinking or creative advertising? You be the judge.

ABOVE: The Car Life test car, clawing its way to some surprisingly good performance numbers. *Road & Track/Hearst Magazines*

RIGHT: Another early 1968 advertisement, intended for dealers to personalize and run in their local newspapers (remember those?) It also references the 427 engine option that would never materialize.

International Airport. Ford's involvement continually pushed Shelby American to become a mass producer of a standardized product instead of remaining a specialty shop that built cars to order.

Adding capacity at Shelby's LAX facilities was not an option, either. While Shelby was preparing to begin 1968 model year production, North American Aviation canceled Shelby's lease, which was set up on a month-to-month basis. The airport owned the property, and zoning regulations stated that any aviation-related industry had top priority. Shelby had no choice but to move. Shelby explored the possibility of leasing property from Southern Pacific Railroad, near Ford's San Jose plant, but that plant was operating at full capacity building regular Mustangs and the plant manager didn't want to interrupt production to build cars for Shelby.

So with Shelby's lease up at LAX, and Ford pushing for standardized production of "their" Shelby Mustangs, Shelby American suddenly became

LEFT WORKSHEET

filled @ 1357 - 14.4 gal
@ 1588 14.9 gal
@ 1741 - 11.8 gal

6/67

R O A D   &   T R A C K
ROAD TEST WORKSHEET

Make & model GT350   Issue _____ Date 3-25-68

odometer mileage 1685   By RW & JTC

SPEEDOMETER CALIBRATION

rpm	ind.	time (sec)	actual
1350	30	3.408	26.4
1750	40	2.496	36.0
2250	50	1.962	45.9
2700	60	1.618	55.6
3150	70	1.377	65.4
3650	80	1.196	75.2
4100	90	1.062	84.7

Odometer: _____ actual = 5.15 indicated

ACCELERATION: 0 to speed in sec

30	3.2	3.0	3.3	3.1		3.2
40	4.3	4.1	4.2	4.0		4.2
50	6.2					6.2
60	7.6	7.6	7.4			7.5
70						
80	12.2	12.5	12.4			12.3
90						
100	21.0	20.7	21.1	21.2		21.0

BRAKING. Panic stop from 80 mph:

ft/sec² 26-24 Control 5000

Comments LR slight lock

Fade: 6 stops from 60 mph:

| 1 | 33 | 3 | 40 | 5 | 42 7.80 |
| 2 | 37 | 4 | 40 | 6 | 62 8.150 |

Comments with P L

Standing 1/4-mile: 16.64 shift weselt
16.35 16.66 16.50 16.61 16.5

ACCELERATION: time to distance in ft

100					
200	5.4	5.6	5.3	5.4	5.6
400	7.9	8.3	7.9	8.2	8.1
600	10.3	10.2	10.1	10.2	10.2
1000	13.6	14.2	13.8	14.0	13.9

Parking: Hold 30% grade? _____

COASTING: from 80 mph:

70 mph 8.2   8.6 9.4
60 mph 10.0   10.1 19.4
50 mph 13.4   12.0 31.1
40 mph 15.2   14.6 14.3

shifts at tach 4800: 1-2 50
2.3 78

on decel in "2" 2nd engage @ 66
" " "1" 2nd @ 18

TOP SPEED: Indicated mph 112 rpm

WEIGHT:
Front 1910
Total 3500
Rear 1600

TACHOMETER CALIBRATION

Indicated	Actual		Indicated	Actual
1000	950		4000	4150
2000	2000		5000	5100
3000	3100		6000	

auto shift: @6900: 1-2 46
2-2 68

RIGHT WORKSHEET

6/67

$1.00   slight lever buzz above 3000; severe when accelerating   37.30 {3.00
carb's 2nd barrels don't open 'til 4500!   40.69
lights on door panels on   w/s washer pisses on full accel in 1st, 2nd

R O A D   &   T R A C K
ROAD TEST WORKSHEET

Make & model Shelby GT 350 rerun   manual shift   Issue June   Date _____

odometer mileage _____   By _____ & _____

SPEEDOMETER CALIBRATION

rpm	ind.	time (sec)	actual
1400	30	35.0	25.7
1850	40	26.5	34.0
	50		
2800	60	140.7	51.2
3250	70	119.8	60.0
3770	80		
4235	90		
4750	100		

Odometer: _____ actual = _____ indicated

ACCELERATION: 0 to speed in sec

30						(avg)
40	3.4	3.2	3.3	3.0	3.4	3.4	3.2
50						
60	5.2	5.2	5.3	4.8	5.3	5.0	5.0
70						
80	8.6	8.1	8.5	8.2	8.6	8.4
90						
100	11.8	13.0	12.2	12.2	11.8	12.5	12.2

BRAKING. Panic stop from 80 mph:

ft/sec² _____ Control _____

Comments _____

Fade: 6 stops from 60 mph:

| 1 | 3 | 5 |
| 2 | 4 | 6 |

Comments _____

Standing 1/4-mile: 14.91 15.07 14.80 15.02 15.1

ACCELERATION: time to distance in ft

(Avg)								
	5.0	200	5.2	4.8	5.0	5.0	5.0	4.9	5.0
	7.2	400	7.2	7.3	7.2	7.3	6.9	7.2	7.2
	9.3	600	9.4	9.3	9.3	9.2	9.3	9.4	9.3
	12.4	1000	12.3	12.5	12.4	12.7	12.4	12.6	12.0

Parking: Hold 30% grade? _____

COASTING: from 80 mph:

70 mph _____
60 mph _____
50 mph _____
40 mph _____

1-2 55 @6000
2-3 76 " "
2-4 100 " "

WEIGHT:
Front 1770 1820
Total 3465 3495-160
Rear 1675 1665

1st @ 10 3250
2nd " 2400
3rd " 1800
4th " 1400

TACHOMETER CALIBRATION

Indicated	Actual		Indicated	Actual
1000			4000	
2000			5000	
3000			6000	

TOP SPEED: Indicated mph _____ rpm

ABOVE LEFT: The hard facts from R&T's performance testing of the automatic 1968 GT350. In spite of the new lo-po 302 engine and lazy automatic it still went 0 to 60 in 7.5 seconds, an impressive number at the time. *Road & Track/Hearst Magazines*

ABOVE RIGHT: Even more impressive were the times laid down by R&T's Paxton S/C 1968 GT350 four-speed test car: 5.0 second average 0 to 60 times! But the notes at the top are the best part: "w/s washer pisses on full acceleration . . ." and "carb's 2nd barrels don't open 'til 4500 RPM!" *Road & Track/Hearst Magazines*

RIGHT: Carried over from 1967 were the upper and lower side scoops and the roll bar with retractable shoulder harnesses, all visible here. The hubcaps were new for 1968.

three separate companies, each with an individual focus. It was simple evolution and a predictable move. Starting with the 1968 model year, all production Shelby Mustangs would be overseen by the new Shelby Automotive, Inc., based about 2,000 miles east of LAX in Livonia, Michigan. Actual assembly of the cars was subcontracted by Ford to A. O. Smith in Ionia, Michigan.

A. O. Smith had recently lost its contract to assemble Corvettes for General Motors and was interested in filling that revenue hole. John Kerr, Shelby's general manager, was friends with a Smith employee named George McCellan, and he put McCellan in touch with the people from Ford. Ford realized that having A. O. Smith assemble Shelby Mustangs would be a perfect opportunity to get a handle on Shelby production costs and improve quality control. Combined with a decrease in shipping costs when working with an in-state partner, it meant that every Shelby Mustang Ford sold would have a higher profit margin.

Another change, this one at Ford, had a serious impact on the relationship between the company and Carroll Shelby. Ford had poached Semon E. "Bunkie" Knudsen from

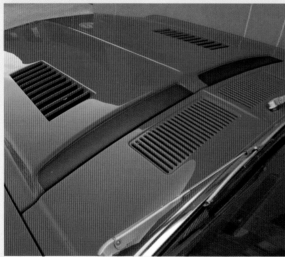

TOP: Gone was the aluminum trim of 1967, replaced with the finest sticky wood known to Detroit. The console now continued to the dash, with integral oil pressure and ampere gauges. Also new was the heavily padded parts bin steering wheel that had both tilt and a vacuum-operated swing-away feature. Fancy stuff for a sports car.

ABOVE LEFT: The new 1968 hood had twin scoops at its leading edge, extraction vents aft, and these black vinyl decals to add some detail at the rear.

ABOVE RIGHT: With the GT350 one could still see the ground through the engine compartment and easily access all regular maintenance items, even with power steering and smog equipment. The same cannot be said for the GT500.

SHELBY COBRA GT 350/500
SPECIFICATIONS & FEATURES

All-new GT 350 and GT 500 convertibles feature integral overhead safety bar, many other performance, handling, safety and comfort features

Get behind the wheel of a Shelby Cobra GT and you command a new motoring dimension. Carroll Shelby has worked a bit of car magic on the Ford Mustang. Result? The Shelby Cobra GT . . . a **true** road performer that rivals Europe's finest limited-produced cars—but for thousands of dollars less. ☐ That's not all the news. Now you can own a Cobra GT 350 or GT 500 **convertible!** These great features as the famed GT 350 and GT 500 fastback 2+2 coupes. ☐ If you love driving, you'll appreciate the pleasure of C thrilling GT performance and exclusive styling. It's a pleasure you can afford, as your Shelby Cobra dealer will gladly prove.

ENGINE SPECIFICATIONS

GT 350

Standard: All new OHV 302 cu. in. V-8; 250 horsepower @ 4800 rpm; 310 lbs./foot of torque @ 2800 rpm; 4.0" x 3.0" bore and stroke; compression ratio 10.5:1; hydraulic valve lifters. Cobra high velocity high volume intake manifold with 4 bbl carburetor with 600 CFM flow rate.

Optional*: Cobra centrifugal supercharger, 335 horsepower at 5200 rpm; 325 lbs./foot of torque @ 3200 rpm.†

NOTE: All Cobra GT engines include high velocity high flow intake manifolds, die-cast aluminum rocker covers, low restriction oval design diecast aluminum air cleaner, chromed filler caps, high capacity fuel pumps.

GT 500

Standard: All new Cobra OHV 428 cu. in. V-8; 360 horsep @ 5400 rpm; 420 lbs./foot of torque @ 3200 rpm; 4.13" x 3.9 bore and stroke; compression ratio 10.5:1; hydraulic va lifters. Cobra high velocity high volume intake manifold w advanced design, 4 bbl Holley carburetor with 600 CFM (flow rate) primaries, 715 CFM secondaries. High capacity fuel pump.

Optional*: All new Cobra hydraulic OHV 427 cu. in. V-8; 400 horsepower @ 5600 rpm; 460 lbs./foot of torque @ 3200 rpm; 4.235" x 3.788" bore and stroke; compression ratio 11.6:1; hydraulic valve lifters, advanced design cathedral float 4 bbl Holley carburetor. High capacity fuel pump.**

YOUR COBRA DEALER

KOONS FORD INC.
7 CORNERS
1051 East Broad St.
Falls Church, Va.

LEFT: This showroom brochure touted the "Race Proven" road cars, and featured the 1968 styling/ engineering prototype car 0139.

ABOVE: The first-ever production Shelby Mustang convertible was understandably big news and well promoted by Shelby.

General Motors and made him corporate president, passing over Lee Iacocca, who at the time was the company's executive vice president. Iacocca was also Carroll Shelby's chief ally within the company.

Bunkie Knudsen? Not so much. Knudsen, who hadn't appreciated having his mighty Corvettes pounded on racetracks around the world by Shelby's humble Cobra, didn't bother to hide his disdain for the flamboyant Texan. One of his first moves at Ford was to begin development of cars that would directly compete with the Shelby Mustang: the Boss 302 and Boss 429. If there was any doubt about Knudsen's intention, the names of the cars removed it—"Boss" was Knudsen's nickname. The Shelby Mustang program had never been especially profitable for Shelby; often it was more trouble than it was worth.

RIGHT: R&T tester sampling the GT350 automatic's interior. Note the high-tech test equipment. *Road & Track/Hearst Magazines*

BELOW LEFT: With its full-sized spare tire there wasn't much room for any junk in the GT350s trunk. And from personal experience I can tell you it isn't any fun wrestling one of those spares in or out. *Road & Track/ Hearst Magazines*

BELOW RIGHT: The Shelby-inspired Mustang GT/CS shown here at its introduction to the California Ford dealer's association. The billboard pictured behind the seating area was used in the California market, Ford's best for Mustang sales. An interesting twist is that just like the Shelby Mustang came back to Ford in 2007, so did the Mustang GT/CS return as an option on 2007 Mustang GTs.

With Ford Motor Company now headed by a man Shelby considered an enemy, he saw no reason to fight to retain control over Shelby Mustang production. The best move, he decided, was to let Ford have control of the car.

Back in California, the newly formed Shelby Racing Company, based in Torrance, would handle Shelby's ongoing racing efforts. Also based in Torrance was another new Shelby company that would handle Shelby's aftermarket parts division, aptly named the Shelby Parts Company.

This also marked the end of the line for US production of the original Shelby Cobras with Ford engines and A.C.–supplied bodies. It was just getting too difficult for a small manufacturer like Shelby to meet all the safety and emissions regulations required by the federal government and various states, especially California. Shelby had developed a Cobra replacement, a mid-engined coupe with a removable roof panel. Rather than a bare-bones racing sports car, this new model, which Shelby called the Lone Star, after his native Texas, would have been a luxurious GT car, like the Shelby Mustang had become. Shelby planned to build the car if he could get the federal government to make safety and emissions exemptions for small manufacturers, but they wouldn't, so he didn't. After just a few years, Shelby was out of the automobile production business.

COBRA MUSTANGS

If there was an upside to this move for the production Shelby Mustangs, it was that 1968 would be the year that the growing pains finally got worked out. With Ford's involvement and resources, plus A. O. Smith's experience in large-scale production work, the new Shelby

BELOW: For most people a 1968 GT350 convertible offered more than enough performance, and even if it was found lacking the styling and ability to drop the top more than made up for it. *David Newhardt*

Mustangs enjoyed their most standardized year yet. In prior years, parts supplier issues, space constraints, and constant development had meant numerous time-consuming and costly running production changes. The 1968 model year was almost devoid of these issues, with very few running changes, and resulted in Shelby's highest production total yet, with 4,451 cars built by the end of the model year.

One notable change to the Shelby GTs was that they featured the word *COBRA* under the snake badges adorning their fenders, between the doors and the wheel wells. The 1967 cars had read either "GT350" or "GT500." Ford now openly marketed the Shelby Mustangs as the Cobra GT350 and Cobra GT500 in promotional literature because, having no further use for it, Shelby had sold the name to Ford . . . for the princely sum of one dollar. Ford's promotional material barely mentioned the name Shelby.

All 1968 Shelbys were built at Ford's Metuchen, New Jersey, plant as knockdown units and then shipped by rail to A. O. Smith in Michigan for final assembly, which included installing all Shelby-specific parts. If you've ever seen an original-paint 1968 Shelby, you'll notice that all Shelby fiberglass parts are usually a different shade than the rest of the body. This is because the body was painted at Ford and the fiberglass parts painted at A. O. Smith.

The redesigned scoops in the fiberglass hood benefitted from some time in Ford's wind tunnel. These units—really a single scoop split horizontally down the middle—moved up toward the

ABOVE: Any Shelby Mustang is a desirable car, and they always draw a crowd on the auction block. Note "Mr. October" Reggie Jackson front and center checking out this 1968 GT350 at Barrett-Jackson. *Jeff Burgy*

ABOVE LEFT: Al Grillo sold a lot of Shelbys at his Ford dealership, enough to warrant Al (center) a visit from Carroll Shelby (left) and sales manager Ed Casey (right) in 1968. Unfortunately, Al Grillo was also involved in other and far less honorable activities than selling new Shelbys, so not long after this photo was taken he was paid another "visit" by some fellows and never seen again. You do the math. *Vern Estes*

BELOW: As soon as Ford had the 428 CJ available in the Mustang, Shelby jumped at the chance to have it in his cars, especially since the 427 he had promised buyers never materialized. The result was the mid-year introduction of the GT500 KR. True to form, Shelby wasted no time in promoting it as this letter shows. Of course, it also includes a little bit of that Shelby snake oil where he states he's "Shelby-ized" the CJ engine for "just a tweak more top-end performance," which, of course, was completely untrue. Not one KR engine was any different than the ones Ford was bolting into their 1968½ Mustangs. But hey, you gotta sell the sizzle with the steak. *Road & Track/Hearst Magazines*

front of the car, right behind the grille, where they could better pull in the fresh air being kicked upward by the car's aerodynamically awful barn door of a front end. A pair of finger-operated Dzus fittings replaced the previous pin-and-clip fittings, taking over the duty of keeping the hood attached to the car at speed. Shelby had good experiences with the Dzus fasteners on Ford's GT40 racing car and adopted them for his Mustangs. The Dzus fasteners also appeared on Ford's new Mach I Mustang. Of course the standard Ford primary and secondary hood latches were fitted as well, in a belt and suspenders move.

Because the opening of the grille was slightly larger for 1968, the car originally looked like a bit of a mouth breather with an open, slack jaw. Ford solved this by simply mounting a pair of SEV Marchal foglights in the opening, but switched to Lucas units midyear because the French-built Marchal lights proved troublesome. (Think about it: "less-troublesome Lucas units." I don't know what this says about the quality of the Marchal units, but, they are French.) To avoid pissing off California's omnipotent DMV, Ford mounted the foglights at the outer edges of the opening rather than together in the center. These rectangular lights filled the space nicely, giving the 1968 cars a face very different from the 1967 versions, with their round foglights, but more importantly, they doubled the lighting power. Since 1939, the US vehicle code had restricted passenger cars to headlights with just 35,000

marketing office

shelby automotive inc.
box 7390, north end station
detroit, michigan 48202

Dear Friend:

Thanks for your request for information about my Shelby Cobra GT cars. The enclosed material should give you a pretty complete idea of what these cars are like.

Please note that my new GT 500-KR is being marketed in addition to the GT 350 and GT 500 described in the color brochure. The GT 500-KR is powered by Ford's fantastic new Cobra Jet 428 cubic inch V-8. I've Shelby-ized it a little, for just a tweak more top-end performance, although it's pretty unbelievable as it is. (The Cobra Jet replaces the 427 engine which was proposed but not produced for '68.)

You'll find a Cobra dealer not too far from you. He'll be glad to answer your questions about prices, trade-ins, terms, delivery, options and equipment...and to give you the pleasure of trying a new Cobra GT 350, GT 500 or GT 500-KR for yourself.

Thanks again for your interest in Shelby cars.

Cordially,

Carroll Shelby
Carroll Shelby

builders of fine sports cars • Cobra GT-350 / GT-500   POWER BY *Ford*

SHELBY COBRA GT 350/500-KR
SPECIFICATIONS AND FEATURES

Get behind the wheel of a Shelby Cobra GT and you command a new motoring dimension. Carroll Shelby has worked his racing magic on the Ford Mustang. Result? The Shelby Cobra GT . . . a completely equipped road performer that rivals Europe's finest limited-production cars—but costs thousands of dollars less.

The all new GT 500-KR is King of the Road. It features Ford's 428 Cobra Jet drag champion engine . . . it's the most exciting road performer going.

That's not all the news. Now you can own a Cobra GT 350 or GT 500-KR convertible! Same great features as the famed GT 350 and GT 500-KR fastback 2+2 coupes.

If you love driving, you'll appreciate the pleasure of Cobra's thrilling GT performance and exclusive styling. It's a pleasure you can afford, as your Shelby Cobra dealers will gladly prove.

All-new GT 500-KR features drag championship 428 CID Cobra Jet V-8, integral overhead safety bar, many other high-performance features.

ENGINE SPECIFICATIONS

GT 350

Standard: All new OHV 302 cu. in V-8; 250 horsepower @ 4800 rpm; 310 lbs./foot of torque @ 2800 rpm; 4.0" x 3.0" bore and stroke; compression ratio 10.5:1; hydraulic valve lifters. Cobra high velocity high volume intake manifold with high-flow 4 bbl carburetor.

GT 500-KR

Standard: All new Cobra Jet OHV 428 cu. in. V-8; 335 horsepower @ 5200 rpm; 440 lbs./foot of torque @ 3400 rpm; 4.13" x 3.984" bore and stroke; compression ratio 10.6:1; hydraulic valve lifters. Revised distributor curve. Cobra high velocity high volume intake manifold with advanced design, 4 bbl Holley carburetor with 715 CFM (flow rate) primaries, 715 CFM secondaries. High capacity fuel pump. Ram air package utilizing twin front hood scoops is **standard.**

NOTE: All Cobra GT engines include high velocity high flow intake manifolds, die-cast aluminum rocker covers, low restriction oval design diecast aluminum air cleaner, chromed filler caps, high capacity fuel pumps.

YOUR COBRA DEALER

The official KR (and mid-year GT350) spec sheet was more exacting in detail.

Surfing, a drive in a GT500KR, or the fair? 02524 proves you can do all three if you play your cards right. *SAAC Archives*

candlepower. Why the federal government felt the need to make it *more* difficult for a driver to see at night remains somewhat of a mystery. Perhaps they didn't want wayward DC-9 aircraft mistaking the highway in front of cars as a runway? Some European cars were using lights two or three times as powerful, but in the United States, antiquated prewar rules were still the order of the day. By mounting the fog lamps, Shelby effectively got his cars up to European lighting standards without violating the Byzantine US rules.

Dropping Top

A new body style joined the Shelby Mustang lineup for 1968: the convertible. Finally fans could get a topless GT without either being Carroll Shelby or marrying Carroll Shelby. Developing a convertible Shelby Mustang proved relatively easy. The standard Mustang convertible top needed very minimal redesigning to fit over the roll bar that was standard equipment. On the convertible the roll bar not only provided a measure of safety, but also a modicum of added chassis stiffness, making the convertible Shelby Mustang structure

arguably the slightest bit more rigid than the pedestrian Ford Mustang convertibles. The convertible Shelbys proved popular, and Shelby produced 1,324 examples for the 1968 model year.

The taillights, derived from the 1965 Thunderbird, operated sequentially—except, of course, for cars sold in California, where the DMV held dominion over virtually every aspect of a car's design. An argent-colored fiberglass surround located the taillights in the time-and-space continuum. In the area between the taillights, the space occupied by the vaguely Native American–looking bird emblem on the donor Thunderbird, Shelby placed the Cobra-logoed pop-off fuel filler cap.

ABOVE: The King of KRs—Cobra Jet power with a top that goes down. With just 517 produced they have always been at the top of the Shelby pecking order. *SAAC Archives*

BELOW: There were 159 "Special Paint" 1968 Shelbys built; 144 of them were this color shown on KR 03777, simply called WT6066 Yellow. Of interest: As WT6066 replaced Sunlit Gold in the color lineup there are no Sunlit Gold GT500 KRs. *SAAC Archives*

The roof pillar–mounted extractor vents returned for one final year, but the inclusion of federally mandated body side-marker lights made the 1968 profile a tad less sleek. As in 1967, the lower scoops ahead of the rear wheels fed cooling air to the drum brakes, which grew increasingly overtaxed as the car continued to gain weight year after year.

On the interior, a little more luxury was added for 1968. Exotic wood trim, made of the finest wood-grained vinyl trees with adhesive-backed bark in all the land, replaced the brushed-aluminum dash inserts of the 1967 cars, a center console that wrapped up to the dash and now housed the Stewart-Warner amp and oil pressure gauges became standard, and both fastbacks and convertibles had roll bars, complete with surfboard tie-down hooks on top of the convertibles' units for trips to the beach. The 1967's three-spoke steering

wheel was replaced by a heavily padded, T-Bird–style, single-spoke affair.

Another T-Bird luxury touch was the tilt and swing-away steering column; when the driver's door was open, the steering column swiveled out of the way for easy entrance and exit. Interiors were offered in two colors: black and saddle.

Trimmed Ponies and Kings of the Road

Under the hood, the GT350 now had a 302-cubic-inch engine with 250 horsepower, replacing the discontinued 289-cubic-inch V-8. Unlike the previous K-code engine, the new 302 featured hydraulic lifters, which were much quieter and never needed to be adjusted. An aluminum intake fed the cylinders air and fuel through a 600-cfm Holley four-barrel carburetor. Initially Ford rated the engine at 235 horsepower at 4,800 rpm, but it quickly upped that number to 250 for what appear to be marketing reasons. Still, this was down 56 horsepower from the 289-cubic-inch engine used the previous year.

Largely this was because of the much more mild hydraulic camshaft and restrictive exhaust manifolds in place of true headers—there was no way the new engine could rev as high and as quickly as its solid-lifter predecessor, which had made its 306 horsepower at a lofty 6,000 rpm, nor was the new 302 as eager to go beyond that speed as the 289 was. Not that anyone cared; the average GT350 buyer just wanted a Mustang that looked like a Shelby.

If a GT350 buyer wanted more power, Shelby still offered the Paxton supercharger as a dealer-installed option. It required a non–air conditioned car because the supercharger was mounted in the same space needed for the air conditioning compressor. The supercharger bumped horsepower to 335, but by this time there was little incentive to order the

TOP: *Car Life* seeing what Shelby's new King of the Road could do against the clock. *Road & Track/Hearst Magazines*

ABOVE: The *Car Life* KR engine with the air cleaner removed. Break out the magnifying glasses, boys. *Road & Track/Hearst Magazines*

Peter Disher is the 1968 Special Paint Guru, and he maintains a phenomenal website chocked full of 1968 Shelby information and history at www. thecoralsnake.com. And this is the car that started Pete's quest for knowledge on Special Paint cars—his GT500KR (03206) in WT5185 Orange. There were only three cars built in this color. Two were GT500KRs with automatic transmissions, Pete's car and its twin 03233, which lives in Sweden. The third car is my WT5185 GT350 four-speed car and lives less than 100 miles from Pete's. The fellow from Sweden needs to move to southeastern Wisconsin if you ask us. *SAAC Archives*

Another great reference photo, this time of the KR's trunk. Note the slightly smaller, due to its lower profile, spare tire and the quad exhaust tips unique to the KR. *Road & Track/Hearst Magazines*

expensive optional supercharger; if a buyer wanted serious performance, he or she stepped up and bought a GT500.

The GT500 had a 360-horsepower 428 Police Interceptor engine with aluminum intake carrying a single Holley 735-cfm carburetor. The big news in power came with the midyear introduction of the GT500KR, *KR* standing for "King of the Road." Shelby had received word that Chevrolet was planning to affix the "King of the Road" moniker to the 396-cubic-inch version of its Camaro, and a man with supersized testes like Shelby could not resist the opportunity to flip Chevrolet the bird and steal the name. Things that happen very slowly at big, bloated, bureaucratic organizations like General Motors happen as quick as lightning at small, rebellious companies like Shelby American. Before Chevrolet could get around to applying the name to the big-block Camaro, Shelby was already using it.

The KR replaced the standard GT500, and the heart of it was the new 428-cid Cobra Jet engine. The main improvement in the new engine was improved cylinder heads, which featured rectangular intake and exhaust ports that were larger than those used on the older 427 Side Oiler racing engine. The Cobra Jet also featured a stronger

TOP: Prototype? Nope. As far as anybody can tell the extra emblems and "COBRA" rocker graphics were added to this GT350 by its owner. *SAAC Archives*

ABOVE: What would a Mustang book be without the ubiquitous "Mustang and a Mustang" photo? Not good, if you ask me! This is GT500KR 04030. *SAAC Archives*

The new Shelby Automotive was no longer a small group of hot-rodders building Shelbys with Mustang features . . .

bottom end with a cast crank, better connecting rods made of high-strength steel, alloy pistons, and a performance camshaft. An even hotter camshaft was available for racing applications. Up top the CJ had a 735-cfm Holley four-barrel with functional Ram-Air that was ducted to the hood scoop via a plenum attached to the underside of the hood. The KR's new engine was rated at 335 horsepower, a bogus number to sway the NHRA factoring of the engine for competition use and likely also to sway insurance premiums for buyers. Insurance companies, which had begun to cancel policies for customers who bought Shelby Mustangs, might have been fooled by the mild horsepower rating, but the NHRA wasn't; it rated the engine at a more realistic 410 to 425 horsepower.

The GT500 KRs featured extra chassis bracing, a bigger-diameter exhaust, and, on four-speed cars, staggered rear shock absorbers to help combat axle hop, resulting in the most civilized Shelby automobiles to date. One company that did appreciate the toned-down nature of the 1968 Shelby was Hertz, which, after a one-year break, added 224 GT350 cars to its Hertz Sports Car Club fleet. No longer a special model like the 1966 GT350H, these were simply standard GT350s. All Hertz GT350s were equipped with automatic transmissions, power steering, power disc brakes, air conditioning, AM radios, fold-down rear seats, tinted glass, and tilt steering wheels.

Transmission choices for all remained the same as in 1967, as did rear axle ratios.

The new Shelby Automotive was no longer a small group of hot-rodders building Shelbys with Mustang features; it was a shop under the direction of Ford, building Mustangs with Shelby features. Unlike years past, there wasn't a race car or race shop in sight. Maybe Simon and Garfunkel should have worried less about Joe DiMaggio and asked where Carroll Shelby went? Lonely eyes looked for the spirit of the original Shelby Mustangs, and it wasn't around by 1968. It was a different world, with far different cars. Performance at all costs was gone, replaced by sporty personal luxury cars with performance looks.

LEFT: This one shows the stable, composed manner in which a high-horsepower muscle car on skinny bias ply tires handles a road course. Oh, wait, that doesn't happen. *Road & Track/Hearst Magazines*

BELOW: Another vintage photo of a magazine guy thrashing a GT500KR. Neat. *Road & Track/Hearst Magazines*

BOTTOM: Not to be outdone by vintage road test drivers, 04030's owner has ditched that P51 Mustang and is seeing just what his KR can do. *SAAC Archives*

While the world was changing in ways that weren't particularly kind to a grizzled racer like Carroll Shelby, the Shelby Mustangs themselves were changing in ways that made them increasingly appealing to car buyers in this brave new world, and sales broke all existing records. When the 1968 model year ended, Shelby American had produced a total of 4,450 GTs, broken down as follows:

BELOW: The well-appointed interior of a KR convertible. *David Newhardt*

BOTTOM: And we're back with a P51 and not one but *two* KRs—03888 and 03463. *SAAC Archives*

GT350 fastbacks: 1,053 (including approximately 230 Hertz cars)	GT500 convertibles: 402
GT350 convertibles: 404	GT500KR fastbacks: 1,053
GT500 fastbacks: 1,020	GT500KR convertibles: 518

1968 Mustang Notchback Engineering Car: The Green Hornet

After 1967's Little Red, another 390-cubic-inch Mustang notchback was pressed into prototype duty in 1968 at Shelby Automotive, now located in Michigan. Originally a Lime Gold car that was used as the Mustang GT/CS prototype, it later became a test mule for some very unique experimental mechanical parts. Externally, it had a 1968 Shelby fiberglass nose and hood, along with the side body scoops and fiberglass trunk lid with ducktail spoiler and matching rear quarter-panel extensions. At the request of Fred Goodell, Shelby American painter Sonny Fee changed the Lime Gold was to a full-custom, almost Candy Apple Green finish with gold metalflake. A spray-on black vinyl top was added, along with white rocker panel stripes with "EXP500" callouts. The interior was dressed up with 1968

Sitting still . . . it looks invincible

Turn it on and let it out and you'll see how that long, low, racy styling dares anything else to come close. When racing expert Carroll Shelby designs a car this way you don't expect him to build very many. He doesn't.

The Shelby GT isn't a car you buy simply because it's handsome and rare. You buy it, of course, to drive it.

Let out the famous ram air 428 Cobra Jet engine in the GT 500, and suddenly you'll know the meaning of the word "power". Wind up the 351 ram air V-8 in the GT 350, and you'll capture the true feeling and excitement of Shelby motion.

Take a corner at speed . . . stab the brakes, and feel how the car is slowed with the force of 11.3" power assisted front disc brakes. Ride through a curve . . . Heavy duty adjustable shock absorbers with competition type springs will keep the fat Polyglass belted tires in firm contact with the road thru all its bumps and dips. A heavy duty front stabilizer bar keeps the body tight and level against the force of cornering.

That's race car handling . . . It's something built into every Shelby GT.

And it's available now at your local Shelby Ford Performance Center.

POWER BY *Ford*

Shelby GT 350/500 SHELBY COBRA

LEFT: This 1969 ad touts the racy styling, low production and solid handling of the Shelby GT350 and GT500 cars. Which nails exactly what they were at this point—an exclusive, good-looking, and great-performing GT car.

BELOW: Not a road test but a PR photo with an attached press release that reads: "A 335-horsepower, 428-cubic-inch Cobra Jet Ram-Air engine powers this 1969 Shelby GT-500. Other Shelby features that insure excellent road performance include an improved suspension system; extra-heavy-duty shock absorbers; strong, low-fad brakes; and E-70 tires on seven inch wheels." *Road & Track Hearst Magazines*

Shelby Mustang trimmings, including a center console. In this trim, the car earned the nickname "Green Hornet," reportedly from Carroll Shelby's friend Bill Cosby.

Now, for the fun stuff: an experimental 428-cubic-inch Cobra Jet engine was installed, with a specially prepared, heavy-duty C6 automatic transmission. *The Green Hornet* was used to test the possibility of an electronic fuel-injection system for production cars, with Shelby eventually settling on the electronic Conelec-built system. It is estimated that with the Conelec EFI, the 428 CJ made roughly 475 horsepower. Under the car, four-wheel disc

brakes were used as was another remarkable engineering feat: an independent rear suspension. While the EFI, four-wheel disc brakes, and IRS failed to make it into any Shelby Mustang, the experiments show the "what if?" forward thinking that lived at Shelby in the 1960s.

The best part about the Green Hornet story is the fact that the car still exists. Like the Little Red prototype, the Green Hornet somehow escaped the crusher at Ford, eventually being sold to an employee at a Ford-company auction in 1971. It is now a part of collector-car auction magnate Craig Jackson's personal collection. Under Jackson's care, the Green Hornet was painstakingly re-restored in 2018 to its exact and historically correct " double prototype" configuration by Jason Billups and his team at Billups Classic Cars. This restoration included properly re-creating the original IRS with newly discovered original parts, having a complete and functional Conolec EFI system fitted and tuned by Chris Long, the son of Conolec creator David E. Long. The best part is the Green Hornet gets to live next to its long lost, yet recently discovered, sibling Little Red, which is also being restored to its precise original specification by Billups. Hollywood couldn't dream of a better reunion story or a better owner to make it all happen.

1968 Ford Mustang GT California Special

Although Shelby American never did build a coupe version of the GT350 or GT500, the two prototypes of the concept, Little Red and the Green Hornet, led to a Shelby-inspired special-edition Mustang called the California Special. At the time, the Los Angeles district was Ford's number-one sales market, and Ford thought that a limited-edition car named for California would further drive sales.

TOP: Roger Morrison purchased this 1970 GT350, 1280, from its original owner in 1974. This photo was taken in 1976 and shows a virtually like-new, six-year-old Shelby. *Roger Morrison*

ABOVE: This ad plays on the status of owning a Shelby, as well as it being a luxury performance machine. Again, a spot-on analysis that spoke to exactly what Shelby buyers wanted in 1969. No more side exhausts or bone-rattling suspensions.

A half year after the introduction of the 1968 model year Mustangs, the Mustang GT/CS coupe was advertised as the car that "California Made Happen" and "The Most Exciting Mustang since Mustang." In practice, it was simply a Mustang coupe with Shelby styling touches. The GT/CS package included foglights in "a wild blackout grille," "wicked looking side scoops with special GT/CS stripes," a louvered hood with integral turn signal indicators, "competition-type hood locks," and a fiberglass trunk lid with a Shelby-style ducktail spoiler, matching fiberglass quarter-panel extensions, and the same Thunderbird horizontal taillights used in the 1968 Shelby Mustangs.

In total, 4,025 California Special Mustangs were produced, all at Ford's San Jose plant. Additionally, 300 almost identical special-edition Mustangs were produced for the Denver, Colorado, sales district and called the High Country Special.

Ducts, Ducts, and More Ducts

When Ford adopted a new-for-1969 Mustang, it meant that the Shelby Mustangs for 1969 would also be all new. Following the trajectory the little Mustang had been on since 1965, this new version was bigger, wider, and heavier than the one it replaced. If you watched the evolution of Elvis Presley throughout his career, the Mustang story will strike you as quite similar. Gone was the young, energetic, trim, edgy version, and in its place was the aged, word-slurring, overweight version that was heavily commercialized. It couldn't run anymore without breaking a sweat, and it was dressed in sequins. And, oddly enough, people didn't seem to mind.

ABOVE: In his role as a professional advertisement guy impersonator, Roger Morrison, complete with his Spirit of 1976 beard, attempts to duplicate the legendary Shelby ad with his GT350. *Roger Morrison*

BELOW: 2244 is unique among all 1969 GT350s as it is the only car to have had a Boss 302 engine installed as original equipment at the factory.

This is the fourth (of five total) 1969 Shelby Trans-Am Mustang. Its actual build, and that of the fifth car as well, was done at Kar Kraft Engineering in Dearborn, Michigan, and not at Shelby in Torrance, California. Chassis number 4 was raced in period by Horst Kwech and Peter Revson, and at the end of the 1969 season was given to Bud Moore Racing. John Gimble raced it in the SCCA Trans-Am series in 1971 and 1972, after which it ended up racing in Mexico with a new owner starting in 1973. It returned to the United States and the ownership of Bud Moore in the late 1970s, later winning the SCCA A/Sedan Championship in 1979 before being reclassified as a GT-1 class car and continuing to compete in SCCA events.

TOP: Peter Revson drives the No. 1 Shelby Racing Company-prepared 1969 Trans-Am Mustang at Watkins Glen, August 1969. Behind him is one of the Bud Moore-prepared cars, either driven by Parnelli Jones or George Follmer. *Carroll Hall Shelby Trust/ Carroll Shelby Licensing, Inc.*

MIDDLE: Despite his best efforts, and a rope holding the exhaust on by mid-race, Revson failed to finish. *Carroll Hall Shelby Trust/Carroll Shelby Licensing, Inc.*

ABOVE: Mark Donohue checks out the Shelby-prepared Boss 302 at Watkins Glen. Of course, Donohue was driving a Chuck Cantwell/Penske-prepared Sunoco Camaro. All of which is quite funny as a few years prior Donohue was driving a GT350 and Chuck Cantwell had helped him prepare it as well! *Carroll Hall Shelby Trust/Carroll Shelby Licensing, Inc.*

With Bunkie Knudsen taking over at Ford and introducing the Boss Mustangs to directly compete with the Shelby Mustangs, it had seemed that the writing was on the wall for the Shelby versions. But Ford marketing recognized the value of having a prestigious name like Shelby associated with the Mustang, and the cars stayed in the lineup, at least for the 1969 model year. Knudsen too recognized the value and told Shelby that the new Shelby Mustangs would be the most distinctively styled and dramatic yet.

Knudsen kept his word. Thanks to input from stylist Larry Shinoda, whom Knudsen had brought with him from General Motors, the design for the 1969 Shelby was flashier than that of any previous version. Along with the new body, streamlined production at A. O. Smith in Michigan, and Ford's basic control of the program came far more capability to create a really unique look for the Shelby Mustang.

The transformation of a pedestrian Mustang into a Shelby GT required the use of 21 separate pieces of plastic and fiberglass. Owens-Corning now supplied the fiberglass panels. Knudsen was familiar with the quality parts produced by Owens-Corning because General Motors had used the company to provide parts for the Chevrolet Corvette. The front fenders and hood were now made of fiberglass and featured an extended nose with a completely different look than the Mustang. In fact, the only body panels that the Shelby Mustang shared with the pedestrian Ford version were doors and roof panels.

A thin chrome bumper wrapped around into chrome trim on the fenders and hood lip to create the grille opening. Rectangular driving lamps were mounted below the bumper, and rather than using the four-headlamp system that the Mustangs did, the Shelbys used two headlamps, each containing both low and high beams. And talk about scoops: the new hood had three scoops at the front and two matching "exit-duct" scoops at the rear. Officially called National Advisory Committee on Aeronautics (NACA) ducts, these triangular scoops represented state-of-the-art jet aircraft technology and had been used to good effect with the GT40 racing program. Plus, they looked wicked cool.

But the five hood scoops were just the beginning. We can't forget about the scoops at the leading edge of each front fender. On the rear quarter panels, brake cooling scoops were fitted, one per side, mounted high on the fastback (now called "Sportsroof" by Ford) and lower on the convertible. These also appeared on the Mach I version of the Mustang, but in that application they were purely ornamental. On the Shelby they were functional and provided cooling air to the rear brakes. The trunk lid was again fiberglass, with an integral rear spoiler and matching quarter-panel extensions. Sequentially activated 1965 Thunderbird taillights were used again in 1969, mounted in a fiberglass tail panel with a center gas cap.

Below the bumper was a cast-aluminum center dual-exhaust exit that used a large cast-aluminum piece behind the rear valance to connect the two tailpipes and direct exhaust gases to the center exit. This was a great-looking item, but it was quickly discovered that it didn't work too well with the vented gas cap right above it. Fourteen cars had gas vapors ignited by the exhaust, and Shelby recalled all cars with the vented gas cap to be converted to a non-vented cap. The gas tank filler neck then had a vent installed in the trunk to direct vapors out of the car via the rear frame rail and far away from any ignition source. Side stripes, by now a Shelby hallmark, were again standard. For 1969 it was a triple stripe: a thick center stripe flanked by two thin stripes that ran the length of the car midway between the side bodylines. GT350 or GT500 callouts were placed within the center stripe, directly in front of the front fender scoops. Stripes were made of 3M reflective material, a unique touch, and offered in white, blue, black, and gold—with colors automatically selected based on the exterior color of the car.

Spinning Wheel

Wheel choices for 1969 were quite simple—you had one. A new Shelby 15x7-inch five-spoke wheel with a cast-aluminum center and chrome rim was the standard wheel. Goodyear E70-15 Wide Oval tires were also standard equipment, with F60-15s available as an option.

Shelby interiors were all based on the Mustang Deluxe interior, with a few additions. A special center console was fitted, with a ribbed lid for the storage compartment, racy-looking toggle switches to activate the driving lights and dome lamps, slots holding the seat belt buckles in place when not in use, and a dual gauge pod in front of the shifter featuring oil pressure and amp gauges. Roll bars with shoulder harness belts were again

Although the Shelby Trans-Am Mustangs were not Boss 302s, they were dressed to look like them. And nobody knew better than Ford that racing (and a racing image) sold cars. In this vintage 1969 Boss 302 ad, the number one Shelby-built Trans-Am Mustang is pictured obviously to inspire consumers to view the new-for-1969 Boss 302 street cars as race cars with license plates.

Wheel choices for 1969 were quite simple— you had one.

TOP: Think newer Shelbys don't race? Think again! This car started life as a 1969 GT500, which was quickly stolen, wrecked, recovered, and sent to a salvage yard by 1971. It was soon sold and transformed into an SCCA legal GT350 race car, with a Boss 302 engine, and raced from 1971–1975. Now painstakingly restored like jewelry inside and out, it is again competing in West Coast vintage events. *Bob Pengraph*

ABOVE: At Coronado the big brute shows you can teach an old dog new tricks—just not necessarily housebreak it. Note the fuel spraying from the tank vent. Lifting a leg and marking its territory? Perhaps! *Bob Pengraph*

fitted to both Sportsroof and convertible versions. Other Shelby touches were placed throughout, such as Shelby emblems on the steering wheel and seat belt buckles.

Mechanically, the GT350 now had Ford's new 351-cubic-inch engine, called the "Windsor" because it was assembled at Ford's Windsor, Ontario, plant. Rated at 290 horsepower, it was fitted with an aluminum dual-plane intake manifold and an Autolite four-barrel carburetor with standard Ram-Air induction. Cobra finned aluminum valve covers were again used for flash.

The GT500 had the 428 CJ engine, rated at 335 horsepower just as it had been in the 1968 GT500KR, although for 1969 this number was closer to the truth. A cast-iron Ford intake was fed by a 735-cfm Holley four-barrel, also fitted with standard Ram-Air induction and finned aluminum valve covers that read "428 Cobra Jet." While the 1969 Shelby Mustangs had more than enough power, the wrath of the EPA was certainly felt industry wide by this point. Emissions controls were strangling muscle cars such as these, and engines were disappearing under miles of spaghetti-like vacuum hoses and clean-air devices like smog pumps. For 1969, there was no longer a GT500 KR option.

Expensive Bodywork Package for a Mach I

The transmission choice was simple: automatic transmissions were Ford's FMX unit for GT350s and C6 unit in GT500s. Two variations of the Ford Toploader four-speed were used: a wide-ratio unit or a close-ratio unit, depending on powertrain and rear axle ratios chosen. Suspension came straight from the regular production Mach I, right down to the Gabriel Adjust-O-Matic shock absorbers and Goodyear F60-15 Polyglas bias-ply tires.

Other than a few Shelby-specific badges, there was as little to separate the Shelby Mustangs from the Mach I Mustangs in the interior of the cars as there was under the hood or in the chassis. A toggle switch below the instrument panel activated 70,000-candlepower Lucas quartz-iodide driving lights below the front bumper, but gauges and trim materials were virtually the same. Not that the standard Mach I interior was a bad place to spend time. Wood-grained plastic adorned the dash panel, premium vinyl covered the seats, and the dash contained a full complement of instrumentation, including an 8,000-rpm tachometer, 140-miles-per-hour speedometer, ammeter, water temperature gauge, and oil pressure gauge.

Once again, the Hertz rental car company wanted some GT350s of their own to rent and ended up ordering 150 cars total. All were Sportsroof cars, equipped almost exactly as they had been in 1968: automatic, air conditioning, fold-down rear seat, tilt wheel, tinted glass, AM radio. All of them also had the 3:1 rear axle ratio and E70-15 tires. These cars were again featured as part of the Hertz Sports Car Club.

Admittedly, the Shelby-specific plastic and fiberglass body panels created a striking profile, and the Shelby Mustangs were among the most attractive cars on the road in 1969, but for all practical purposes, they were really just Mach I Mustangs under that pretty skin. Very, very expensive Mach I Mustangs. A base GT350 listed for $4,434, and the base GT500 listed for $4,700, but good luck finding a stripper 1969 Shelby Mustang. Virtually all Shelby Mustangs sold in 1969 left their dealers' lots optioned to the hilt, and prices were commonly north of $5,000 for the GT350 and $6,000 for a GT500 convertible. By contrast, the base price for a Mach I was $3,122, and it was a lot easier to find a Mach I priced near that amount sitting on a dealer's lot than it was to find a base-priced Shelby. Pretty as the Shelby was, it was difficult to justify spending over 30 percent more to buy one instead of a Mach I.

Ed Casey was a brilliant sales manager for Shelby. One of his favorite marketing "techniques" was to bring a new Shelby and a Playboy Playmate to West Point, and let the soldiers have their pictures taken with the girl and the car. This is Connie Kreski, 1969 Playmate of the Year, with a 1969 GT500 at WestPoint. How many Shelbys do you think this sold for Ed? *Vern Estes*

Speaking of Connie Kreski, did you know for her Playmate of the Year win she received a brand new pink GT500? Well now you do. *SAAC Archives*

End of the Line

As great as the new Shelbys may have looked, sales were disappointing. A number of factors may have contributed to this. Competition had increased from other manufacturers, including Ford's own Boss 302, Boss 429, and Mach 1 Mustangs, which offered the same or better performance for less money. The market for Shelby Mustangs may have been getting saturated as well. Or perhaps the people who had bought Shelbys because of their raw performance edge couldn't relate to the new Shelby-ized Ford that was more style than substance.

Whatever the case, by the end of the 1969 model year, Carroll Shelby had pulled the plug on the Shelby Mustang. Shelby and Ford agreed there would be no new Shelby for the 1970 model year. As a result, the 789 unsold 1969 Shelbys that were still in the production pipeline at A. O. Smith would be slightly updated as "1970" models, assigned new 1970 VINs, and sold as 1970 cars.

For the 1970 version, two black stripes that ran between the two front air scoops and led to the two rear air scoops were added to the hoods. A Boss 302 front chin spoiler was added to the front valence. And under the watchful eye of the FBI, the 1969 VIN tags were removed and replaced with new 1970 VIN tags. The 1969 VIN tags were then destroyed by the FBI. The hidden, stamped VINs in the front fender aprons were left intact, since they were covered by the front fenders and not visible.

After all the dust settled, total 1969 and 1970 production was 3,153 cars, far less than Shelby had sold in 1968 alone. A breakdown of 1969–1970 production is as follows:

1969 Shelby models: 2,361
1970 Shelby models: 789
Barrier test and prototype pilot cars: 3
GT350 fastbacks: 935
GT350 fastback Hertz cars: 152
GT350 convertibles: 194
GT500 fastbacks: 1,534
GT500 convertibles: 335
Total 1969–1970 production: 3,153

1969 Shelby-Prepared Trans-Am Mustangs

It was no secret that Ford threw away the 1968 Trans-Am championship. So, for 1969, Ford wasn't looking to be embarrassed again. The 1969 program would be different. And rather than relying on one shop to build the 1969 Trans-Am Mustangs, Ford would have three shops preparing cars to race.

In January 1969, seven base Mustang Sportsroof cars with 351 engines and four-speed transmissions rolled out of Detroit and were divided up among these three race shops. Kar Kraft in Michigan got one, Bud Moore Engineering in Spartanburg, South Carolina, received three, and Shelby Racing, Inc., in Torrance, California, received the last three cars.

LEFT: By 1969, no matter how brightly colored the exterior was, the interiors were even more luxurious than prior years. The closest thing you could get to a hot-rod Thunderbird! *David Newhardt*

PREVIOUS PAGES: Yellow might be the color of cowards but not when it is Grabber Yellow on a GT500. Then people give you the respect you deserve. *David Newhardt*

Shelby, as always, built his cars to within the letter of the law for Trans-Am competition. That isn't to say some loopholes weren't exploited or some rules weren't interpreted other than as intended by those who wrote them, but the cars were legal. They were lightened by more than 350 pounds by using tricks like thin window glass, aluminum window regulators, and many other proven techniques to get the cars from their original 3,300 pounds to just over the minimum legal race weight of 2,900 pounds. Street cars in looks alone, every mechanical aspect of the Shelby Trans-Am Mustangs was purpose-built, from the suspension to the roll cage.

Ford supplied Shelby with full-race-spec versions of the new Boss 302 engine, which made almost 500 horsepower in race trim. On the exterior, Shelby's cars were painted a dark navy blue with white Boss 302 stripes.

By the end of the season, however, the cars from Shelby's rival, Bud Moore, had a better record. An announcement came from Ford at the end of the season that the racing budget for 1970 would be a mere fraction of what it was for 1969. As a result, the company chose Moore, not Shelby, to field the only factory Trans-Am team for 1970. And with that decision, Carroll Shelby decided it was a really good time to retire from racing—which is exactly what he did.

Of course the ever-popular convertibles continued for 1969/1970. Shown here is the extra-strength version, the GT500. *David Newhardt*

Shelby de Mexico

We all know about Shelby's chili, but did you know about his salsa? One of the big Texan's more unique business ventures has to be that of Shelby de Mexico S.A.

Eduardo Velazquez was a car enthusiast of the first order, and also the son of a well-to-do Mexican diplomat. After going to school in Europe and enjoying a successful career in law, he decided to follow his first love and get into the automobile aftermarket business. With the introduction of the new Ford Mustang in 1965, Velazquez, knowing that Ford of Mexico produced its own version right in his backyard, contacted Shelby American to get set up as the exclusive Mexican distributor for Shelby American parts. At the end of 1965, Velazquez was the largest single purchaser of Shelby parts, and in January 1966 he decided to buy a Mustang of his own through Shelby to race in Mexico. What he received is believed to be one of the 1965 Mustang notchback coupes that were used for GT350 chassis development at Shelby American. Velazquez decided to

ABOVE: This promotional photo of a new Shelby de Mexico GT350, was taken in November 1968 on the dealership lot. The Mexican GT350 was quite a different animal than the GT350 that Shelby was marketing in the United States that same year.

TOP: All 1970 Shelbys are simply re-tagged (under the watchful eye of the FBI) 1969 models. But besides the 1970 VINs they also received black stripes on the hood to differentiate them as this Grabber Blue car shows. *SAAC Archives*

The Cobra Jet 428 remained essentially unchanged for 1969/1970.

send this car to Lew Spencer and Carroll Shelby's dealership, High Performance Motors, for full race preparation.

When he returned about a month later to pick up the race car, Velazquez met Carroll Shelby. The two became fast friends, and soon the idea to form Shelby de Mexico S.A. was hatched. Shelby and Velazquez would be partners in the venture, and Shelby de Mexico would sell special Mexican-made Mustangs with Shelby American parts and accessories in Mexico, starting in 1967. Since the only body style produced in Mexico was the notchback coupe, all Shelby de Mexico cars would use this body style. Also interesting to note, Mexican law dictated that all cars manufactured in Mexico needed at least 45 percent domestic (Mexican) parts content. To that end, all Mustangs produced in Mexico had parts like the well-known Ford Mexican 302-cid engine forged at Ford of Mexico in place of the 289-cid from the United States, rear axles from Dana Corporation's Mexican plant, and even Goodyear tires molded in Mexico.

The 1967 and 1968 Shelby de Mexico cars bore a striking resemblance to the Little Red Shelby prototype. All were based on the GT coupe and equipped with Ford's HD export suspension fitted with Shelby modifications and Koni shocks, metallic brakes, 15-inch Shelby 10-spoke alloy wheels, full Cobra engine dress-up kits, Shelby aluminum intake manifolds with Holley 715-cfm four-barrel carburetors, Shelby tri-Y exhaust headers, Shelby three-spoke wooden steering wheels, 1966 GT350-style tachometers, 1967 Shelby GT350/GT500 taillights, fiberglass body panels, GT350 emblems, and GT350 rocker panel stripes that gave the cars an appearance very much like that of the 1968 California Special Mustangs.

A total of 169 Shelbys de Mexico were produced in 1967 and 203 in 1968.

The 1969 Shelby de Mexico cars were very similar, although based on the new-for-1969 Mustang coupe body. The biggest visual difference was the addition of fiberglass sail panels that extended back from the rear window area and into the rear quarter panels, giving a unique fastback look to the cars. A vinyl top then covered the works. Again a fiberglass trunk lid with integral spoiler and matching end caps was installed, along with 1969-style Shelby sequential taillights (originally lifted from the 1965 Thunderbird). The front ends were dressed just like the 1969 Mustang Mach 1, and again Shelby 10-spoke alloy wheels were installed. Shelby GT350 stripes and emblems completed the package.

Total production of the 1969 Shelby de Mexico was 306.

One 1969 Shelby de Mexico race car was built by Velazquez. He wanted to have a presence in Mexican race events to help drive sales. This car was an all-out effort, lightened to within an inch of its life, with fiberglass body panels everywhere: doors, fenders, hood, trunk lid, and nose. Subframe connectors were installed and tied into a carefully engineered roll cage. The engine, however, was the secret weapon. A Ford experimental race engine, a 302-cid unit with an actual displacement of 377 cid, was obtained with Carroll Shelby's help. It was fitted with Gurney-Weslake cylinder heads and four Weber carburetors, and it made over 450 horsepower at 7,000 rpm. As could be expected, this car did exceptionally well racing in Mexico, winning multiple championships.

In 1970, a similar race car was built for the same use, although this one featured a 351 Windsor-based engine. It too was nearly unbeatable. No 1970 Shelby de Mexico production cars were produced.

For 1969 and 1970 the GT350 used Ford's new 290-horsepower 351-cubic-inch Windsor engine with standard Ram Air induction.

TOP: Fine, one more Mustang-and-a-Mustang photo. But that's it. You're cut off. *SAAC Archives*

ABOVE LEFT: Not many things are more era-correct for a 1969 car than Black Jade paint with a white interior. *David Newhardt*

ABOVE RIGHT: Grabber Green was another killer hue available to buyers of Shelby Mustangs. *SAAC Archives*

For 1971, Shelby de Mexico production started again, using the new 1971 Ford Mustang as a base. It was called the GT351, and unlike the prior Shelby de Mexico products, it was more of an appearance package than a wholesale performance makeover.

Mechanicals were stock Ford with a Shelby engine dress-up kit installed. Also installed were Shelby alloy wheels, front and rear spoilers, rear window louvers, and strobe stripe decals down the sides and on the hoods. Truth be told, the 1971 GT351 used as many aftermarket parts from Superior Industries as it did from Shelby. Production numbers are not known, but Velazquez estimates that roughly 250 were built.

By the end of 1971, Shelby was out of the aftermarket parts business. That meant his partnership with Eduardo Velazquez came to an end as well. The Shelby de Mexico connection is indeed one of the more unique business ventures that Carroll Shelby had during the heyday of Shelby American. Thus began a decade-long period in which Shelby was more or less out of the automobile business.

ABOVE: The Shelby de Mexico GT350 race car that dominated the racing scene south of the border in 1969 and 1970.

TOP: Of note here is the cast aluminum center exhaust outlet that caused Ford so much grief when the fuel tank vent was causing fumes to ignite from the exhaust heat. A recall was done to move the gas tank vent away from the hot exhaust outlet. *David Newhardt*

Chapter 6

The Second Coming

ABOVE: While the 2007 Shelby GT-H really got things rolling again at Shelby American, it wasn't until 2008 that the general public could buy their own modern Shelby. That happened with the 2008 Shelby GT, which featured all the good stuff of the GT-H but with an available five-speed manual and not a rental contract or damage waiver in sight. *David Newhardt*

BELOW: More big news for Shelby in 2008 was the Hertz order for GT-H convertibles. A truckload of them is being unloaded here. *David Newhardt*

By the end of the 1970 model year the Shelby Mustang was a mere shadow of its 1965 race-car self. It had morphed into a gentleman's express, a luxurious car with sporting intentions rather than a sports car with no luxury intentions whatsoever. But they were still Shelby Mustangs, and you could still go buy a new one. Then, they were gone. And as we all know, within a few years every other performance car even worth talking about was gone as well. Gas prices, insurance premiums, and emissions and safety regulations made it impossible for any manufacturer to build, let alone sell, anything that even approached exciting.

And that's when the phenomenon began. Owners of good Shelby Mustangs knew they couldn't trade up to new cars that would offer them what their Shelbys did, so they kept them. And demand for used performance cars in the secondary market was outpacing supply, especially for those who wanted a clean, straight Shelby Mustang. It didn't take long for the 1965–1970 cars to reach cult status and become true collector cars. The old school of thought that a collectible had to be over 25 years old was out the window; by 1975 people were hunting early Shelby Mustangs and paying almost as much as they'd

cost when new for like-new examples. And the people who were lucky enough to get their hands on them felt a certain kinship with other Shelby owners. Clubs, such as the Shelby American Automobile Club (SAAC), were formed and an entire subculture of Shelby owners took root.

In these pre-Internet days, the exchange of information on proper care and feeding for these special cars, along with events in which to use them and a network of like-minded people to help share ideas, parts sources, and yes, even Shelby-themed t-shirts, formed the core of these groups and only helped cement the value of Shelbys as collectible cars. From this came the SAAC Registry, where designated registrars kept track of every Shelby they could by serial number, creating a database that remains invaluable today. There isn't another enthusiast group that has such important information at their fingertips, and it has become the watchdog for all Shelbys, keeping the fakes and frauds out while protecting the identities of the real cars.

So while Carroll Shelby may have been on to other projects, those who were faithful to his cars remained so in his absence and truly kept the flame alive. Which is good, because

Under the hood the GT consisted of the stock 4.6L with a Ford Racing Performance parts kit that included a cold air intake, FRPP exhaust, and a special FRPP "flash cal" tool that put a performance tune into the ECU. Also included was a FRPP "handling package" that brought a strut tower brace and a set of new coil springs. *David Newhardt*

This GT-H convertible is getting its performance tune downloaded. Note the tuning device plugged into the OBD-II port under the dashboard. *David Newhardt*

for about 13 years after the last Shelby rolled out of A. O. Smith the most notable product Carroll Shelby produced was his famous chili mix. And when Shelby cars once again became available, they were cars of a most unexpected variety. Shelby had followed his old friend and benefactor Lee Iacocca to Chrysler Corporation. Iacocca had held Chrysler back from bankruptcy in the early 1980s, but he did so by producing boring economy cars. To rectify the situation, Iacocca once again turned to Shelby. Shelby did return excitement to the Dodge brand, first in the form of the 1983 Shelby Charger, which at the time was as pedestrian a front-wheel-drive transportation appliance as was imaginable. Shelby tuned the Charger's carbureted 2.2-liter four-cylinder to gain 13 horsepower, swapped in a shorter final drive ratio in the transaxle, lowered the suspension on stiffer springs, added quick-ratio steering, used bigger brakes, and employed other subtle mechanical tweaks using existing parts. Sound familiar? Over the next six years Shelby-ized Dodges became quite potent machines, with even another familiar trick thrown in: a Shelby rental car, the CSX-T, for "Thrifty," as in the Thrifty rent-a-car brand. As they say, a leopard just doesn't change its spots. Shelby is also credited for helping give birth to what many considered to be the second coming of the Cobra, the Dodge Viper. But something just never seemed right about Carroll Shelby being with Dodge, did it?

Series 1

After Dodge, Carroll Shelby struck out in an attempt to build his own modern Cobra. He began developing the Shelby Series 1 in 1996, hoping to produce it as a 1999 model year vehicle. But the world of the 1990s was a very different place than the world of the 1960s. Production constraints, EPA/DOT red tape, and corporate politics at Oldsmobile managed to stall the project.

Shelby's Las Vegas Speedway location was buzzing in 2008. *David Newhardt*

They stacked Mustangs waiting for the Shelby GT conversion deep. *David Newhardt*

Still, Shelby found a way and started building the Shelby Series 1 after being granted a small-volume airbag-exemption by the FHWA and EPA. Shelby found no shortage of buyers willing to place hefty deposits for the proposed $85,000 1999 car, only to see the base price jump to $98,000, then $113,000, and later nearly $140,000. Performance results fell short of the expected 12.8-second quarter-mile times and 4.4-second 0-to-60 sprints. A number of cars tested also suffered embarrassing mechanical failures, which is of course typical for a built-from-the-ground-up, newly-created American muscle car. Shelby equipped the Series 1 with the same Oldsmobile Aurora engine that had been cleaning up on the racetracks of America.

The Costly Accoutrements of the Shelby Mustang World

As a Shelby guy, I am addicted to all the little trinkets that went along with Shelby's promotion of the cars I love. And like any good junkie, I know a guy . . . and that guy is Vern Estes, a young man who has been on a mission to know everything there is about Shelby memorabilia. So I cornered the kid in a dark room, under a bright light, and quizzed him on the subject. Here are Vern's notes on what memorabilia matters, year by year, for all five years of original Shelby Mustang production.

1965

Shelby memorabilia from 1965 is the rarest and most desirable of all. Apparent in many of the earliest pieces is the fact that Shelby American didn't have their GT350 specifications or printed materials figured out, nor was the specific formula for their advertising campaign completely in place. What did clearly show through, however, was the genius design influence of Pete Brock, who perfected, with the help of the late George Bartell, the now famous Cobra advertising and sales materials. Over the course of 1965, a wide variety of items was produced. While some sales brochures are considered common and go for around $100, other sales brochures based on the magazine tests of the day have become so rare that they command upwards of $750. Of course, during the year there was also a choice of many jackets, key chains, lighters, tie tacks, and everything else that Ol' Shel could make a dime on; however, most all those items were branded as "Cobra" items for 1965.

Another unique aspect of the 1965 materials is the existence of some items created by the larger Shelby dealerships. While perhaps unknown to even some serious collectors, custom GT350 brochures were produced by Carroll Shelby's and Lew Spencer's Hi-Performance Motors and by Jack Loftus Ford in the greater Chicago area, among others.

Of course, no write-up on '65 materials would be complete without mentioning the two holy grails for every collector. For the year, it is rumored that only half the cars received owner's manuals from the factory, with only half of *those* cars getting a full owner's manual packet. This manual has become so rare that car owners and collectors alike look for years, often offering up their first- and second-borns in exchange for the privilege of ownership. [Author's note: Of an owner's manual!]

And, if a '65 manual is rare, then you may as well give up on the idea of ever owning an original factory postcard. Having a '65 postcard is comparable to having a Daytona coupe. [Author's note: That you can't

drive.] If you have one, you have reached the top of the food chain. Very few exist today and those who own them are understandably hesitant to even take pictures of them for fear of reproductions being made.

1966

The encore year for the Shelby Mustang brought on quadruple the total production of cars. With the cars becoming more refined and comfortable GT cars, as opposed to hardcore race machines, so too was the promotional effort refined. While still retaining the masterful touch of Pete Brock, marketing materials for the new cars began to become more uniform in design. After a year of seemingly producing promotional materials on the fly, Shelby American was now a large company at the LAX facility and the marketing efforts of the company began to show the influence of the Ford Motor Company corporate machine, just like Shelby's 1966 GT350s did. Showroom brochures were reasonably standardized, and Shelby's GT350s enjoyed promotion in some of the most widely distributed magazines in the country, such as *Playboy* and *Sports Illustrated*.

Gone, for 1966, were the days of full-page, simple-type ads with a single picture and specifications. Notable ads from 1966 included detailed and [imaginative] scenes of the GT350 being portrayed as a gentleman's GT car. Some ads portrayed the car as the American alternative to more expensive Italian variants, while others painted the car as the star of a Hollywood blockbuster. Regardless of the hardcore characteristics of the 1965 GT350 promotional materials, Ford was beginning to hammer home that the GT350 for 1966 was a performance car that everyone could enjoy, a car for the sophisticated young man who needed to get where he was going quickly.

That said, there was no shortage of rare items produced for 1966, and those items that have now become most desired followed much the same formula of 1965 pieces. Among the rarest items are press kits, rarer "magazine reprint" sales brochures, and GT350H Hertz Sports Car Club pieces, just to name a select few.

1967

With 1967 being the final curtain for Shelby American, it also served as the final year that marketing materials would show the design touches that had become synonymous with the Shelby American brand since 1962. For 1967, Shelby American advertised "The Road Cars," as they were called, and welcomed in the brand new big-block GT500. Over the course of the year, while the promotional materials continued to show signs of Ford uniformity, pieces also continued to show the influence of the unstoppable duo of George Bartell and Peter Brock.

As a matter of fact, one of the absolute holy grails of all 1967 Shelby items is a poster produced by Shelby American as a showroom poster that prominently featured a George Bartell painting of a 1967 Shelby and "The Road Cars" slogan. This poster had a sister poster, which instead featured "The 1967 Version of the World Champion" 427 Cobra. During 1967, the promotional photography also continued to become more and more similar to those photographs that were used by Ford to promote their more pedestrian Mustangs and other models.

Over the course of 1967, the rarest items mostly have to do with dealer-only materials, such as a dealer sales packets, press kits, and salesman's booklets. By the third year of Shelby American GT production, rare iterations of sales literature had all but disappeared with the exception of a few pieces. Most of what was handed out at dealers included common pieces such as postcards and specification sheets. Without doubt, however, most Shelby collectors and historians remember 1967 as the last year where Shelby marketing materials truly were Shelby-inspired as opposed to being pumped out according to the wishes of Ford Motor Company.

1968

With the move to Michigan, Shelby Automotive essentially became an arm of Ford Motor Company. Gone were the days where Shelby American produced more creative PR and marketing materials to exemplify their company. Days of structure had come to Shelby and the literature and memorabilia distributed and sold by Shelby Automotive tended to reflect that ideal. In fact, with Ford's purchase of the "Cobra" name from Carroll in late 1967, the Shelby Mustangs were now referred to as "Cobra GTs" in the promotional materials as opposed to "Shelby Mustangs." Of course, regardless of Ford's corporate influence, 1968 materials are highly desirable and can bring the big bucks. In fact, there are as many diehard collectors who focus on 1968 and later years as those who focus on Shelby American–related materials.

Some very rare pieces were produced by Shelby Automotive. For example, 1968 saw the production of 24 Shelby Cobra–branded Heuer Carrera 45 Dato 3147 chronographs, which were produced to be handed out at the 1968 New York Auto Show to executives who attended. This was the first branded Carrera ever produced and, today, is one of the most sought-after pieces of Shelby memorabilia in existence. I am personally hopeful that one day I can find one for myself. The year 1968 also saw the production of an extensive Shelby GT350/500 dealer kit, which included an oversized press kit along with colorful window hangings that were to be used in the showroom. Those kits bring big money when they come to market. Finally, 1968 also saw the introduction of a Professional Sales Club, comprised of the best Shelby salesmen in the country. The award pen holder given to club members is among the rarest pieces in existence and is only seen in the finest of collections. Overall, it is fair to say that the volume of rare individual pieces did go down in 1968; however, those items produced in 1968 that are considered rare do bring the same strong money as rare items from any other year.

1969–1970

The years 1969 and 1970 were very similar years to 1968. Corporate culture for Shelby Automotive did not change in any material sense, so the materials still reflected more of Ford's desire to bang out performance GT cars for the masses than produce hardcore, specialized driving machines for the chosen few sports car enthusiasts. Again, the vast majority of pieces from 1969 and 1970 are standard showroom items; however, those items that were produced in low quantities are highly sought by today's collectors.

For example, a penguin lighter was produced in 1969 that was inscribed "1969 Shelby Intro" on the back and was handed out to executives at the introduction of the car. During my time in the hobby, I have owned three of those lighters but have known only three others to exist, making a total of six. For 1969, however, there was an increased emphasis on accessory and trinket sales from Shelby Automotive and Ford. Over the course of 1969 and 1970, Ford began to realize that the need for Shelby Automotive as a car company was dwindling. However, Ford did see the branding potential of the Shelby name. Over the course of 1969 to 1970, more Shelby- and Cobra-branded items—such as jackets, key chains, patches, pilsner beer glasses, and cufflinks—were sold than any other year because Ford and Shelby stood to gain financially from the high profit margins of such items. From Ford's perspective, the sale of Shelby cars was becoming less and less important to them; it was the branding opportunities that the Cobra name offered that stood to affect Ford's pocketbook, and it is there, in the branding, where Ford began to focus most of its efforts—something readily apparent by looking at the printed promotional materials of the day.

ABOVE: Ford certainly wasn't out of the Shelby Mustang-building business in 2007, either, with the introduction of their new GT500. *David Newhardt*

OPPOSITE TOP: The new GT500s 5.4L V8 with 500 ponies was big horsepower, and big news, at the time. They have since continued to raise that bar! *David Newhardt*

OPPOSITE BOTTOM LEFT: As luxuriously appointed as any Mustang could be, the optional Décor group with red seat trim added that extra pop many buyers wanted. *David Newhardt*

OPPOSITE BOTTOM RIGHT: Rocker panel stripes and a snake on the fender pay homage to the Shelbys of old. *David Newhardt*

Shelby, despite these roadblocks, delivered the first production Series 1 in 1999. Soon, a supercharged version was offered, with a base price of around $180,000. By the end of the Series 1 project in 2003, 249 Series 1 cars had been built and sold.

1965 All Over Again

While the Series 1 did have a lot going for it, the rough and tumble experience of manufacturing his own car in this brave new world showed Shelby that the only way to build a pre-titled car was to partner with an established manufacturer. This time he turned once again to Ford. The first sign that Ford and Shelby had renewed their partnership came in the form of the Cobra concept car, a modern interpretation of Shelby's original 427 Cobra roadsters, unveiled at the 2004 Detroit Auto Show. The idea was to create a pure performance car with no frills like air conditioning, power windows, or even a radio. Carroll Shelby summed it up in a Ford press release: "It is a massive motor in a tiny, lightweight car."

The engine was a front-mounted V-10, created by adding two cylinders to Ford's 4.6-liter modular V-8 for a total of 6.4 liters. It was a trick piece, with dry-sump lubrication and 10 Weber-esque velocity stacks poking through the car's hood scoop, covering 10 individual slide plate throttle bodies and multiport electronic fuel injection. The engine made 605 horsepower, which it sent to a Ricardo six-speed transaxle in the rear.

For the automatic Shelby GT-H and GT cars, Shelby American swapped out the standard 3.25:1 rear axle assembly for a factory-fresh 3.55:1 unit to perk up off-the-line performance. *David Newhardt*

While the GT-H cars had their own unique hoods, the GT cars received this 1965–1966-style hood scoop that was riveted on. Unfortunately these scoops were the cause of much trouble; they just didn't hold up the way Shelby had hoped. *David Newhardt*

BELOW: The year 2008 also saw Ford introduce the GT500KR, an $80,000, 540-horsepower monster, to celebrate the 40th anniversary of the original GT500KR. *David Newhardt*

The following year Ford showed the Shelby GR-1 concept car, a tribute to Shelby's 1965 Cobra Daytona Coupe. It was formed over a virtually identical chassis and the 6.4-liter, 605-horsepower V-10 of the Cobra concept. The GR-1 was named, according to Ford, for "Group Racing" and was unveiled as a design study at the Pebble Beach Concours d'Elegance in August 2004 before hitting the 2005 auto show circuit. The GR-1 captured the true essence of the original Cobra Daytona Coupe that inspired it. Unlike the bare-bones Cobra concept that preceded it, the GR-1's interior was focused on high-tech performance and driver comfort. Like the Cobra concept, the GR-1 was purely an engineering study and concept car, or, as Ford called it, "A salute to performance art." But Shelby fans wouldn't have to wait too much longer to buy an actual production Shelby.

Return of the Shelby Mustang

The concept cars were just teasers; the meat in the Shelby-Ford sandwich would be a new Shelby Mustang. Or, rather, a series of new Shelby Mustangs. But for this to happen, agreements would need to be reached with Ford, and Shelby did so. The first production car to feature Shelby's involvement was the limited-production Ford GT supercar, but everyone knew that what the world wanted was a new Shelby Mustang. By 2005 the decision had been made to build a new Shelby GT500.

But before that car hit the streets, Ford and Shelby produced a somewhat unexpected Mustang—a new Shelby GT-H. Forty years after the original 1966 GT350 Hertz cars, Shelby once again made a deal with Hertz (the first since the late 1960s) to provide a limited edition "Shelby" Mustang for its rental fleet. This car was the 2006 Shelby GT-H Mustang. It was a fitting tribute to the original Shelby rent-a-racer from the rental car giant. Using a standard Mustang GT fastback, Shelby Automobiles in Las Vegas built 500 specially prepared GT-H cars for Hertz. All were finished in black with gold "Shelby GT-H"–labeled stripes; they were fitted with a new, aggressive front fascia and body side scoops (later used on the 2007 Mustang GT/CS), a special Shelby hood with hood pins, and a standard Mustang GT rear deck lid spoiler. Five-spoke wheels with black-painted centers were lifted from the Mustang *Bullitt* edition and used on the GT-H. All interiors were finished in dark charcoal gray, with Shelby touches limited to doorsill plates that proclaimed "Hertz Shelby GT-H" and a serialized Shelby GT-H dash plaque mounted between the center dash vents.

Ol' Shel' took a great deal of pride in his Carroll Shelby Engine Company venture, and customers buying new Cobras certainly appreciated being able to buy a Shelby-built engine for their new Shelbys. *David Newhardt*

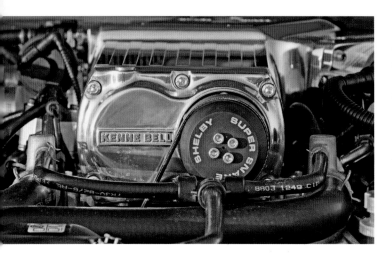

TOP: If the standard 500 horsepower GT500 wasn't good enough for you, Shelby American was happy to turn it into a Super Snake. Shelby's Gary Patterson is seen here exercising a 725-horsepower 2008 model. *David Newhardt*

ABOVE: And here's one major component of the Super Snake package: a huge Kenne Bell blower to shove as much air as possible through the 5.4L V8. *David Newhardt*

As delivered from Ford, the GT-H had the standard Mustang GT 4.6-liter, 300-horsepower engine fitted to a five-speed automatic transmission. Once at Shelby, they were up-fitted with a Ford Racing Performance Parts cold-air intake, a FRPP exhaust, and a special FRPP computer tune that adjusted fuel mixture and ignition timing to properly take advantage of this new breathing potential "flashed" into the car's computer. All of this resulted in a gain of 25 horsepower and 10 lbs-ft of torque, along with one hell of a great V-8 soundtrack through the open element air intake and free-flowing exhaust. Although the standard Ford rear axle ratio for all automatic-equipped Mustang GTs was 3.25:1, Shelby swapped out the rear axle for 3.55:1-geared units like those fitted to five-speed manual cars, which really woke up the GT-H's performance.

To get the right "stance" and also make the GT-H cars handle like a true Shelby, an FRPP "handling package" was used on all cars. It featured special dampers, stiff springs that lowered the car significantly, beefier anti-roll bars, and a strut tower brace in the engine compartment.

For 2007, there was again another special Hertz Shelby GT-H, but this time it was topless. Gone was the fastback coupe, and for 2007 all GT-H cars were convertibles. Equipment was identical to the 2006 GT-H, except for the addition of a decorative "roll bar" and minor trim changes. Just 500 of these were produced as well.

While some companies may have taken the easy way out and just slapped on some decals on such a "tribute" car, the GT-H had no such mockery. It was a true Shelby performance package, installed at Shelby. Customers really were "Renting a Legend," as the Hertz ads of 2006 and 2007 claimed. Once retired from rental duty, these GT-H cars were sold off at wholesale auctions, just as they had been in 1966, and are now on the

In 2008, Team Shelby organized an epic meet for Shelby owners and enthusiasts in Terlingua, Texas, one of Shelby's favorite places on earth. It was a sold-out event. *David Newhardt*

secondary market. With just 1,000 total built, one can only assume they will be collectible in the future, or at least far more collectible than any other rental car sold since the last Hertz Shelby of 1969.

A New Kind of Shelby

Before customers could buy a new Shelby Mustang at their local Ford dealerships, Shelby offered something completely different. Always on the cutting edge of performance trends, Carroll Shelby did not fool himself into thinking that fuel mileage and vehicle costs were minor factors for today's performance car buyers. After all, look at the huge popularity of import tuner-type cars, the fastest-growing automotive aftermarket segment out there. One could say that tuner cars are the modern equivalent of yesterday's muscle cars.

With that in mind, Shelby took a hard look at making big horsepower from engines other than V-8s. One result was the 2006 Shelby CS6 Mustang. Using a base Mustang V-6 coupe, Shelby engineered a balanced performance package that surrounded a Paxton-supercharged, 350-horsepower V-6. With numerous options available, the CS 6 package was sold as a kit for owners to install themselves or installed either by Shelby Automotive in Las Vegas or through its network of authorized installers.

Starting Small

The basic work done to create the GT-H gave Ford and Shelby a platform for a Shelby Mustang that they could sell while they developed the GT500. And there was a market for such a car. After the introduction of the Hertz-only GT-H model, Shelby and Ford were overwhelmed with people requesting a "civilian" version. And just like that, the Shelby GT was born. Based on the GT-H, a few differences separated the GT from its rental-car brethren. First, and perhaps most importantly, a five-speed manual transmission was available, and in the GT it was fitted with a Hurst short-throw shifter.

LEFT: Shelby's Gary Patterson and the legendary Bob Bondurant keep an eye on the performance stages. *David Newhardt*

BELOW: Of course Gary Patterson, Shelby's chief test driver, had to hop on the runway and show people how it is done. *David Newhardt*

Gone was the GT-H hood, and in its place was a standard Mustang hood with a 1966 GT350–style hood scoop riveted on for a vintage look. Only available in a coupe for 2007, and in either white or black, the Shelby GT had a base price of $36,970. In spite of this being within spitting distance of the 500-horsepower GT500, a remarkable 5,632 Shelby GTs were sold in 2007.

For 2008 the Shelby GT returned, now with both coupe and convertible models available. Two new colors were also available: Vista Blue and Grabber Orange, the latter available only in limited markets. Base price of the coupe was $38,970, with $43,970 required to drive home a Shelby GT convertible.

Return of the Big Boys

Hot on the heels of the Shelby GT-H, Ford brought back another famous Shelby name attached to a new performance Mustang: GT500. Unlike the GT-H, this was not a Shelby-modified car, but rather a car for which Carroll Shelby served as a performance consultant to Ford during its development. Working with Ford's Special Vehicle Team division, Shelby and Ford's goal was to build a true performance car that excelled on all levels: power, handling, and comfort.

The most impressive feature of this new GT500 was its 5.4-liter, 32-valve, supercharged engine, which produced 500 horsepower, the highest horsepower ever in a production Mustang. The only transmission available was a special heavy-duty Tremec TR6060 six-speed manual with a GT500-specific clutch. The suspension was carefully developed by the SVT team and transformed the base Mustang into an extremely capable handler. Brembo brakes were fitted at all four corners, along with Goodyear F1 tires specific to the GT500.

Carroll Shelby and his Terlingua Edition Shelby Mustang. *David Newhardt*

Both coupe and convertible body styles were offered. Body modifications were designed to mimic the original 1968 GT500, including aggressive front upper and lower fascias with a Shelby-styled mesh grille, Shelby snake emblems, and a special ducted hood. Rocker panel stripes with GT500 callouts were standard, and Le Mans stripes were optional on the coupes. At the rear, a special fascia with an under-bumper air splitter was used, and "Shelby" lettering was applied to the deck lid under a special rear spoiler. Other retro-Shelby styling cues were used on the exterior as well. Seven exterior colors were offered, along with various options for stripe colors.

The interior was loaded up with special GT500 seats and a few buckets of Cobra snake emblems as well for good measure. Special instrumentation was fitted, with the tachometer and speedometer switching sides from the standard Mustang gauge cluster. Interiors were available in either dark charcoal or a two-tone charcoal and red combination.

With its retro styling and 500 horsepower offering performance like 0 to 60 in 4.5 seconds, all for just over $40,000, the new GT500 was heralded as the performance car buy of the year in 2007. What a novel concept: good styling, big horsepower, and a reasonably affordable price.

LEFT: Spike's popular show *Bullrun* was there to help owners put their cars through their paces. They also handled staffing the flag stations. *David Newhardt*

Return of the King of the Road

Another Shelby-Ford 40th anniversary was reached in 2008: the 40th anniversary of the original 1968 Shelby GT500 KR. What better way to celebrate this than make a 2008 version of the KR? Starting with production 2008 GT500s shipped to Shelby's Las Vegas factory, the KRs were upgraded by Shelby employees with a Ford Racing Performance Package for the engine that raised supercharger boost, then fitted with a cold-air intake that breathed through a special, KR-only, composite-carbon-fiber hood with functional hood scoops styled just like those on the 1968 KRs. Of course, each car received the required performance retuning of its computer. Post-combustion, all the hot air exited through a special KR-only exhaust system developed by Shelby. The result: 540 horsepower. All this went through the same Tremec 6060 six-speed transmission, fitted with a short-throw Ford Racing shifter, and ended up at the KR-only 3.73:1-ratio rear axle. Other KR upgrades included special forged-alloy Alcoa wheels with specially developed KR-only Goodyear tires, lowered suspension, unique GT500 KR badges and striping, and a host of other appearance upgrades.

The KR was a true Shelby project, with considerable design and development done by both Shelby and SVT teams. It is also an honest-to-goodness Shelby Automobiles–modified car. Just 1,000 were produced for 2008, with an additional 746 units planned for 2009. Only 571 of the 2009 model year KRs are intended for the US market, with the remainder being produced for export. That makes a grand total of 1,571 KRs, and if that number sounds familiar, it should; that's the number of original KRs produced by Shelby in 1968. All of this exclusivity does not come cheap; the base price of a KR was some $40,000 higher than a standard GT500. That's about $1,000 per additional horsepower, or in the $85k range total for those keeping score.

Return of the Super Snake
2007–2009

Another Shelby alternative to the drudgery of a plain old 500-horsepower GT500 was the Super Snake Package. The new Super Snake was named after the original GT40 427-powered 1967 GT500. This modern Shelby upgrade was available to owners of any 2007 to 2009 GT500 via Shelby in Las Vegas, and two versions were available: a 605-horsepower base model or a 725-horsepower version.

GT500 Super Snake awaits its turn to turn it loose. *David Newhardt*

Sam Smith:
Does Generation X Care? This One Does

First things first: I don't own a Shelby Mustang. I mention this only because I wish I did—I'm one of those people who could probably swing a good '65 GT350 if I sold absolutely everything and ate ramen noodles for the rest of my life, but then I'd have no house or things to put in said house and nothing to eat but noodles. And probably no wife and kids either. I like my wife and kids. So, I can't sell everything and buy the Shelby of my dreams.

But that doesn't mean I haven't seriously considered it.

What is it about the man's work that just makes so much sense? The Mustang was a mere style exercise, an economy car in wolf's clothing, before Carroll and his guys got to it. After a handful of changes, it became something bigger. History and countless imitators have proven that the appeal is more than just hot-rod parts or race wins. It's in the charm of Shelby the salesman, Shelby the Le Mans captain, Shelby the guy who hired Remington and Brock and Miles and the rest. Peter Brock once told me that Carroll's greatest quality wasn't salesmanship, as most people think, but being a talent scout, and I think he's right—the people make the stories, and the stories make the car. And no one's Mustang stories are better than the ones that began at 1042 Princeton.

Perspective helps. I'm fortunate enough to drive a lot of stuff for my day job, but surprisingly, most of it leaves me cold. (Don't tell the PR guys I said that. Supercar X is great, guys, I promise!) Power is nice, but it's not everything, and the more seat time you get with neat machinery, the more you realize that truly great cars—soul, a connection to the road, a sense of history—are few and far between. You also see pretty quickly that there's no set recipe for greatness, nor an easy-to-explain appeal. Ever try to tell someone why an R Model matters? You get either enthusiastic nodding (the faithful) or a blank stare. It's like Louis Armstrong once said about jazz: "If you have to ask, you'll never know."

Me, I've wanted a Shelby Mustang for as long as I can remember. I'm 38 as this book goes to press, which makes me too young to have been there in the '60s but old enough to remember when anyone could afford one. In the eighth grade, I tried like crazy to convince my father to cash in his 401(k) and buy two '65 350s. Twenty-five years later, those cars would've made the same cash in a fund look like chump change, but I digress. (At least he regrets it now. And he once bought a 2012 Boss 302 as partial absolution.)

That was as close as I got until six years ago, when the evil author of this book let me drive his ex–*Sports Car Graphic* Shelby/Paxton-supercharged '65 GT350. It's one of the nicest and most sorted 350s on earth, and he knew I already wanted one, knew that drive would put me over the edge.

It did. Six months later, there was a '65 fastback in my garage, a GT350 "tribute" car that began life as a Primrose Yellow two-barrel

After driving his Shelby-ized 1965 Mustang to Shelby American's Las Vegas facility, Sam Smith attempts to soak it all in before taking another step. *Michael Darter*

289 but sported Wimbledon White paint and the usual Shelby mods. It was nothing special, but I sold a near-perfect 1988 BMW M3 and a much-loved Honda CB400F to make it happen, and I loved it. (My Gen X friends told me I was crazy, but got it when they experienced the car.)

My fastback was missing that actual Shelby magic, but it helped scratch the itch. It made the right noises and felt about right; and at the core, it touched what's great about the Fords that Carroll built. I ended up selling my car after a few years, right before I moved my family west in a rare moment of adulting. But I miss it, and what it represented. Shelby Mustangs are hot rods—hot rods that do the work of sports cars, sure, but hot rods nonetheless. And hot-rodding ties into that great American notion of constant reinvention. We do it with our cities, our culture, and the things we create, but I'd argue that it's never more inspiring than it is with cars. And Mustangs in particular.

Some people contend we're in a bubble, that the values of real Shelby Mustangs have to come down. I know they aren't right, but selfishly, I secretly hope they are. Because one day, I'm going to put something from 1042 Princeton Drive or that LAX hangar in my garage. In the meantime, I'll make do with a wife, two great kids, real food on the table, great memories of a GT350-esque Mustang Fastback, and not pawning off the contents of my house.

Yet.

Ramen noodles don't taste that bad, right?

—Sam Smith
Editor at Large, *Road & Track* magazine

2011–2014 Shelby American GT350

Ford updated the Mustang's sheet metal for the 2010 model year. The Shelby GT500 retained the same supercharged 5.4-liter engine, but power rose to 540 horsepower. Otherwise, not much changed, other than body panels.

The following year, Shelby offered a new sort-of model: the 2011 GT350. To get one of these, a customer had to buy a standard Mustang GT and bring it to Shelby American's Las Vegas facilities to be converted to a Shelby GT350.

The raw material was solid. For 2011, Ford gave the Mustang GT its new 5-liter Coyote engine, named in honor of the Ford 32-valve racing engine used by A. J. Foyt's 1969 Indy car racing team. The new-for-2011 all-aluminum Coyote engine used chain-driven double-overhead camshafts to operate four-valve cylinder heads with variable valve timing to produce 412 horsepower. Once at Shelby's facilities, this engine was tuned to produce 430 horsepower in normally aspirated form, or the owner could opt for a Whipple supercharger, which bumped power to 525 horsepower. An R version took that number to 624 horsepower.

As one would expect, the Shelby GT350 came with all the badges, special trim, and unique bodywork bits and pieces found on any modern Shelby, along with a tuned suspension. None of it came cheap: the normally aspirated conversion cost buyers $26,995

The modular Ford motors are very stout and respond incredibly well to performance upgrades. And Shelby American has figured out how to get as much HP as anybody out of them through the use of upgrades like this huge polished blower that adds boost while also creating a cooler intake charge. It's a win-win.
David Newhardt

on top of the price of the donor Mustang GT. At $33,995, the supercharged version virtually doubled the price of the donor Mustang. Tuning the supercharged version to R specifications was a relative bargain, costing just another $750. The Shelby American GT350 was dropped after the 2014 model year as Ford introduced its 2015-up GT350.

ABOVE: Carroll Shelby was understandably thrilled to introduce the 2011 GT350. So thrilled, in fact, that this was the image he used for Cleo and his 2010 Christmas card! *David Newhardt*

OPPOSITE TOP: With Shelby American located at the Las Vegas Speedway, it would have been a crime to not have them use a new GT350 as their official pace car. *David Newhardt*

OPPOSITE BOTTOM: The new GT350 took advantage of the return of the 5.0L in the 2011 Mustang GT, and supercharged it all the way to 525 horsepower. *David Newhardt*

The Last Carroll Shelby Shelby Mustang

Overall, not much happened with the Shelby Mustangs in the early years of the second decade of the twenty-first century until the introduction of the 2013 GT500. By this time, the Camaro ZL1 had upstaged the Shelby GT500 by featuring a 580-horsepower supercharged V-8 engine. So, for 2013, Shelby got busy.

To beat the Camaro, Ford replaced the 5.4-liter engine with a new aluminum 5.8-liter engine. Thanks to the 14 pounds of boost produced by the Twin Vortices Series (or TVS) 2300 supercharger, the 2013 Shelby GT500 pumped out an astounding 662 horsepower and torque increased to 631 pounds-feet, resulting in a genuine 200-mile-per-hour supercar. To handle all that power, Ford's SVT engineers upgraded virtually every component in the car. A stronger Tremec six-speed transmission with a dual-disc clutch transferred power to the live axle out back through a one-piece carbon-fiber driveshaft. An optional performance package added a Torsen differential and stiffer suspension bits.

Like all the modern Shelby GT500s, this was a Ford product, designed by the SVT crew and built on Ford's assembly lines, but that didn't mean Carroll Shelby wasn't involved. This was very much his baby, and he had a hand in almost every aspect of its development. It

turned out that this would be his last hurrah. On May 10, 2012, Shelby finally succumbed to the heart problems that had derailed his racing career 50 years earlier, making the 2013 Shelby GT500 the last car to receive input from the man himself.

More Super
The Super Snake returned yet again for the 2015–2019 model years, based on the new Mustang 5.0L GT. It featured upgraded suspension, brakes, and a standard 670-horsepower supercharged engine with over 750 horsepower as optional through 2017. For 2018–2019, the base Super Snake offered 710 horsepower with over 800 horsepower optional. A top spec Super Snake can run 0–60 in 3.5 seconds and the 1/4 mile in 10.9 seconds. Super indeed!

A Shelby for Every Taste and Budget
The new Shelby American really shines in continually churning out exciting new Shelby Mustang variants for every taste and budget. The options run from relatively modest modifications to sky-is-the limit conversions.

Take, for example, the Shelby GTS. Introduced in 2011 and applicable to 2011–2014 V-6-powered Mustangs, Shelby adds a special hood and front fascia, Billet Black upper grille, upgraded brakes, a Ford Racing suspension package, Borla Performance exhaust,

The 2013–2014 GT500 Super Snake is capable of 10 second ¼-mile times right out of the box. And that's with the "small" 850 horsepower engine. *David Newhardt*

continued on page 226

ABOVE: It is really something when a stock, 550-horespower GT500 looks tame, isn't it? What a world we live in! *David Newhardt*

LEFT: For 2011, Ford introduced an all-aluminum version of their monstrous 5.4L engine in the GT500. With 550 horsepower and a convertible top, this is what I call a hair drier. *David Newhardt*

BELOW: With over 800 horsepower on tap, the 2018–2019 Shelby Super Snakes pictured here certainly have the power to back up their impressive, muscular looks. You have to respect machines that can not only talk the talk but also walk the walk! *Shelby American*

ABOVE: Showing they know no limits, in 2009 Shelby and Don Prudomme came up with the idea for a purpose-built drag car based on their history of doing drag cars together. Vince LaViolette at Shelby worked out the details and the result is what you see here: an 800 horsepower, fully caged, flip front end, drag car. Just seven were built. *David Newhardt*

LEFT: Clearly the Prudomme-edition drag car is not your usual late-model Shelby Mustang. *David Newhardt*

OPPOSITE TOP: The 2012 Shelby GTS was Shelby American's successor to the very popular Shelby GT. Designed to be affordable, buyers can spec their GTS from a base V-6 with no performance options all the way through a supercharged 5.0L. *David Newhardt*

OPPOSITE BOTTOM: How do you make a GT350 even meaner? Make it black with gold stripes. *David Newhardt*

TOP: Unlike most modern cars, Ford gives you a full viewing privileges. No reason to cover all those horses up with plastic covers and gingerbread. *David Newhardt*

ABOVE: One of the coolest details of the GT500 has to be the very Hurst-esque cue ball shifter knob with factory Le Mans stripes. *David Newhardt*

continued from page 222

Shelby badging, and of course the obligatory Le Mans racing stripes and Shelby numbered dash plaque and engine plate. Many options are available, including a Procharger supercharger that bumps power from the V-6 engine to 475 horsepower.

Of course, the Shelby GT and Shelby GT/SC packages have continued as well, for both the original 2006–2009 Shelby GT and GT-H cars as well as the 2011–2014 cars, or as a conversion that starts with a Ford Mustang GT as a donor car.

Starting in 2012, the Shelby 1000 package was made available for 2012–2014 GT500s. While you might think that "1000" refers to horsepower output, you would be wrong, since actual output is 1,100 horsepower. The option list for this beast is fairly limited, consisting only of an optional Kenne Bell supercharger that bumps output to "if you have to ask . . ." and a Shelby wide-body kit. Every component of the Shelby 1000 is beefed up to handle the extra power.

The rest of the car is much like the Super Snake, with additional upgrades. In 2017, the Shelby 1000 package returned but using 2015–2018 Mustang 5.0L GTs as the jumping off point—yet being no less wicked as a result.

Hertz So Good

In 2016, for the 50th Anniversary of the original 1966 Shelby/Hertz collaboration, the two companies decided to celebrate the same way they had for the 40th Anniversary: with a new Shelby GT-H Mustang. This one was based on the S550 chassis, of course, and certainly the most aggressive-looking Hertz Mustang yet. Until the 60th, I presume.

The E Is for Everywhere

For 2017, Shelby rolled out the all-new Shelby GTE, an outgrowth of the Shelby GT and GT-H programs, to deliver legendary Shelby style and performance in a sophisticated, global-

ABOVE: Three generations of Shelby Hertz Mustangs: 1966, 2006, and 2016. I bet even 'ol Shel himself would not have guessed that when he inked that groundbreaking Hertz deal in 1966 that he was creating a legacy that would continue for fifty years and beyond. *Shelby American*

LEFT: Based on the world-class S550 Mustang, the 2017-up Shelby GTE was designed by Shelby American from the outset to be tailored to the individual tastes of owners worldwide. From 2.3L Ecoboost to supercharged 5.0L Coyote power, stick or automatic, just about any performance modification you can think of can be specified. *Shelby American*

market focused package. With a base 2.3L Ecoboost four-cylinder engine delivering 335 horsepower or the optional 456 horsepower 5.0L Coyote engine, and a nearly limitless options list to deliver everything from suspension upgrades to superchargers, the GTE offers a great and very affordable gateway to the Shelby lifestyle that can be optioned from mild to wild, for customers around the world.

The GT Returns

In 2019, the iconic Shelby GT model returned, with a 480-horsepower, naturally aspirated 5.0L engine, but when optioned with the Ford Performance supercharger, that number grew to a whopping 700-plus. And you could also get it in convertible form . . . how's that for a speedy way to a tan?

TOP: At Shelby's location just off the Las Vegas strip, things are busier than ever. Here's a bird's-eye view of just part of the massive facility to give you an idea. *Michael Darter*

ABOVE: Here is a Race Red 2014 GT350 nearing completion in the shop.

2015-Up Ford Shelby GT350 and GT350R

When the new S550 Mustang was introduced in 2015, it was met with rave reviews. But that didn't stop Ford from dropping hints of a track-focused Shelby variant for months, finally releasing details in early 2015. Honoring the original 1965 Shelby GT350, the new Shelby GT350 and GT350R brought back a name that had been long dormant with Ford. And like that original GT350, the new one was all business, starting with Ford's "Voodoo" 5.2-liter flat-plane crank V-8 that produced 526 naturally aspirated horsepower and shrieked to 8,250 rpm with a sound unlike anything a traditional cross-plane crank V-8 can muster. A six-speed manual transmission transferred power to the Torsen limited-slip differential with 3.73 gears, while large Brembo brakes gave it incredible stopping power. MagneRide adjustable dampeners offered state-of-the-art high-end chassis tuning, adjusting to conditions in milliseconds. Beyond the top-shelf hardware, new exterior styling was introduced with GT350-specific sheet metal, an upgraded interior, and numerous other tweaks. The new GT350 was Ford's BMW M4 and Porsche 911 killer.

The 2013 GT500 upped the ante again with an increase to 5.8 liters and, get this, 662 horsepower. Stock. Off the showroom floor. With a warranty. And throw on the optional Performance Package like this car has (as evidenced by the dark argent wheels and special side stripes) and you have a car that can clean the clock of supercars costing many multiples as much. The world's first 200-mile-per-hour production Mustang needs a lot of fuel, and a lot of cooling, at that incredible speed. As such, Ford engineers removed portions of the grille to increase airflow through the multiple fluid coolers. This is exotic stuff, boys and girls. *Joshua Taff*

RiGHT: A 2018 Ford Shelby GT350 R in its happy place: being exercised on a racetrack. These are immensely capable and thrilling machines, not even factoring in the incredible flat-plane-crank music that blasts from the exhaust which on the R is even louder thanks to the lack of the exhaust resonators found on the standard GT350. *Ford Motor Company*

BELOW: A trio of 2017 GT350s shows a Grabber Blue version in the foreground with a Lightning Blue GT350 R to the left and a Ruby Red GT350 R to the right. Note the distinguishing visual cues that identify the hardcore R models: carbon-fiber wheels, red brake calipers, red badging, a red outline on the factory stripes (if so equipped), and the large "horseshoe" rear spoiler. *Ford Motor Company*

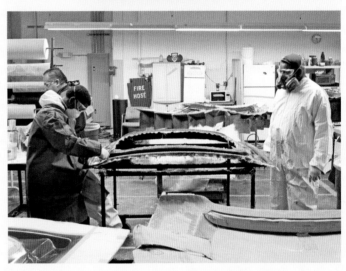

But the real story was the track-focused GT350R. Gone were the aluminum-spoke wheels replaced by full carbon-fiber wheels, a first for a major manufacturer, and saving a total of 52 pounds of unsprung weight. The back seat was deleted, a large front splitter added, and a special carbon-fiber wing at the rear replaced the smaller lip spoiler of the Technology or Track Pack equipped standard GT350s. The radio and air conditioning were removed to save weight, but they became extra-cost options if you didn't want to sweat on the way to the track.

In either GT350 or GT350R spec, these were widely praised as the best road or track Mustangs ever created. And while they are officially 2016-model-year-and-up production cars, when the GT350 and GT350R were revealed in 2015, Ford announced that it would build 137 2015 model year GT350s for Ford executives and VIP customers. The breakdown was 50 Track Pack cars, 50 Technology Pack cars, and just 37 GT350Rs for 2015, making this unofficial model year for the new GT350 the one I'm sure collectors will seek out for years to come.

2020-Up Ford Shelby GT500

So, if you're Ford, how do you top the stellar world-beating GT350 and GT350R? Well, in the fall of 2019, that question will be answered when the new 2020 Mustang Shelby

continued on page 234

TOP LEFT: Just in case anybody at Shelby should forget their most important partner.

TOP RIGHT: While Shelby American saves most take-off parts and resells them, there were a few dumpsters full of stuff I'm sure restorers in the year 2065 would kill for.

ABOVE LEFT: A GT500 undergoing a wide-body conversion.

ABOVE RIGHT: Shelby builds many components in-house, including body panels. It is one way to definitively control quality.

Jim Farley: Ford's Future

It is hard not to compare Jim Farley, Ford's president of Global Markets, to two of his legendary Mustang predecessors: Lee Iacocca and Carroll Shelby. Think that's a stretch? Ponder the facts. Farley joined Ford in 2007 as an outspoken 40-something executive who wasn't going to let politics get in the way of his passion for the brand. And like Shelby and Iacocca, Farley doesn't pull any punches. He speaks his mind; rather than telling people what they want to hear, he tells them what they need to hear. As part of his job of steering Ford into the future, Farley needs to not only know what people want but then to actually build it. And that's a job Farley doesn't take lightly.

So even if you may not know of Farley, trust me: if you're a Ford person, be glad he is there. Don't let the suit and the fancy title fool you; Jim Farley is one of us. To prove it, I subjected myself to a full cavity search (twice), a retina scan, and a full background check to get close enough to him to ask a few questions.

Q: Jim, you're a young guy and have already amassed a hell of a resume in the auto industry. After 17 years at Toyota—by all accounts as their in-house rock star, in charge of everything from trucks to Lexus to creating the Scion brand—you left to sign on at Ford in 2007. Besides dragging your family from California to Michigan, that's a huge move. Why did you do it?

A: I've always loved cars. My parents never had a moment where they said, "We wonder what Jim wants to do . . ." And I always wanted to be in business, but I really struggled with combining the two. I didn't want the car business to ruin my love of cars. I went to IBM, was looking for a job, and one day met Briggs Cunningham. He sent me over to Hill and Vaughn, Phil Hill's restoration company. So, there I was, riding my bike to Hill and Vaughn, working my way through grad school, and falling in love with cars on this much deeper level. Restoring and learning about the European coach-built cars. I loved it.

When the job came up at Toyota, I took it for the opportunity to run the Lexus brand. It was great, exciting, but after a while, it was more of a job and less of my passion. I've always been a Mustang guy. I even drove them all through my time at Toyota, which was quite awkward, actually, and they let me know it. [laughs]

When the opportunity at Ford came up, I looked at it and thought, I'm getting older, my family has a long history with Ford—and I didn't want to look at my grandkids one day and tell them I never took a risk. Plus, Ford was in trouble and I didn't want to look back and think I could have helped them and didn't. Not to mention I was driving a Prius as a company car and it was killing me inside. I really needed a Mustang as a company car. And, well, Ford is Ford. You can't beat that.

Q: You've owned 1965 and 1966 GT350s, a factory Comp 289 Cobra, a 427 Cobra race car, a 1990s Mustang Trans-Am race car, an early Bronco and even an original GT40, among others. I've watched you find these cars, restore them, and drive or race the wheels off them. Clearly, you love this stuff—or are you just the world's best method actor?

A: The cars are really what it is all about. Don't get me wrong; I love the people in this hobby, but I am just crazy about cars. I'm all about how they sound. How they look. How they work. But most importantly, how they drive. I know what I spend on them to make them work is irrational, but if you can't drive the cars, what good are they? I don't want to own 20 cars. Maybe five street cars and some dedicated race cars. Ten cars max. That's not to say I wouldn't love to own a hundred, but that just isn't practical. I want to stay a driver and not become a hoarder.

Q: So, these old cars that we both agree were not technical marvels, even when new, have this intangible thing, this magic that makes them among the most desirable cars ever built. We have technology today that nobody could ever dream of 50 years ago, or even 10. The most pedestrian car of today, on pure numbers, can run with a 1965 GT350, but yet nobody cares because they are boring. So as a manufacturer today, how hard do you work to get that soul, that special not-boring something that seems to be so hard to capture, into your new performance cars?

A: Make no mistake; we work on this literally every day. We could re-create a 427 Cobra or a 1965 GT350, but that isn't the right thing to do. It isn't sustainable. Our job is to get the cycle right, have a performance car for everybody, all the time, and not just one every 10 years. That's why we built the current GT350, the Raptor, the Ford GT, the upcoming GT500, but also the Edge and Explorer STs. Being retro isn't good enough. Throughout my career, people have always asked, "Why are you so intense?" It comes from visualizing guys like us on the other side. Thinking of all the people who want us to push the envelope and make them a better car. It's this passion for the cars that changes the way we work and the end result. In other words, our math may be different, but the result is the same—the product is one people want because it isn't boring.

Q: Big Brother: He's everywhere. Buy a soda at the gas station and 10 minutes later Google emails you a coupon for your next one. The old joke used to be, "If this car could talk . . ." Well, now they can. How long before that info changes how we are allowed to use our cars, especially performance cars?

A: People are smart. Everybody expects more transparency these days across the board. Cars are no exception. And everybody knows the street isn't where you go fast; it just isn't logical. That's why we see so many customers buying cars for track day use, or country club–type racetracks. You can buy a new GT350 or GT500, drive it to the track, spend the day going as fast as you want, and drive home. Big Brother

When Jim Farley isn't at Ford finding ways to build 200-miles-per-hour Mustangs, you can usually find him at the track trying to go 200 miles per hour in one of his race cars. This is Jim with his Comp Cobra, CSX2513, at the Monterey Motorsports Reunion in 2012. *Ford Motor Company*

can't stop you from doing something that is legal. And consumer data is really important for the industry; it helps us build better cars, safer cars. With things like 911 Assist, we can help you if your airbags are deployed and we know your car is upside down in a ditch. Of course, as a consumer, you can always opt out of all of it too.

Q: *To that point, the upcoming 2020 GT500 will have well over 700 horsepower. The last one had 662 horsepower. Clearly, at some point soon these numbers have to start going the other way, right?*

A: Does it have to? A 700-plus horsepower 200-mile-per-hour Mustang feels right to me!

Q: *Shelby American went from being a manufacturer building Shelby Mustangs in 1965 to basically being a styling package built by Ford and then to being a pre-title manufacturer of Mustangs again in 2006, and now Shelby American is again a post-title mod shop for your new cars. Just how close is the relationship between Ford and Shelby American these days? Do the guys at Ford look at the 1,000-horsepower monsters Shelby American transforms your Mustangs into and go, "Hell yeah!" Or do they say, "Oh Hell no!"?*

A: Shelby and Ford have an important relationship. We all remember our conversations with Carroll about his ideas and expectations. He always had a target. A quick look into the Ford executive garage will tell you all you need to know. We're all car guys at heart. Just like Carroll was.

Q: *Ford's 2015-up Shelby GT350 was met with rave reviews. It's a BMW and Porsche killer. Your new Shelby GT500 promises groundbreaking*

technology and performance in a Mustang. Ford has announced its move away from passenger cars but is clearly keeping the Mustang. So, what are Ford's plans for the Shelby brand going forward?

A: We need to be true to the idea, the heritage, but also relevant and a manufacturer of affordable performance cars for a global audience. We want to build cars that true car people want and can relate to. We firmly believe in not just investing in the product but also the hobby and its enthusiast groups, like SAAC and the MCA. The Mustang brand is iconic, as is the Shelby name, and we embrace them both.

Q: *There has been a lot written lately about the end of car collecting being near, relatively speaking, and how kids today just aren't interested in old cars. You're a car collector, a parent, and somebody who monitors the future of the automobile in general on a daily basis. Obviously, it is our job to teach the next generation(s) about the cars we love, but will it work? Is this just the same doom-and-gloom prediction some collectors propagated in the 1950s when they said nobody would care about Duesenbergs in 20 years?*

A: I think about this a lot. There have always been collectors, starting with Roman chariots, I guess? I'm optimistic. I see my son's enthusiasm and car-spotting ability. His nickname is GTO Jaimo; he loves the Judge. Isn't a 275 GTB four-cam or a Ford GT40 the same thing as a Monet or a Renoir? The appeal is universal. Even if the numbers are smaller, I don't worry. I think we're in really good shape.

TOP: Another mean-looking wide-body GT500 awaits completion on the factory floor.

LEFT: Speaking of quality control, each car undergoes OE-level inspections throughout the build process at Shelby American.

BELOW: A completed GT350 aims itself towards the door, just waiting to run. I love the color and the satin wheels.

There is a huge problem we discovered with the 2014 Shelby GT/SC: The rear tires are defective. *Michael Darter*

continued from page 230

GT500 hits the streets. With a supercharged 5.2-liter V-8 producing more than 700 horsepower and capable of mid-three-second 0–60 mph and sub-11-second quarter-mile scores, this new Shelby GT500 features the best Mustang track times and also the best cornering and the largest brakes of any domestic sports coupe thanks to tech transfer from the 2017-up Ford GT and Mustang GT4 racing programs, including a segment-first dual-clutch seven-speed transmission. Ford declares it "the pinnacle of any pony car ever engineered by Ford Performance—delivers on its heritage with more than 700 horsepower for the quickest street-legal acceleration and most high-performance technology to date ever offered in a Ford Mustang" while Jim Farley, Ford president of global markets, simply calls it "a takedown artist."

"With its supercar-level powertrain, the all-new Shelby GT500 takes the sixth-generation Mustang to a performance level once reserved only for exotics," said Hermann Salenbauch, global director of Ford Performance vehicle programs. "As a Mustang, it has to be attainable and punch above its weight. To that end, we've set a new standard among American performance cars with our most powerful street-legal V-8 engine to date, plus the quickest-shifting transmission ever in a Mustang for all-out precision and speed."

And the specs bear all of this out: 16.5-inch two-piece brake rotors up front with six-piston Brembo calipers, an available Track Package with 20x11-inch front and 20x11.5-inch rear carbon-fiber wheels wrapped in sticky Michelin Pilot Sport Cup 2 tires, and extended aero equipment. This new GT500 should indeed set the standard for modern pony car performance. I know I can't wait to drive one.

The Future?

Ford has clearly proven that the Mustang and Shelby names remain revered in Dearborn. With incredible new Ford Shelby Mustangs like the 2015-up GT350s and the 2020-up GT500 offering cutting-edge technology and supercar performance we couldn't have dreamt of even fifteen years ago, the future certainly looks bright for us Ford fans.

Shelby American sells 1,000-horsepower street cars that you can drive every day. They pass emissions. You can drive them to the store. One. Thousand. Horsepower. I bet nobody in 1964 saw this coming. *David Newhardt*

And the folks at Shelby American's Las Vegas facilities will continue to focus on taking Mustangs that customers buy from Ford ("post-title" in industry speak) even one step further by converting them into any number of Shelby American models. Think of this as an evolution of the original coach-built automobiles of an earlier era, where lavish, exclusive automotive works of art rolled out of fabled companies such as Pininfarina and Zagato.

As proof that this time-honored concept still works, Shelby American's facilities just off the Las Vegas Strip are working at capacity to keep up with demand for Mustang conversions and simply buzzing with activity from the production floor, to the museum, and even in the substantial gift shop, which, by the way, also sells Shelby go-fast parts over the counter. And judging by what I saw during a recent visit to the shop, there is no shortage of power-hungry Mustang owners and modern Shelby fans.

While we may never see Shelby American return to automobile manufacturer status, we still have the Shelbys Carroll created in his lifetime: the Cobras, Dodges, Series 1s, and of course all of those amazing Shelby Mustangs. Since 1965, it has been the perfect symbiotic relationship. Shelby very well may have saved the Mustang brand, and in so doing, the Mustang may have very well saved Shelby American. It is a story even Hollywood couldn't have dreamed of, and I bet anything that if you're holding this book, you're as happy as I am that Lee Iacocca talked Shelby into making a racehorse from that pretty little mule.

ABOVE: The upcoming 2020 Ford Shelby GT500 is based on the 6th-generation Mustang motivated by Ford's most powerful engine to date (over 700hp) all surrounded by the latest in performance technology, much of it gleaned from Ford's GT4 Mustang race program. Just look at this thing. Can you say "badass"? *Ford Motor Company*

LEFT: The tech and killer design continues in the new GT500's interior. Multi-screen configurable LCD displays with data available from every parameter imaginable, along with the cutting-edge connectivity today's supercar buyers demand make this one heck of a cockpit. And while purists may lament the lack of a clutch pedal, the GT500's state-of-the art dual-clutch gearbox is not only NOT an automatic—it is also shared with the Ford GT Supercar. Yes, the same one that won Le Mans. *Ford Motor Company*

Index

Page numbers in italics indicate an item that appears in a photograph or caption.

A. O. Smith, *164*, 167, 171–172, 186, 204
AC Car Company, 13, 18
Arning, Klaus, *18*, 34, 39
Atzbach, John, *72*
Austin-Healey, 13

Bachelor, Dean, 104
Bartell, George, 206–207
Billups, Jason, 184
Bishop, John, 30–31, 39, 45, 52, *151*
Bondurant, Bob, 34, *215*
Bridgehampton Raceway, 66
Bristol Aeroplane Company, 13
Brock, Peter, *21*, 39, 45, *50*, 51–53, 58, 91, 139, 206
Buddy Bar Casting Company, 51
Bud Moore Engineering, 193–194
Burgy, Diane, 99
Burgy, Jeff, 106–107

Cantwell, Chuck, 39, 40, 44-46, *50, 55, 62, 145, 186*
Car and Driver, 85, *151*
Car Life, 91–92, 104, 109, *166*
Carroll Shelby Children's Heart Foundation, 107
Carroll Shelby Engine Company, *211*
Carroll Shelby School of High Performance Driving, 13
Carroll Shelby Sports Cars, 12
Casey, Ed, *145*
Castrol, 33
Chevrolet, 178
Chrysler Corporation, 204
    CSX-T, 204
      Dodge Viper, 204
      1983 Shelby Charger, 204
Colby, Bob, *136*
Competition Press & Autoweek, 52, 107
Coronado Naval Air Station, *71*
Cosby, Bill, 154, 183
Cowan, Andrew, 23
Cragar, 53
Cramer, Peyton, 45, 113
Cunningham, Briggs, 39, 51–52

1965 Daytona races, 62
Dearborn Steel Tubing (DST), 128
2004 Detroit Auto Show, 208
Disher, Peter, *178*
Donohue, Mark, 46, 67, *186*
Droste, Harold, 49

Estes, Vern, 206–207
Evans, Dave, 13

Farley, Jim, 232–233, *233*
Farrer, Joe, 139
Fee, Sonny, 182

Ferrari, Enzo, 30
Ford, Edsel, II, 211
Ford, Henry, II, 8
Ford Motor Company
    Boss 302, 169, *186*, 189
    Boss 429, 169, 189
    2004 Cobra concept car, 208
    Falcon, 8, 19–20, 54
    Ford of Mexico, 195–196
    future of, 232–233
    Galaxie, 34
    GT40, 129, 135, 139
    2007–2008 GT500, 216–217
    GT supercar, 211
    Mach 1 Mustang, 189
    Mustang (stock), 18–20, 33, *84*
    Mustang 351 Sportsroof, 193–194
    Mustang development, 13, 18, *20*
    Mustang GT/CS, *170*
    Shelby GR-1 concept car, 211
    Special Vehicle Team, 216
    T-5, 23
    Trans-Am SCCA series, 158–160, 193–194
Frey, Don, 8, 22, 151

Geddes, Ray, 28, 40, 45
General Motors, 13, 30
George May Ford, 78
Gillis, Randy, *118*
Goodell, Fred, 146–147, 151, 154, 182
Goodyear, 33, 146–147
Gorman, James, 148
Green Valley Raceway, 45, *72*
Gurney, Dan, 34

Hadden, James, 148
Healey, Donald, 13
Herb Tousely Ford, *94*
Hertz, John, 113
Hertz Sports Car Club, *92, 93, 102, 103, 104, 105, 110,* 112–113, *113,* 115–116, *115*, 189, 206
Hidalgo, David, *109*
High Performance Motors, 196
Holcomb, Jud, 44
Hoopingarner, Eric, 53

Iacocca, Lee, 8, 9, 22, 28, 31, 39, 45, 169, 204

Jack Loftus Ford, 206
Jackson, Craig, 151, 153, 155, 184
Jeanes, William, 211

Kar Kraft Engineering, *186*, 193–194
Kemp, Charlie, *75*
Kemper, Bill, 107
Kerr, Alex "Skeet," 51
Kerr, John, 167
Kingston Trio, *111*
Knudsen, Semon E. "Bunkie," 167, 169, 186

Kopec, Rick, 66–67, *67,* 68, *70*
Kreski, Connie, *189*
Kwech, Horst, *186*

Laguna Seca raceway (check), 67
Los Angeles Times, *33*
LaViolette, Vince, *225*
Long, Chris, 151, 184
Long, David E., 151, 184

Maier, Bill, 106
Maier Racing, 106
McCain, Don, 70, 73, 78, 148
McCellan, George, 167
McHose, Charles "Chuck," 124, 128–129, 135–136, 139
McNamara, Robert, 8, 22
Mel Burns Ford, 148
Miles, Ken, *14–15,* 33–34, 39, 45–46, *72, 92, 96*
1966 Minneapolis Auto Show, *94*
Moffat, Allan, 20
Moir, Bill, 53
Moon, Dean, 18
Moore, Bud, *186,* 194
Morrison, Richard, 140–141
Motor Trend, *24–27*
Muhleman, Max, 70
Mulholland, Joe, 19

Nance, Jim, 141
National Advisory Committee on Aeronautics (NACA) ducts, 187
National Hot Rod Association, 70, 73
Neerpasch, Jochen, 69
1968 New York Auto Show, 207
North, Tim, 140–141

Onken, John, 19, 22–23
Owens-Corning, 186

Pardee, Howard, 107
Passino, Jacques, 28, *151*
Patterson, Gary, *212, 215*
Paxton superchargers, 104, *108,* 109, 177
2004 Pebble Beach Concours d'Elegance, 211
Performance Associates, 74
Pike, Don, 46
Playboy, 206
Pontiac GTO, 8
Portland International Raceway, 107
Proctor, Peter, 23
Prudomme, Don, *225*

Ram Rod, 71
Remington, Phil, 33, 37, 115–116
Revson, Peter, *186*
Ritchey, Les, 74
Riverside International Raceway, 13, 46, 92, 156
Road & Track, *166, 167*

SAAC World Registry of Shelbys and Cobras, 107, 203
Salvadori, Roy, 12
SCCA. *See* Sport Car Club of America (SSCA)
1956 SCCA National Championship, 12
Schwarz, Jerry, 45
Shane, Bob, *111*
Shelby, Carroll Hall
    1967 models and, 135, 139
    Chrysler Corporation and, 204
    death of, 222
    Edsel Ford II and, 211
    GT350 development, 33–34, 36–38, 40–41, 47–49
    GT350 racing, 62, 65
    KR models and, 178
    "Little Red" and, 154
    pictured, *151*, *159*, *173*, *200*, *211*, *216*, *220*
    racing career of, 12
    SCCA and, 28, 30–31, 39, *151*
    Semon "Bunkie" Knudsen and, 169, 171
    Shelby de Mexico S.A. and, 195–197, 199
    Shelby Owner's Association/SAAC and, 107
    Shelby/Paxton superchargers, 104, 109
    Super Snake and, 146–147
Shelby American, 9, 34
    Cobra, 18, 28, 30, 34, 66, 171
    2004 Cobra concept car, 208
    Cobra "Dragonsnake," 70
    Cobra kits, *118*
    CS6 Mustang, 214
    CSX3056, 107
    Daytona Cobra Coupe, 30, 51, 211
    future of, 235–236
    impact of, 9
    2007 GT, 216
    2007 GT500, *209*
    2008 GT, *202*
    2019 GT, 228
    2008 GT500 Super Snake, *212*
    GTE, 226, 228
    2006 GT-H, 211–213, 214, 216
    2008 GT-H convertible, *202*, *204*
    2007 GT-H convertible, *202*, 212–213, 216
    GTS, *225*, 226
    GT supercar, 211
    Lone Star, 171
    memorabilia, 206–207
    PR materials, *34*
    Prudomme edition Mustang, *225*
    Series 1, 204–205, 208
    Shelby GR-1 concept car, 211
    Southern Pacific Railroad facility, 166
    Terlingua Edition Shelby Mustang, *216*
    See also Shelby GT350; Shelby GT500.
Shelby American Automobile Club (SAAC), 107, 203

Shelby American Collection museum, 90
Shelby Automotive, Inc., 167, 180, 207, 214
Shelby de Mexico S.A., 195–197, *199*, 199
Shelby GT350
    5R002, *58*, *62*, *72*, *73*, *77*, *79*
    5S003, *48*, *49*, *50*, 52–53
    1966 models, 98, 101–102, 104
    1967 models, 124, 128–129, *128*, *129*, 135–136, *136*, *137*, 144–146, 150–151, 153
    1968 California Special coupe, 154, 184–185
    1968 Convertible, *169*, 175–177
    1968 models, *168*, *169*, *182*
    1969 models, 185–188, *185*, 189, 193
    2011–2014 models, 219–220, 226
    2015 and up, 228–229
    alterations for mass market, 82, 85–86, 89–91
    Changeover (1965 1/2) cars, 91, 93, 98, *100*
    Cobra-badged 1968 models, 171–173, 175
    Color options (1966), 98, 101
    1966 Convertibles, *110*, *111*, *117*, 117
    CSX 2000, 18
    CSX 2002, 18
    development of 1964/64 models, 19, 34, 36–41, 47–49, 51–52, 54–55
    Factory Drag Cars, 68, 69, 70, 73–74, 76, 78
    Group II racers, *94–95*, 158–160
    Hertz rental models (350H), *92*, *102*, *103*, *104*, *105*, *110*, 112–113, *113*, 115–116, *115*, 189
    magazine reviews/track tests, *14–15*, *24–27*, *91–92*, *130–134*, *166*, *167*
    PR materials, *29*, *84*, *87*, *88*, *125–126*
    Racing models, *58*, 58, *59*, *60*, *62*, *63*, *64*, 65–68, 78, *98*
    Special Paint models (1968), *176*, *178*
    spec sheets, *83*
Shelby GT500
    1968 California Special, 154
    1968 California Special coupe, 154, 184–185
    1968 Convertible, *153*, *169*, *171*, 175–177
    1968 Convertible prototype (0139), 155–156, 158, *160*, *161*
    1968 Fastback prototype (0100), 155, *158*
    1968 models, *169*, 182
    1969 models, 185–188, *185*, 189, 193
    2008 Mustang GT500KR, 217
    2010 models, 226
    2013 models, 220, 222
    2012–2014 models, 226
    2020 and up, 230, 235
    Cobra-badged 1968 models, 171–173, 175
    GT500KR, *173*, *174*, *175*, *177*, 177–178, *178*, *179*, 180, *181*, *182*

GT500KR convertibles, *176*, *180*
    introduction of (1967), 142, *143*, 144–146, *144*, 150–151, 153
    magazine reviews/track tests, *130–134*
    prototype "Little Red" (0131), 153–155
    prototype "Green Hornet," 151, 182–184
    PR materials, *125–126*
    sales from, 164
    Special Paint models (1968), *176*, *178*
    Super Snake (1967), 146–148, 150
    Super Snake package (2007–2009), 217
    Super Snake package (2015–2019), *222*, 222
    1969 Trans-Am cars, *186*, *187*, 193–194
Shelby Owner's Association, 106
Shelby Parts Company, 171
Shelby/Paxton superchargers, 104, *108*, 109, 177
Shelby Professional Sales Club, 207
Shelby Racing Company, 160, 171, *186*, 193–194
Shinoda, Larry, 186
Smith, Dick, 46
Smith, Sam, 45, 218
Smith, Steve, 85
Spencer, Lew, 196
Sports Car Club of America (SSCA), 9, 23, 28, 30, 45, 52, 58, 158–160
Sports Car Graphic, *14–15*, 65, 85, *130–131*, *151*
Sports Illustrated, 12, 206
Stacey, Pete, 139
Stroppe, Bill, *37*
Sullivan, Don "Sully," 51

Thompson, Tommy, *70*
Titus, Jerry, *14–15*, 46, *53*, *59*, *60*, *61*, 65, *67*, *130–131*, *151*
Tonkin, Marv, *100*
1964 Tour de France endurance race, 23
Trans-Am SCCA series, 158–160, 193–194
24 Hours of Le Mans, 129

Velazquez, Eduardo, 195–197, 199
Ventrella, James, 156, 158

Wagner, Gerry, 107
Waterford Hills raceway (Clarkston, MI), 19, 22
Wegner, Chuck, *71*
West Imperial Highway facility, *22*
Whitton, Kelly, *109*
Willow Springs Raceway, 33, 39, 45, *62*
Wolfe, Ray, 46

Young, Ken, 107

Inspiring | Educating | Creating | Entertaining

Brimming with creative inspiration, how-to projects, and useful information to enrich your everyday life, Quarto Knows is a favorite destination for those pursuing their interests and passions. Visit our site and dig deeper with our books into your area of interest: Quarto Creates, Quarto Cooks, Quarto Homes, Quarto Lives, Quarto Drives, Quarto Explores, Quarto Gifts, or Quarto Kids.

First Published in 2014 by Motorbooks, an imprint of The Quarto Group,
100 Cummings Center, Suite 265-D, Beverly, MA 01915, USA.
T (978) 282-9590 F (978) 283-2742 QuartoKnows.com

New Edition published in 2019.

Motorbooks titles are also available at discount for retail, wholesale, promotional, and bulk purchase. For details, contact the Special Sales Manager by email at specialsales@quarto.com or by mail at The Quarto Group, Attn: Special Sales Manager, 100 Cummings Center, Suite 265-D, Beverly, MA 01915, USA.

23 22 21 20 19   1 2 3 4 5

ISBN: 978-0-7603-6597-7

Digital edition published in 2019
eISBN: 978-0-7603-6598-4

Library of Congress Cataloging-in-Publication Data

Names: Comer, Colin, author.
Title: Shelby Mustang : fifty years / Colin Comer.
Description: Beverly, MA : Motorbooks, [2019] | Includes index.
Identifiers: LCCN 2019018882 (print) | LCCN 2019021186 (ebook) | ISBN
   9780760365984 (E-Book) | ISBN 9780760365977 (pbk.)
Subjects: LCSH: Mustang automobile--History. | Shelby, Carroll, 1923-2012. |
   Muscle cars--United States--History.
Classification: LCC TL215.M8 (ebook) | LCC TL215.M8 C65 2019 (print) | DDC
   629.222/2--dc23
LC record available at https://lccn.loc.gov/2019018882

Acquisitions Editor: Darwin Holmstrom
Art Directors: Cindy Samargia Laun and Rebecca Pagel
Page Design: Chris Fayers and Rebecca Pagel

Frontis: Author collection
Title page: photo by Michael Darter
Front cover: photo by David Newhardt
Back cover: Ford Motor Company, photo by Andrew Surma

Printed in China